Copyright © 2023 by Anthony of Boston
All rights reserved. No part of this publication may be reproduced, distributed, or transmitted in any form or by any means, including photocopying, recording, or other electronic or mechanical methods, without the prior written permission of the publisher, except in the case of brief quotations embodied in critical reviews and certain other noncommercial uses permitted by copyright law.

Table of Contents

Volume I:
US Dollar Prediction Algorithms

Volume II:
Stock Market Prediction Algorithms

Volume III:
Bitcoin Research Prediction Algorithms

Astrology

Market Prediction Algorithms
for the US Dollar, the Stock Market and Bitcoin

Anthony of Boston

Author's Note

The contents of this book were extracted from the book "Ares Le Mandat", which was written by the same author, Anthony of Boston. The writings here were copied from chapters 21, 25, 48, and 50. The stock, bitcoin, and forex historical data came from investing.com

Introduction

Market Prediction Algorithms for the US Dollar, the Stock Market and Bitcoin

Below is a quick demonstration on how the Dow Jones is affected by the position of the Sun, Moon, and Lunar node (Eclipses 360). This quick demonstration will lay the groundwork for understanding the rest of this book which was simply extracted from the book "Ares Le Mandat"

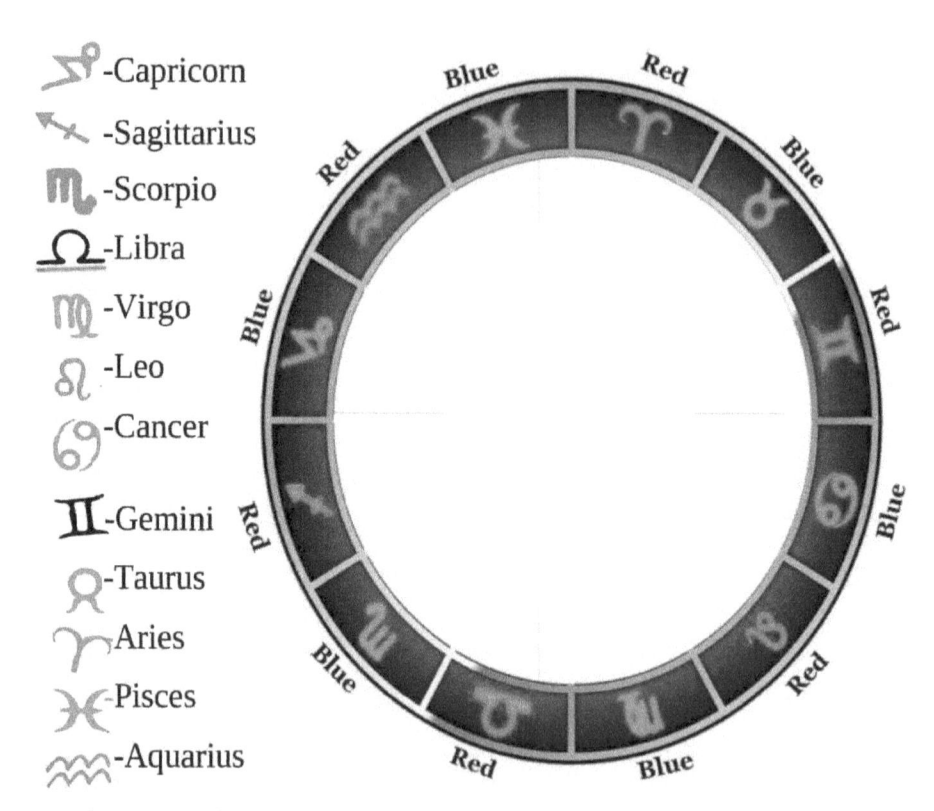

- ♑ -Capricorn
- ♐ -Sagittarius
- ♏ -Scorpio
- ♎ -Libra
- ♍ -Virgo
- ♌ -Leo
- ♋ -Cancer
- ♊ -Gemini
- ♉ -Taurus
- ♈ -Aries
- ♓ -Pisces
- ♒ -Aquarius

Notice the colors of each symbol representing a zodiac sign alternating between red and blue. For example Aquarius's symbol being red and Pisces's symbol being blue, and then back to red for Aries's symbol. This is done to indicate an opposite effect that takes place in one sign compared to the other and how what is explained for one red symbol should be exactly how it is defined for all Red zodiac symbols with the opposite explanation for the blue symbol being applied to all blue symbols. For example, the moon within 1 degree of the degree of the Sun in any blue zodiac symbol would be the opposite of what happens when the moon is within 1 degree of the degree of the Sun in any red zodiac symbol. **Please note that the degree of the Sun is applied as if the Sun is in every zodiac sign. This also applies to the lunar nodes with the degree of the lunar node being applied to every sign.** In the Case of the stock market, historically, when the moon gets to within 1 degree of the degree of the sun in any of the Zodiac signs marked blue, the stock market rises and when its within 1 degree of the degree of the sun in any red zodiac sign, the market drops. The definition for each parameter holds true until the moon lines up into what defines another parameter that has another meaning. When using eclipses there are a number of parameters applied. The first is the one I gave about the moon being within 1 degree of the degree of the sun bringing the market up when in a blue sign and bringing it down when in a red sign---on average historically. The zodiac signs are classified into 4 elements: Fire, Earth, Air and Water. The Fire signs are Aries, Leo and Sagittarius. The Earth Signs are Taurus, Virgo, and Capricorn. The Air signs are Gemini, Libra, and Aquarius. The Water signs are Cancer, Scorpio, and Pisces. You'll notice in the example chart coming up that the Fire and Air signs are colored Red, while the Earth and Water signs are colored Blue. **That's is the main significance of the distinctions, not the fact that red and blue colors are used. Red and Blue is only used to provide some clarity in explaining how the parameters for the Fire/Air signs are essentially opposite from the parameters for the Earth/Water signs.** On the next page are the 7 parameters when using Eclipses360 to see how it correlates to the daily Stock Market(Dow Jones and S&P) movements. We'll label it **Figure 1.** First calculate the astrology chart using the timeframe in which the Stock Market is open in New York on a given day.

Figure 1. – Keep this page referenced to follow how the 7 parameters are applied to the Dow Jones prediction example

1. When the moon is within 1 degree of the degree of the sun in a blue sign, the market tends to go up.

2. When the moon is within 1 degree of the degree of the sun in a red sign, the market tends to go down.

3. When the moon is within 3 degrees of the degree of the lunar node in any sign(blue or red), the result is that the market drops.

4. when the moon is within 1 degree of the degree of the lunar node after it has passed the degree of the sun in a blue sign, the market tends to drop.

5. when the moon is within 1 degree of the degree of the lunar node after it has passed the

degree of the sun in a red sign, the market tends to rise.

6. When moon is within 3 degrees of the degree of the Sun in a blue sign, the result is a drop

for the market.

7. When the moon is within 3 degrees of the degree of the Sun in a red sign, the market tends to rise.

PLEASE NOTE: When seeing how the moon, sun, and lunar nodes apply daily to the stock market movements, the effects that are defined by one parameter apply at the time it happens and all the way until another parameter comes into effect. For example, as the moon travels and goes into 1 degree of the degree of the sun, that resulting effect would stay in effect until one of the other parameters come about.... such as the moon going to within 3 degrees of the degree of the lunar node. Until the next is there, the previous parameter applies...whatever it may have been.

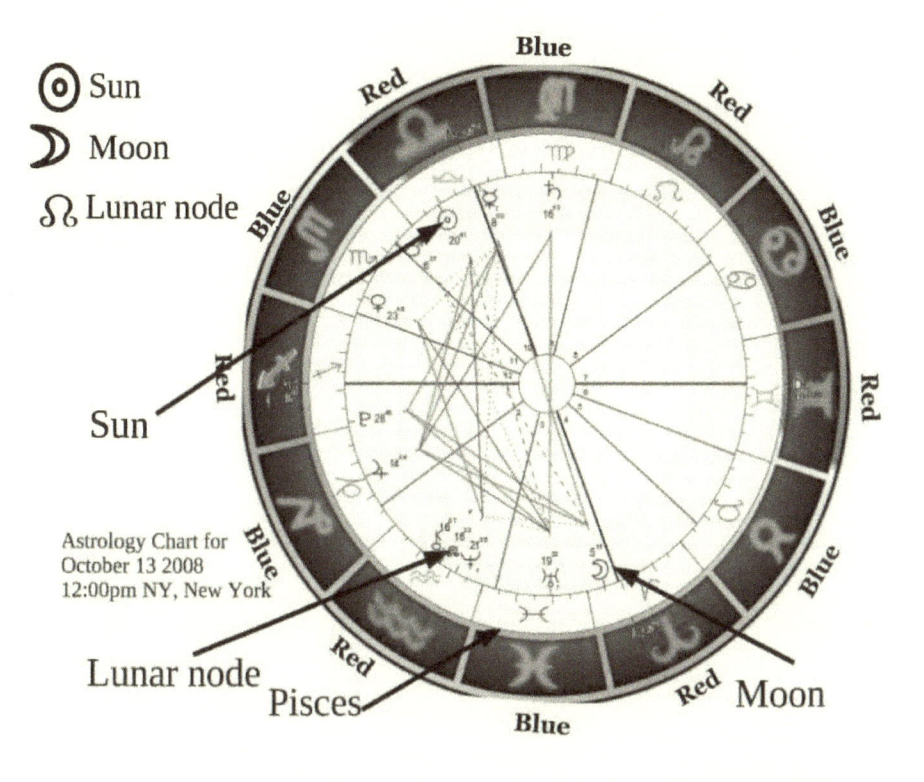

Notice the moon at 5 degrees of Aries. To interpret the meaning of how this predicts where the stock market will go that day, first look to see if the moon follows any of the 7 parameters listed in **Figure 1**. We can see at 5 degrees along with the Sun at 20 degrees and the lunar node at 16 degrees, the moon doesn't follow any of the Parameters in **Figure 1** at first glance, so what we do is interpret based on the last parameter that took place in this chart. Since the Sun's degree is at 20 degrees, which applies to the 20th degree mark in every sign, the last parameter that would have been applied would be the moon within 1 degree of the degree of the sun in the blue sign of Pisces as it states in the 1st parameter in **Figure 1**. This would indicate a likelihood of the market rising from that point until the next parameter comes about. The Dow Jones was up 976 points that day. These instructions apply for any time you calculate the chart for that day. I used 12:00pm in my example, but the instructions apply for all market hours, so if a new parameter comes about an hour after the market opens, then one has to take that into account when doing the daily forecast with Eclipses 360. While these parameters result in a some degree of accuracy when predicting the daily movements of the stock market, daily and historically, they don't result in 100 percent accuracy.

On the next page are the 9 parameters that will be used to see how eclipses line up with past EUR/USD price movements. Since the EUR/USD is the highest concentration of volume for any financial instrument, it has to be considered a strong overall representation of the global economic mood for the day. The Eur/usd is usually 24 hours starting Sunday evening and going all the way till Friday late afternoon. I will calculate the astrology chart using 12pm New York time and base the prediction from the parameters which apply around that time on how the EUR/USD will perform for that entire day. We will call these 9 parameters **Figure 1a.**

Volume I:

US Dollar Prediction Algorithm

Figure 1a – Keep the Figure 1a pages referenced to follow how the 9 parameters are applied to the EUR/USD predictions

Figure 1a

1. When the moon is within 1 degree of the degree of the sun in an Earth or Water sign, the value of EUR/USD tends to go up. For instance, the zodiac goes as follows: **aries, taurus, gemini, cancer, leo, virgo, libra, scorpio, sagittarius, capricorn, aquarius, and pisces**. The Earth and Water signs are Taurus, Cancer, Virgo, Scorpio, Caricorn, and Pisces.

2. When the moon is within 1 degree of the degree of the sun in an Fire or Air sign, the value of EUR/USD tends to go down. For instance, the zodiac goes as follows: **aries, taurus, gemini, cancer, leo, virgo, libra, scorpio, sagittarius, capricorn, aquarius, and pisces**. The Fire and Air signs are Aries, Gemini, Leo, Libra, Saggitarius, Aquarius.

3. When the moon is within 3 degrees of the degree of the lunar node in any sign, the result is that the EUR/USD drops.

4. When the moon is within 1 degree of the degree of the lunar node in the sign that that the lunar node is in and every other sign after that one, the value of the EUR/USD tends to drop. For instance, the zodiac goes as follows: **aries, taurus, gemini, cancer, leo, virgo, libra, scorpio, sagittarius, capricorn, aquarius, and pisces.** If the lunar node is in aries, the sign after the next sign is gemini, and after the next sign from gemini would be leo. This parameter regarding the moon being within 1 degree of the

Figure 1a *cont'd*

degree of the lunar node would apply to the sign that the lunar node is in and every other sign from that point. So if the lunar node is in Aries, this parameter would apply to the moon in aries, gemini, leo, libra, sagittarius, and aquarius. If the lunar node is in taurus, this parameter would apply to the moon in taurus, cancer, virgo, scorpio, capricorn, and pisces. If the lunar node is in Sagittarius, this parameter would apply to the moon in sagittarius, aquarius, aries, gemini, leo, and libra.

5. when the moon is within 1 degree of the degree of the lunar node in the sign next to the sign that the lunar node is in and every other sign from that point, the value of the EUR/USD tends to rise. For example, if the lunar node is in aries, this parameter would apply to the moon in taurus and every other sign from there. So taurus, cancer, virgo, scorpio, capricorn, and pisces. If the lunar node is in taurus, this parameter applies to the moon in aries, gemini, leo, libra, sagittarius, and aquarius.

6. When the moon is within 3 degrees of the degree of the sun in an Earth or Water sign, the value of EUR/USD tends to go down. For instance, the zodiac goes as follows: **aries, taurus, gemini, cancer, leo, virgo, libra, scorpio, sagittarius, capricorn, aquarius, and pisces**. The Earth and Water signs are Aries, Gemini, Leo, Libra, Saggitarius, Aquarius.

7. When the moon is within 3 degrees of the degree of the sun in an Fire or Air sign, the value of EUR/USD tends to go up. For instance, the zodiac goes as follows: **aries, taurus, gemini, cancer, leo, virgo, libra, scorpio, sagittarius, capricorn, aquarius, and pisces**. The Fire and Air signs are Aries, Gemini, Leo, Libra, Saggitarius, Aquarius.

Figure 1a *cont'd*

8. When the moon is within 1 degree of the degree of Mercury in the sign of the Lunar node and every other sign after that one, the market tends to drop. For instance, the zodiac goes as follows: **aries, taurus, gemini, cancer, leo, virgo, libra, scorpio, sagittarius, capricorn, aquarius, and pisces**. If the Lunar node is in aries, the sign after the next sign is gemini, and after the next sign from gemini would be leo. This parameter regarding the moon being within 1 degree of the degree of the Mercury in the sign of the lunar node would apply to the sign that the lunar node is in and every other sign from that point. So if the lunar node is in Aries, this parameter would apply to the moon in aries, gemini, leo, libra, sagittarius, and aquarius. If the lunar node is in taurus, this parameter would apply to the moon in taurus, cancer, virgo, scorpio, capricorn, and pisces. If the lunar node is in Sagittarius, this parameter would apply to the moon in sagittarius, aquarius, aries, gemini, leo, and libra.

9. When the moon is within 1 degree of the degree of mercury in the sign next to the sign that the lunar node is in and every other sign from that point, the market tends to go up. For example, if the lunar node is in aries, this parameter would apply to the moon in taurus and every other sign from there. So it would be the moon in taurus, cancer, virgo, scorpio, capricorn, and pisces. If the lunar node is in Taurus, this parameter applies to the moon in Aries, gemini, Leo, libra, Sagittarius, and Aquarius.

PLEASE NOTE: When seeing how the moon, sun, mercury, and the lunar nodes apply daily to the market movements, the effects that are defined by one parameter apply at the time it happens and all the way until another parameter comes into effect. For example, as the moon travels and goes into 1 degree of the degree of the sun, that resulting effect would stay in effect until one of the other parameters come about.... such as the moon going to within 3 degrees of the degree of the lunar node. Until the moon takes you to a point where a new parameter can be applied, the previous parameter continues to apply...whatever it may have been. Here is what the lunar nodes look like in a astrology chart. ☊ ☋

To demonstrate this algorithm, I will calculate the astrology chart using 12pm New York time and base the prediction from the parameter which applies around that time on how the EUR/USD will perform for that entire day since the prices listed on the next page show where the value of the EUR/USD actually finished that day. We will use the month of October 2008 for our example. See the next page.

Market Prediction Algorithms for the US Dollar, the Stock Market and Bitcoin

10/01/2008 - 10/31/2008

Date	Price	Open	High	Low	Change %
Oct 31, 2008	1.2733	1.2855	1.2897	1.2668	-1.36%
Oct 30, 2008	1.2908	1.2965	1.3295	1.2803	-0.42%
Oct 29, 2008	1.2963	1.2768	1.2994	1.2627	1.95%
Oct 28, 2008	1.2715	1.2475	1.2744	1.2330	1.99%
Oct 27, 2008	1.2467	1.2549	1.2686	1.2333	-1.24%
Oct 24, 2008	1.2624	1.2973	1.2980	1.2498	-2.74%
Oct 23, 2008	1.2980	1.2828	1.3003	1.2727	0.98%
Oct 22, 2008	1.2854	1.3065	1.3078	1.2773	-1.57%
Oct 21, 2008	1.3059	1.3332	1.3355	1.3051	-2.14%
Oct 20, 2008	1.3344	1.3403	1.3532	1.3286	-0.48%
Oct 17, 2008	1.3409	1.3483	1.3518	1.3387	-0.58%
Oct 16, 2008	1.3487	1.3467	1.3539	1.3346	0.20%
Oct 15, 2008	1.3460	1.3620	1.3685	1.3453	-1.20%
Oct 14, 2008	1.3624	1.3594	1.3771	1.3586	0.23%
Oct 13, 2008	1.3593	1.3559	1.3683	1.3458	1.33%
Oct 10, 2008	1.3414	1.3589	1.3652	1.3259	-1.35%
Oct 09, 2008	1.3597	1.3631	1.3785	1.3580	-0.24%
Oct 08, 2008	1.3630	1.3630	1.3758	1.3544	0.08%
Oct 07, 2008	1.3619	1.3486	1.3741	1.3481	0.96%
Oct 06, 2008	1.3490	1.3665	1.3676	1.3443	-2.04%
Oct 03, 2008	1.3771	1.3818	1.3907	1.3704	-0.34%
Oct 02, 2008	1.3818	1.4026	1.4027	1.3745	-1.45%
Oct 01, 2008	1.4021	1.4124	1.4176	1.3976	-0.59%

These are the prices for the EUR/USD for the month of October 2008

Highest: 1.4176 Lowest: 1.2330 Difference: 0.1846 Average: 1.3286 Change %: -9.7206

We will look at the most negative and positive days in October and see how they correlate to the placement of the moon based on our 9 parameters. Starting on the next page is the chart for October 2nd, a day in which, as we can see above, the Eur/Usd fell – 1.45%.

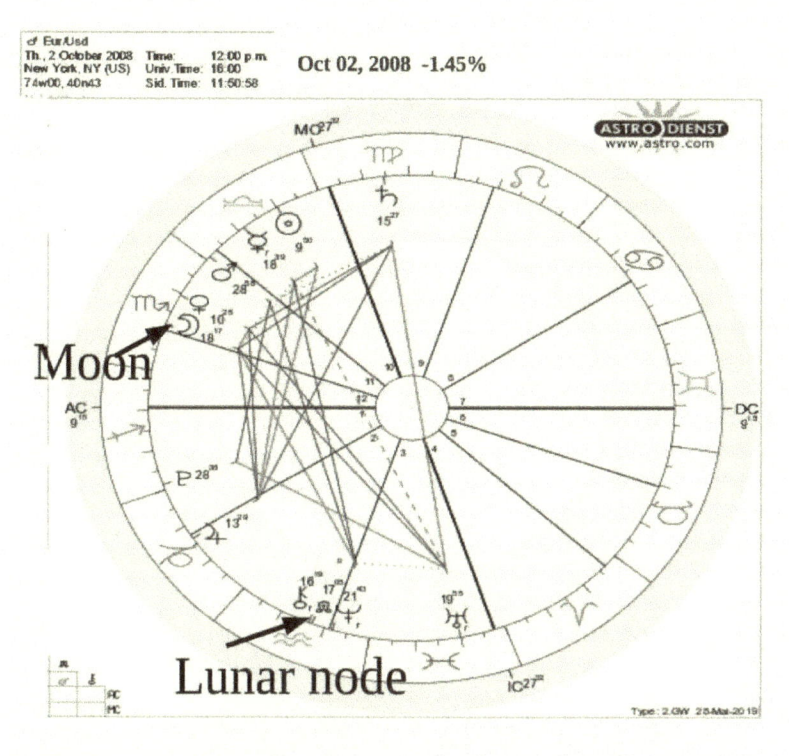

♂ Eur/Usd
Th., 2 October 2008   Time: 12:00 p.m.
New York, NY (US)   Univ. Time: 16:00   **Oct 02, 2008 -1.45%**
74w00, 40n43   Sid. Time: 11:50:58

So we have the chart for October 2, 2008 at 12pm New York. With the moon at 18 degrees Scorpio. The last parameter that would apply would be parameter 9 as written in **Figure 1a**. However, that would make the prediction wrong because in parameter 9, it says when the moon is within 1 degree of the degree of mercury in the sign next to the sign that the lunar node is in and every other sign from that point, the eur/usd tends to go up. The Eur/Usd actually dropped this day. The lunar node is in Aquarius. So counting every other sign from pisces bring us to the moon scorpio. So here we have a wrong assessment. However, if we calculate the chart to about a few hours before to about 7am, we have parameter 3 in **Figure 1a**. to reference which would indicate a drop for the EUR/USD during that timeframe when the moon is traveling within 3 degrees of the degree of the lunar node.

♂ Eur/Usd
Mo., 6 October 2008   Time: 12:00 p.m
New York, NY (US)   Univ. Time: 16:00
74w00, 40n43   Sid. Time: 12:08:44

Oct 06, 2008 - 2.04%

Moon

Lunar node

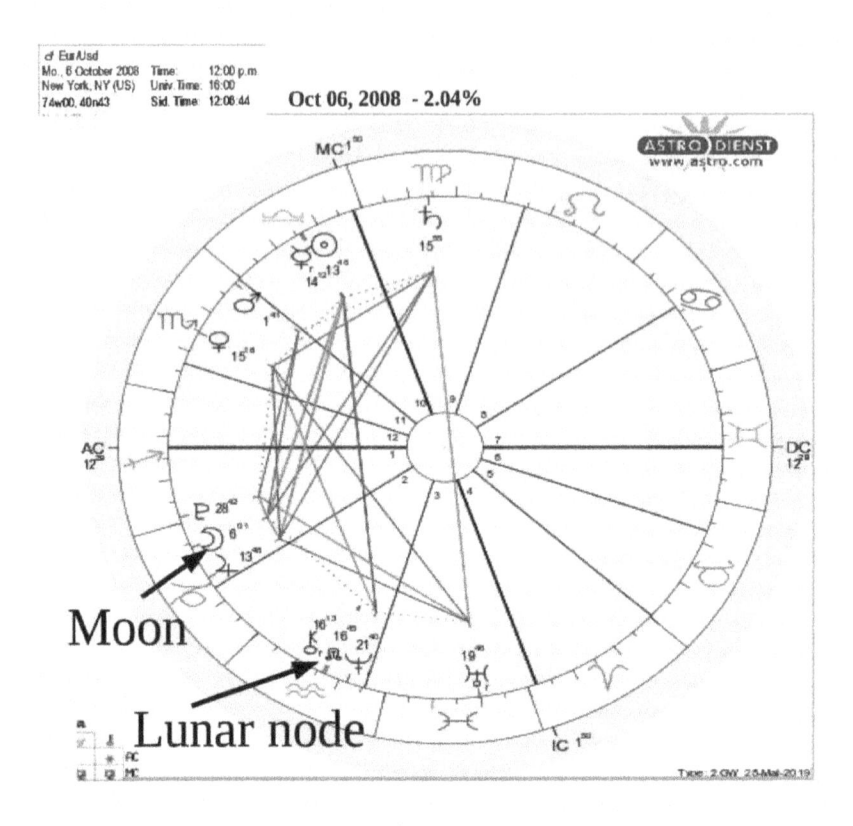

For October 6, 2008, the moon is at 6 degrees Capricorn and we can see clearly that parameter 4 in **Figure 1a** would be the last to apply, which says the moon being within 1 degree of the degree of the lunar node in the sign that its in and every other sign from that point drops the value of Eur/Usd. So, if we count every other sign from the sign that the lunar node is in, which is Aquarius, we are eventually taken to Sagittarius, which is where the last parameter would have applied and still apply at 12pm that day. Since that parameter states that the EUR/USD drops when that happens, we therefore have a correct assessment of the EUR/USD that day, as it dropped − 2.04%

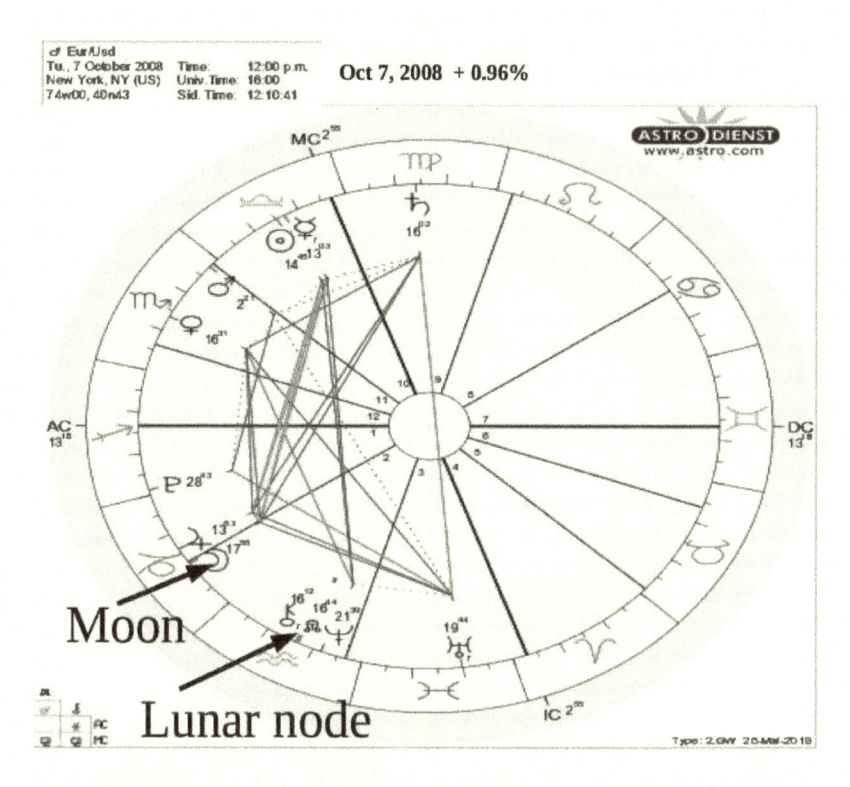

Market Prediction Algorithms for the US Dollar, the Stock Market and Bitcoin

Oct 7, 2008 + 0.96%

For October 7, 2008, the moon is at 17 degrees Capricorn. The last parameter that applies is parameter 5 in **Figure 1a**, which says the moon being within 1 degree of the degree of the lunar node in the sign next to the sign that the lunar node is in and every other sign from that point makes the EUR/USD rise. So since the lunar node is at 16 degrees in aquarius, the sign next to that is pisces and counting every other sign from that point brings us to the degree of the lunar node in Capricorn. When the moon hit within 1 degree of that degree of the lunar node, a rise was expected for the EUR/USD as indicated in parameter 5 in **Figure 1a**. So in looking at the overall outcome of the EUR/USD rising +0.96 that day, we have a valid assessment based on that parameter.

The EUR/USD then dropped significantly on October 10 2008. See the next page

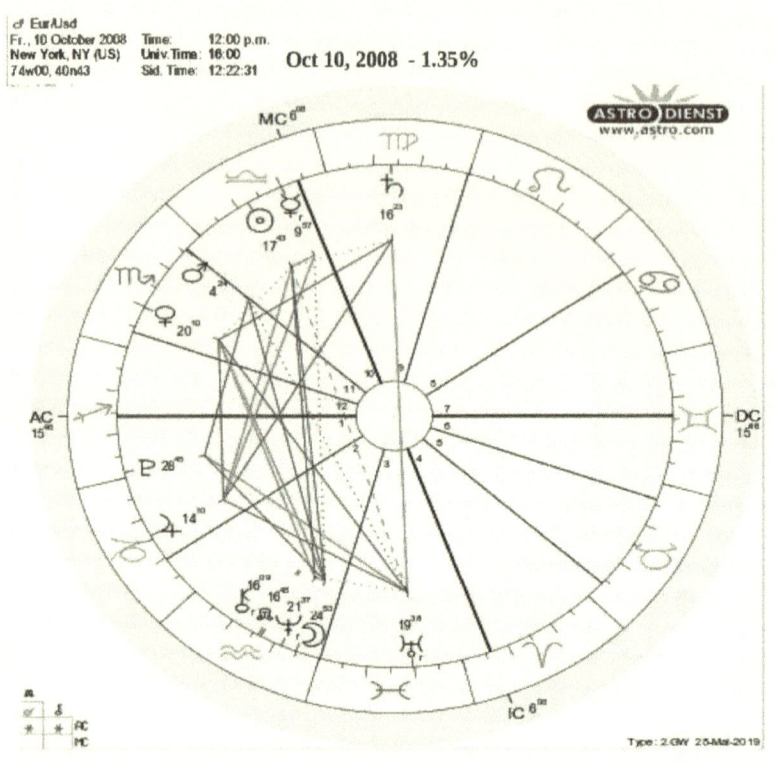

♂ EurAUsd
Fr., 10 October 2008   Time: 12:00 p.m.
New York, NY (US)   Univ. Time: 16:00
74w00, 40n43   Sid. Time: 12:22:31

Oct 10, 2008 - 1.35%

For October 10, 2008, the EUR/USD dropped. Since the moon is at 24 degrees aquarius, the last parameter that would have applied would have been parameter 2 in **Figure 1a**, which says the moon being within 1 degree of the degree of the sun in an Fire or Air sign brings the Eur/Usd down. Since Aquarius is an air sign, and the Sun is at 17 degrees in Libra, the degree of the sun in Aquarius would be 17 degrees. When moon was within 1 degree of that, parameter 2 in **Figure 1a** defined it as a drop in the value of EUR/USD, which did occur as the EUR/USD dropped 1.35% that day.

On the next page is the chart for October 13th 2008.

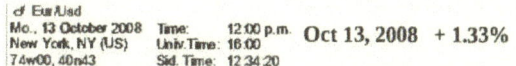

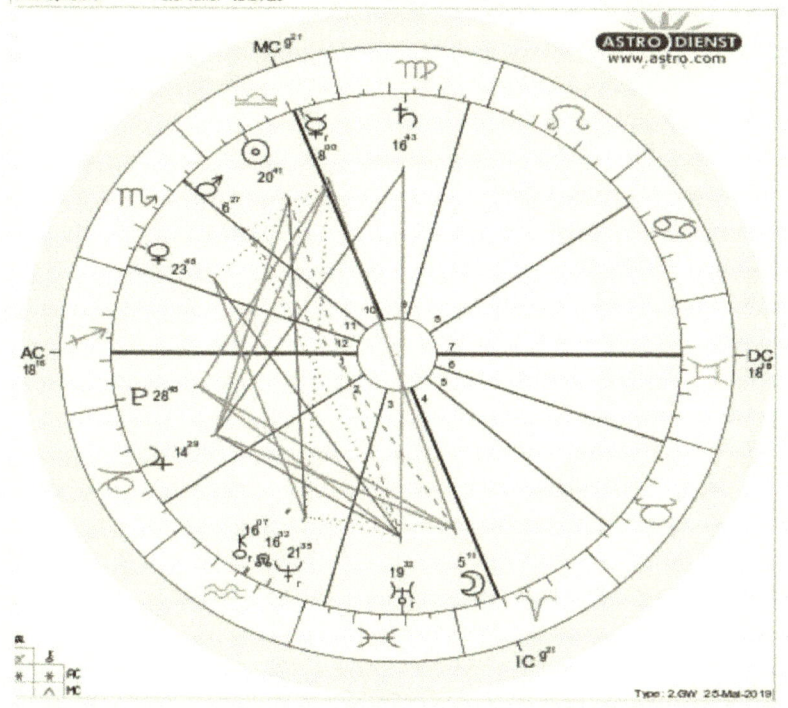

Market Prediction Algorithms for the US Dollar, the Stock Market and Bitcoin

Oct 13, 2008 + 1.33%

For October 13, 2008, the moon was at 5 degrees Aries. The last parameter that would have applied would be parameter 1 in **Figure 1a,** which says the moon being within 1 degree of the degree of the sun in an Earth or Water sign brings the value of Eur/Usd up. Pisces, which is before Aries and the sign where the last parameter took place, is also a Water sign. So, when the moon was within 1 degree of the degree of the sun in that sign at 20 degrees(The Sun is in Libra at 20 degrees so thus the degree of the sun is 20 degrees),the parameter thus defined the EUR/USD to rise. Which it did. The EUR/USD was up +1.33%. The next significant drop takes place on October 15 2008. See the next page

Oct 15, 2008 -1.20%

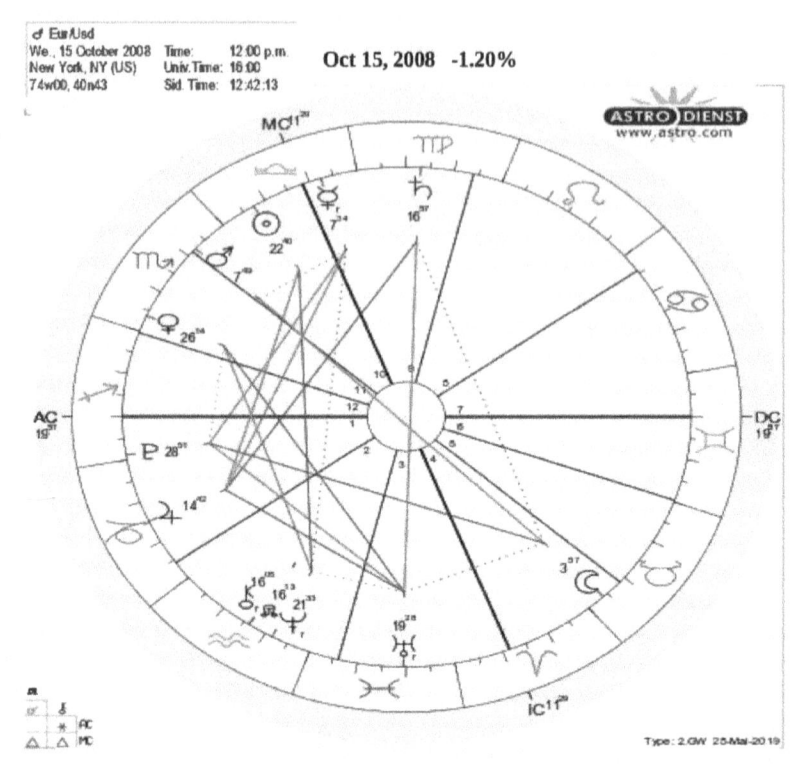

For October 15, 2008, the moon was at 3 degrees Taurus at 12pm. The last parameter that would have applied would be parameter 2 in **Figure 1a,** which says the moon being within 1 degree of the degree of the sun in a Fire or Air sign brings the value of EUR/USD down. Since Aries is a fire sign and the sun is at 22 degrees in Libra, the degree of the sun would be 22 degrees for Aries. When moon was within 1 degree of that point in Aries, the parameter defined the EUR/USD to drop, which it did. The EUR/USD fell -1.20% that day.

The next significant moves were drops which occurred on October 21 and 22. See the next page.

Oct 21, 2008 -2.14%

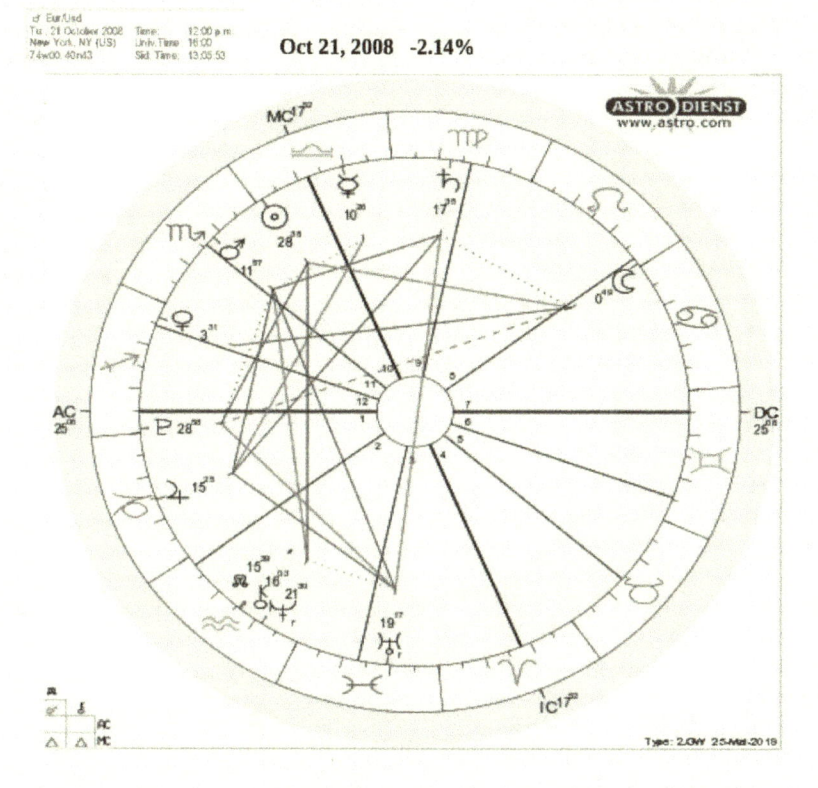

For October 21, 2008, the moon is at 0 degrees Leo. The last parameter that would have applied would be parameter 2 in **Figure 1a**, which says the moon being within 1 degree of the degree of the sun in a fire or air sign brings the value of Eur/Usd down. Since the degree of the Sun is 28 degrees, that last parameter would apply to the 28th degree mark of Cancer. Since we round off to the next sign at 24 degrees, the 28th degree mark is thus assigned to the sign of Leo. Since Leo is a fire sign, the moon within 1 degree of the degree of the sun at that 28th degree mark in Cancer interpreted to Leo is thus defined by parameter 2 in **Figure 1a** to bring the value of EUR/USD down. The EUR/USD dropped -2.14% that day.

Oct 22, 2008 -1.57%

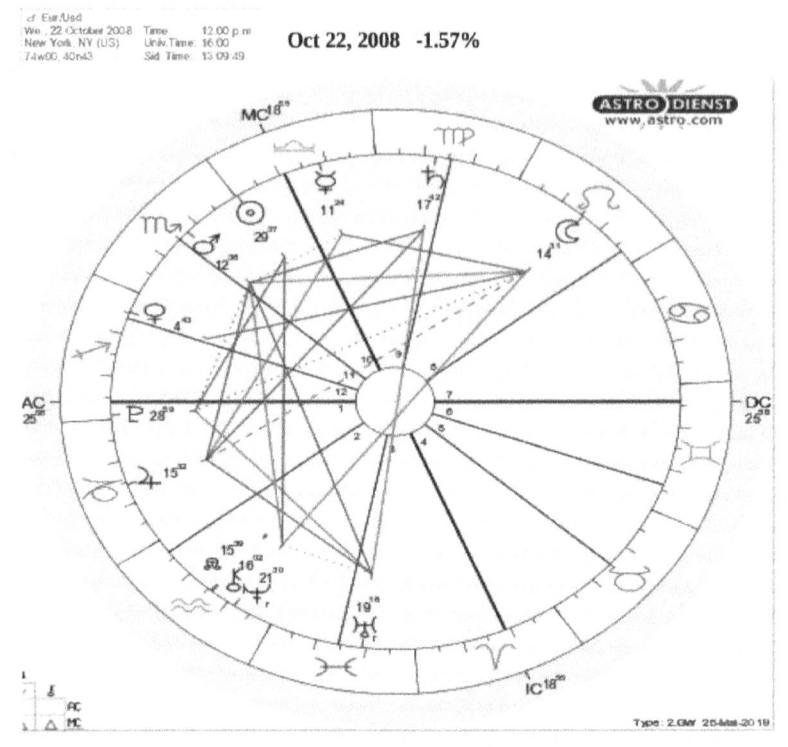

For October 22, 2008, the moon is at 14 degrees Leo. The last parameter that would have applied would be parameter 3 in **Figure 1a**, which says the moon being within 3 degrees of the degree of the lunar node in any sign brings the value of Eur/Usd down. The degree of the lunar node is 15 degrees, so this parameter became invoked when the moon was within 3 degrees from that point in Leo. We can see that the moon is also entering into its next parameter, which is parameter 4 in **Figure 1a**, which states that when the moon is within 1 degree of the degree of the lunar node in the sign that the lunar node is in and every other from that point, the value of EUR/USD drops. Since the moon is at 14^{31} degrees and the lunar node is at 15^{39} degrees, parameter 4 would be invoked within minutes as the moon would move to exactly 1 degree of the degree of the lunar node. Both parameters indicate a drop and thus fulfill what occurred that day. The EUR/USD dropped -1.57%.

Oct 24, 2008 -2.74%

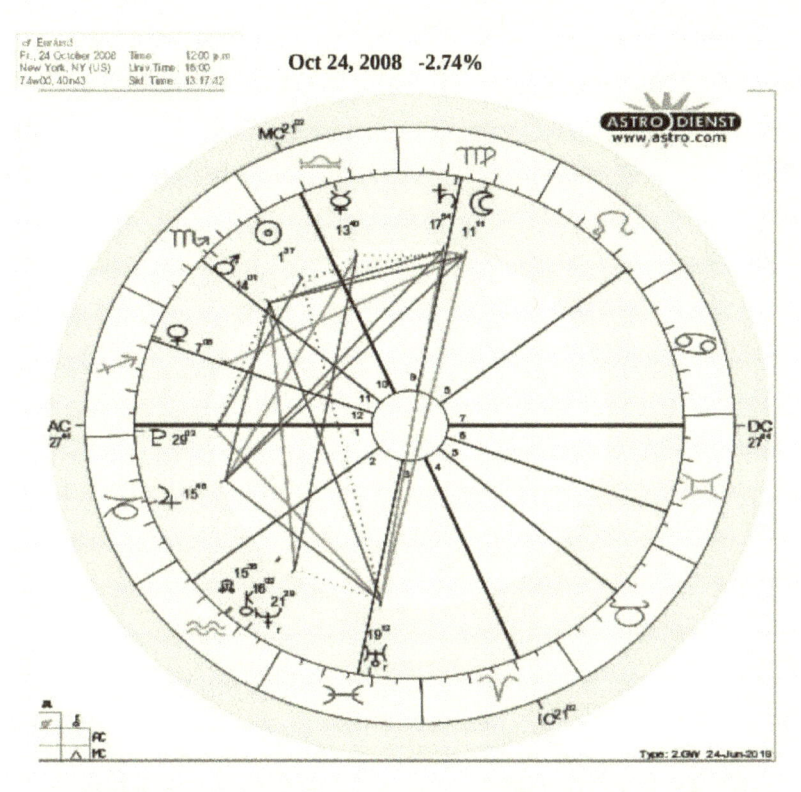

For October 24, 2008, the moon is at 11 degrees Virgo. The last parameter that would have applied would be parameter 1 in **Figure 1a** which says the moon within 1 degree of the degree of the Sun in an earth or water sign brings the Eur/Usd up. With the moon in Virgo, it would have last been within one degree of the degree of the sun in an earth sign, since Virgo is an earth sign. However, since the Eur/Usd was actually down on this day, the prediction using that parameter would have been wrong. There is also no way to potentially justify the correct analysis as the next parameter involving the moon within 1 degree of the degree of mercury would still not apply to what actually happened.

Oct 27, 2008 -1.27%

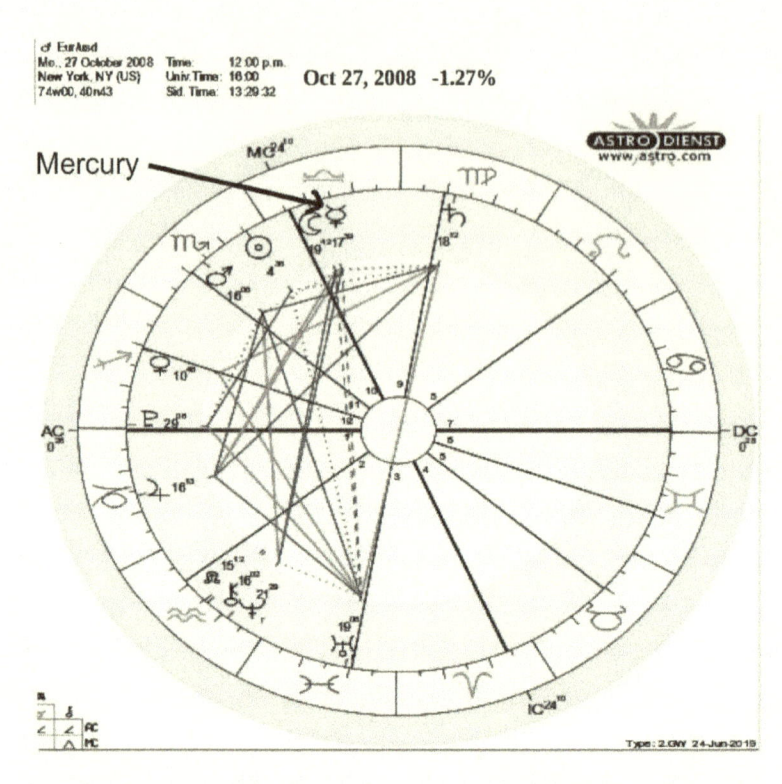

For October 27, 2008, the moon is at 19 degrees Libra. The last parameter that would have applied would be parameter 8 in **Figure 1a** which says the moon being within one degree of the degree of mercury in the sign of the lunar node and every other sign from that point brings the Eur/usd down. The moon is at 19 degrees Libra and would have been within one degree of the degree of mercury in the sign of Libra, which is on the path of every other sign from the sign the lunar node is located, which is Aquarius. That assessment would be correct for this day since the Eur/usd dropped -1.27%

Oct 28, 2008 +1.99%

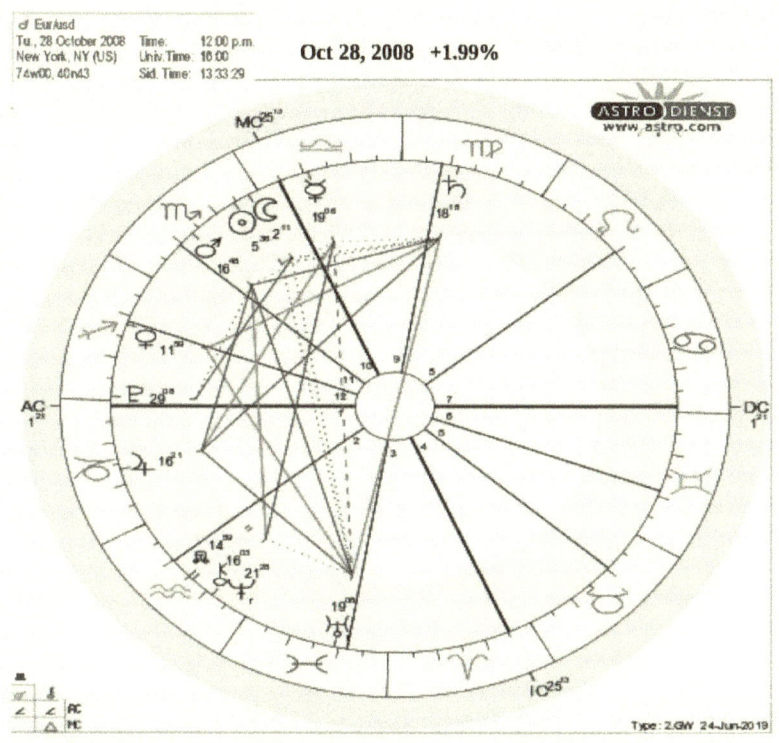

For October 28, 2008, the moon is at 2 degrees Scorpio. The last parameter that would have applied here would be parameter 8 in **Figure 1a** which says the moon being within one degree of the degree of mercury in the sign of the lunar node and every other sign from that point brings the Eur/usd down. The moon is at 2 degrees Scorpio and would have been within one degree of the degree of mercury back in the sign of Libra, which is on the path of every other sign from the sign in which the lunar node is located(Aquarius). However, that assessment would be wrong for this day since the Eur/usd was up +1.99%. Another parameter, in this case parameter 6 in **Figure 1a**, could be justified as applicable as the moon is close to being within 3 degrees of the degree of the sun in an earth or water sign. However, that parameter would still not apply to the price of Eur/usd rising on this day as parameter 6 also predicts the Eur/usd to fall.

Oct 29, 2008 +1.95%

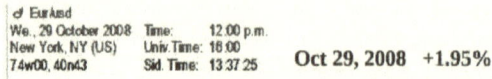

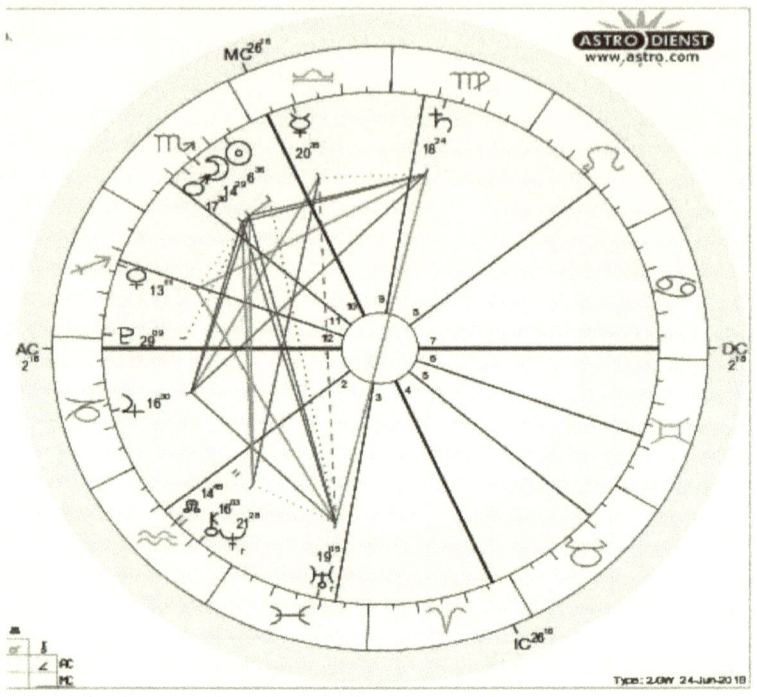

For October 29, 2008, the moon is at 14 degrees Scorpio. The last parameter that would have applied here would be parameter 5 in **Figure 1a** which says the moon being within 1 degree of the degree of the lunar node in the sign next to the sign that the lunar node is in and every other sign from that point brings the EUR/USD up. Here, the lunar node is 14 degree aquarius. The sign next to aquarius is Pisces. Every other sign from Pisces eventually takes us to the location of the moon's degree in scorpio at 14 degrees, which is within 1 degree of the degree of the lunar node. The Lunar node's degree is the 14th degree. This assessment turns out accurate as the Eur/Usd rose +1.95% this day.

Oct 31, 2008 -1.36%

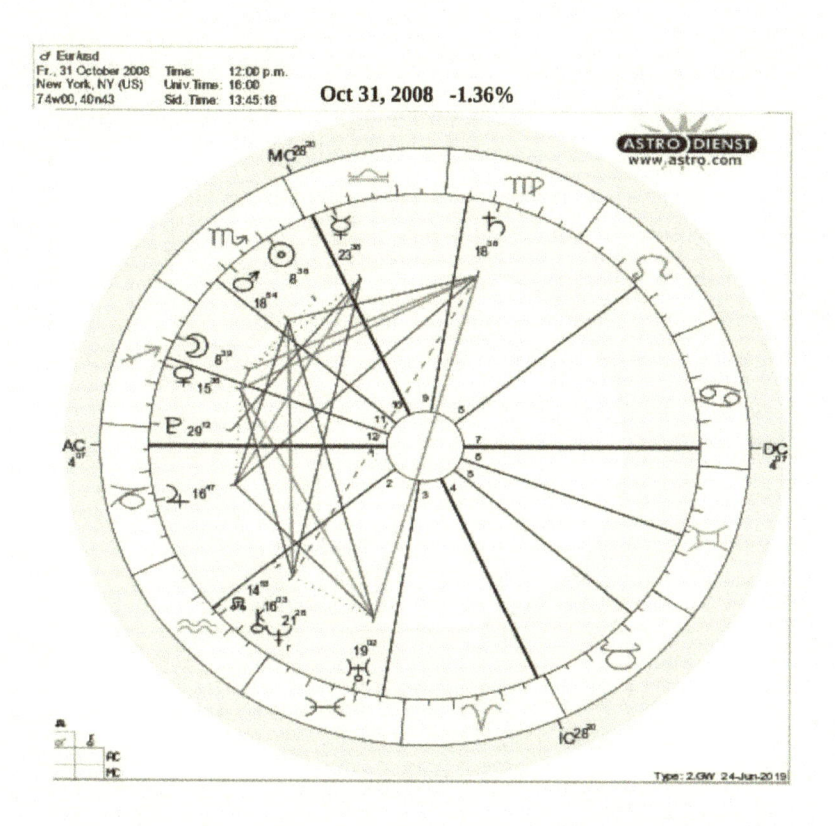

For October 31, 2008, the moon is at 8 degrees Sagittarius. The last parameter that would have applied here would be parameter 2 in **Figure 1a** which says the moon being within 1 degree of the degree of the sun in air or fire sign brings the value of Eur/Usd down. The degree of the Sun is 8 degrees and the Moon is at 8 degrees Sagittarius, which is a fire sign. This meets the conditions for parameter 2 to be the last parameter to apply which therefore provides us with an accurate assessment as the Eur/Usd dropped -1.36% on this day.

We can see in our demonstration of applying a fixed set of parameters for predicting the eur/usd for the month of October 2008 has provided us with some accurate predictions, and also a few non-accurate predictions. While the few errors hurt our confidence about the value of the entire algorithm, those errors have to be weighed against the algorithm's historical correlation. We will see how in November, the correlation of those same fixed parameters to the eur/usd keep us from drawing a conclusion that the algorithm doesn't satisfy quantitative analysis. Below are the eur/usd prices for November. We will use the significant days only.

Date	Open	Low	High	Close	Change
Nov 28, 2008	1.2698	1.2904	1.2961	1.2647	-1.51%
Nov 27, 2008	1.2893	1.2881	1.2970	1.2859	0.00%
Nov 26, 2008	1.2893	1.3064	1.3073	1.2821	-1.26%
Nov 25, 2008	1.3058	1.2929	1.3081	1.2805	1.12%
Nov 24, 2008	1.2914	1.2592	1.2930	1.2568	2.65%
Nov 21, 2008	1.2581	1.2447	1.2643	1.2425	0.99%
Nov 20, 2008	1.2458	1.2502	1.2595	1.2456	-0.52%
Nov 19, 2008	1.2523	1.2616	1.2814	1.2517	-0.78%
Nov 18, 2008	1.2622	1.2649	1.2700	1.2567	-0.20%
Nov 17, 2008	1.2647	1.2534	1.2742	1.2513	0.10%
Nov 14, 2008	1.2634	1.2787	1.2830	1.2617	-1.53%
Nov 13, 2008	1.2830	1.2505	1.2855	1.2389	2.87%
Nov 12, 2008	1.2472	1.2530	1.2636	1.2470	-0.38%
Nov 11, 2008	1.2519	1.2755	1.2801	1.2506	-1.68%
Nov 10, 2008	1.2733	1.2821	1.2930	1.2719	-0.05%
Nov 07, 2008	1.2739	1.2718	1.2853	1.2654	0.29%
Nov 06, 2008	1.2702	1.2961	1.2967	1.2702	-1.93%
Nov 05, 2008	1.2952	1.2980	1.3118	1.2792	-0.63%
Nov 04, 2008	1.3034	1.2631	1.3038	1.2527	3.09%
Nov 03, 2008	1.2643	1.2750	1.2900	1.2596	-0.71%

Change %: -0.2749

Nov 4, 2008 +3.09%

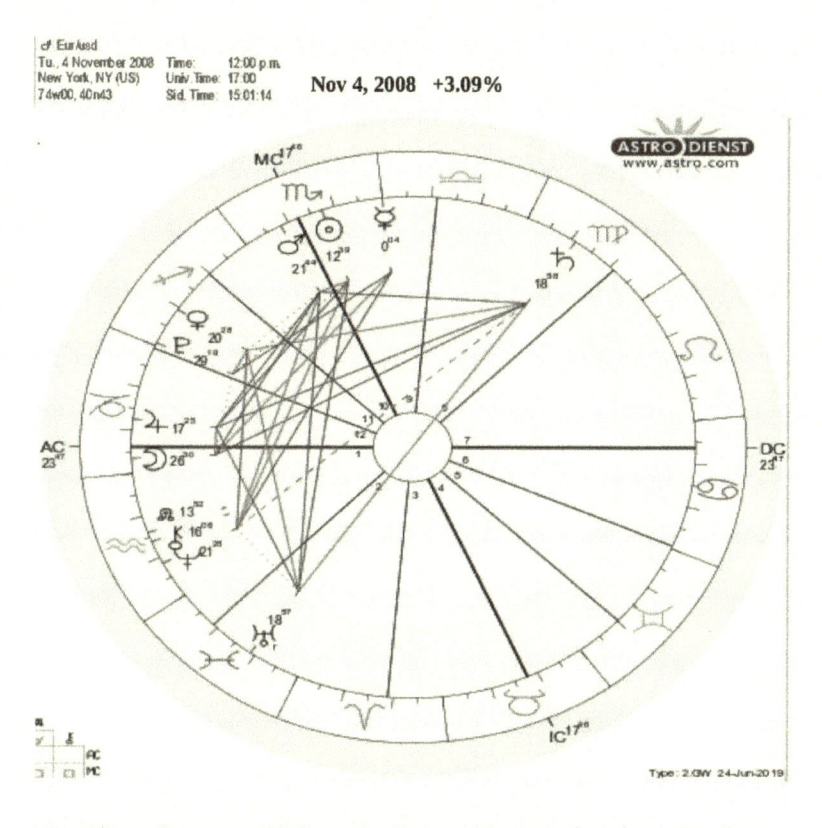

For November 4, 2008, the moon is at 26 degrees Capricorn. The last parameter that would have applied here would be parameter 5 in **Figure 1a** which says the moon being within 1 degree of the degree of the lunar node in the sign next to the sign that the lunar node is in and every other sign from that point makes the eur/usd rise. The moon at 26 degrees Capricorn would have last passed within 1 degree of the 13th degree in Capricorn, which would be the degree of the lunar node. Capricorn is on the path related to every other sign from the sign that's next to the sign that the lunar node is in. With the lunar node in Aquarius, the sign next to it is Pisces and every other sign from Pisces eventually takes us to Capricorn. Therefore, the conditions for that parameter are fulfilled and the prediction of the eur/usd going up as a result is correct. The eur/usd was up +3.09%

Nov 6, 2008 -1.93%

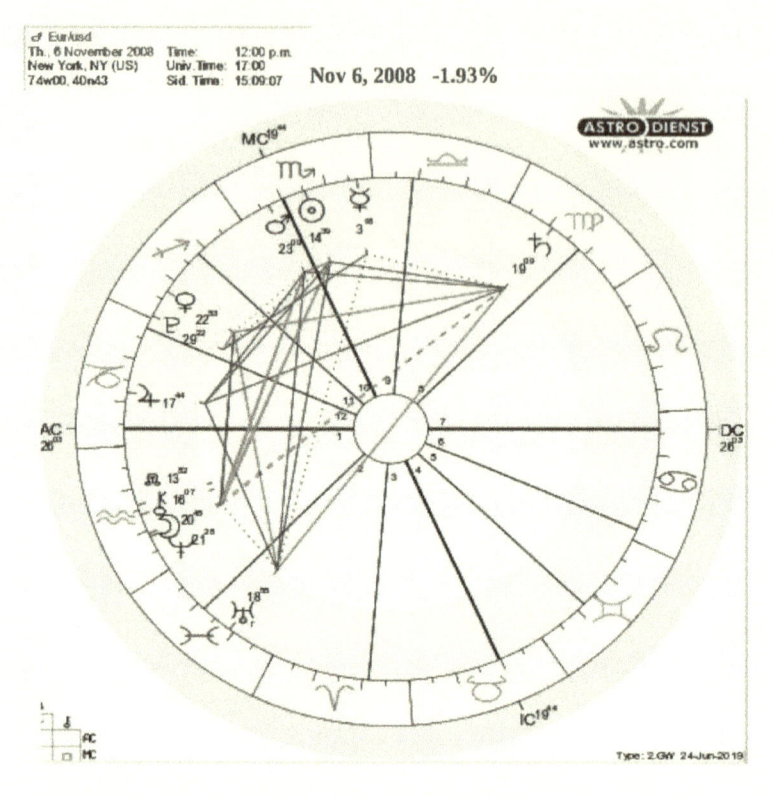

For November 6, 2008, the moon is at 20 degrees Aquarius. The last parameter that would have applied here would be parameter 2 in **Figure 1a** which says the moon being within 1 degree of the degree of the sun in an air of fire sign brings the value of Eur/Usd down. Since the moon is at 20 degrees Aquarius, it would have last passed within 1 degree of the Sun's degree(which is the 14th degree) in Aquarius, which is an air sign. This fulfills the conditions of parameter 2 and therefore makes the prediction of a Eur/Usd drop turn out correct. The Eur/Usd was down -1.93% on this day.

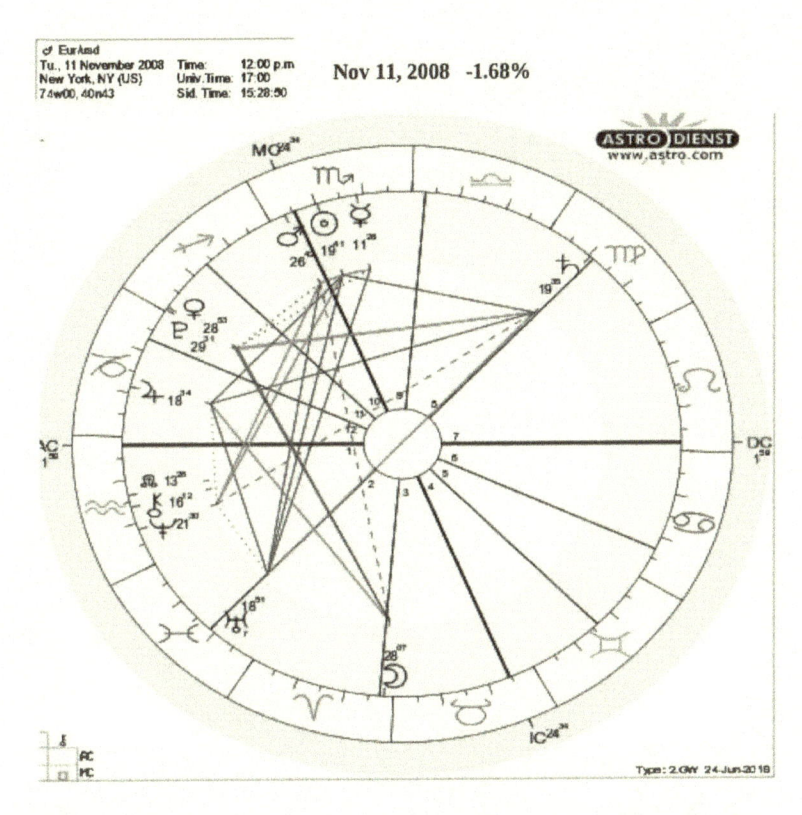

Nov 11, 2008 -1.68%

For November 11, 2008, the moon is at 28 degrees in Aries. The last parameter that would have applied here would be parameter 2 in **Figure 1a** which says the moon being within 1 degree of the degree of the sun in an air or fire sign brings the value of Eur/Usd down. Since the moon is at 28 degrees Aries, it would have last passed within 1 degree of the Sun's degree(which is the 19th degree) in Aries, which is a fire sign. This fulfills the conditions of parameter 2 and therefore makes the prediction of a Eur/Usd drop turn out correct. The Eur/Usd was down -1.68% on this day.

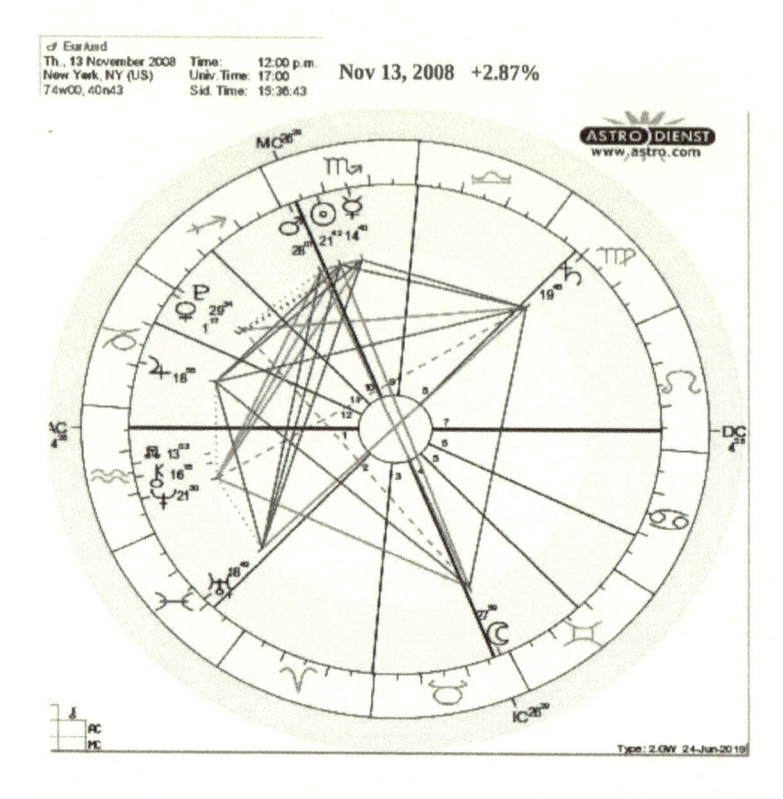

♂ EurAusd
Th., 13 November 2008   Time: 12:00 p.m.
New York, NY (US)   Univ. Time: 17:00   Nov 13, 2008 +2.87%
74w00, 40n43   Sid. Time: 15:36:43

For November 13, 2008, the moon is at 27 degrees in Taurus. The last parameter that would have applied here would be parameter 1 in **Figure 1a** which says the moon being within 1 degree of the degree of the sun in an earth or water sign brings the value of Eur/Usd up. Since the moon is at 27 degrees Taurus, it would have last passed within 1 degree of the Sun's degree(21st degree) in Taurus, which is an Earth sign. This fulfills the conditions of parameter 1 and therefore makes the prediction of a Eur/Usd rise to turn out correct. The Eur/Usd was up +2.87% on this day.

Nov 14, 2008 -1.53%

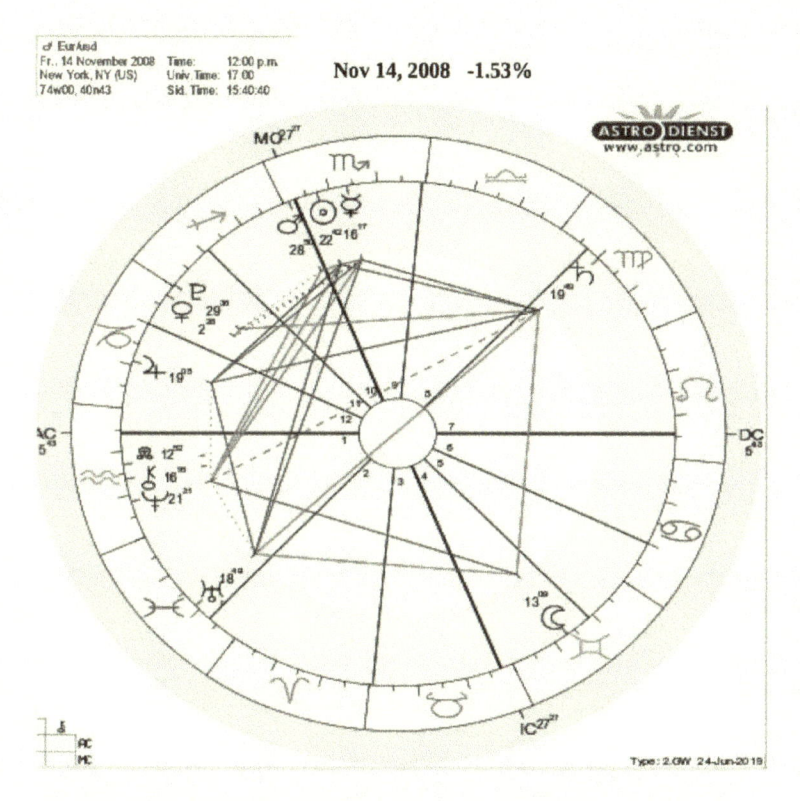

For November 14, 2008, the moon is at 13 degrees in Gemini. The last parameter that would have applied here would be parameter 4 in **Figure 1a** which says the moon being within 1 degree of the degree of the lunar node in the sign that that the lunar node is in and every other sign after that one brings the value of the EUR/USD down. Since the moon being within this 1 degree of the degree of the lunar node would have taken place in gemini and gemini is on the path of ever other sign from the sign that the lunar node is in(lunar node is in Aquarius), the conditions of the parameter 4 are fulfilled and the prediction from parameter 4 turns out correct. The Eur/Usd was down -1.53% this day.

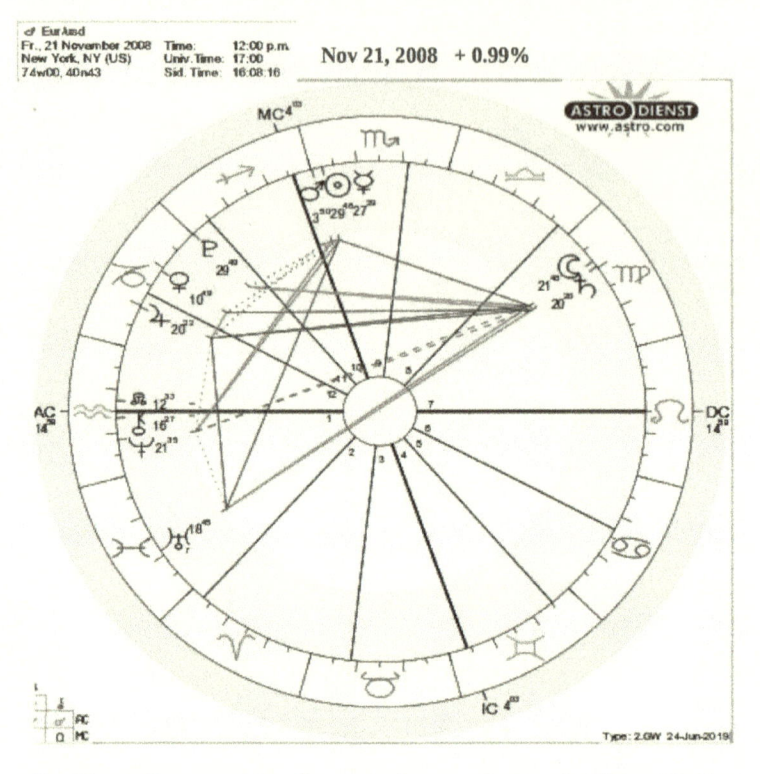

For November 21, 2008, the moon is at 21 degrees in Virgo. The last parameter that would have applied here would be parameter 5 in **Figure 1a** which says the moon being within 1 degree of the degree of the lunar node in the sign next to the sign that the lunar node is in and every other sign from that point makes the EUR/USD rise. The moon at 21 degrees virgo would have last passed within 1 degree of the 12th degree in virgo, which would be the degree of the lunar node. Virgo is on the path relative to every other sign from the sign that's next to the sign that the lunar node is in. With the lunar node in Aquarius, the sign next to it would be Pisces and every other sign from Pisces eventually takes us to Virgo. Therefore, the conditions for that parameter are fulfilled and the prediction of the eur/usd going up is correct. The Eur/Usd was up +0.99% this day.

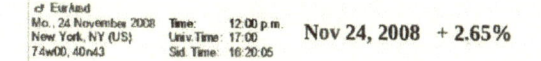

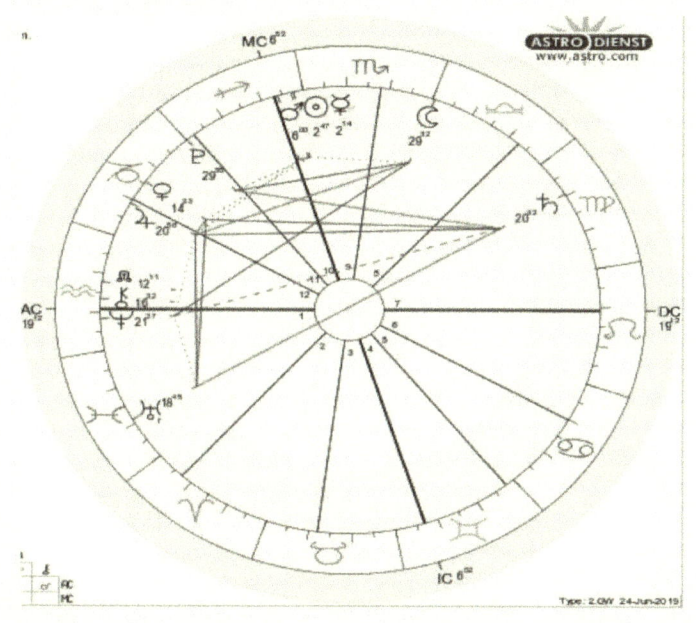

Market Prediction Algorithms for the US Dollar, the Stock Market and Bitcoin

Nov 24, 2008   + 2.65%

For November 24, 2008, the moon is at 29 degrees in Libra. The last parameter that would have applied here would be parameter 4 in **Figure 1a** which says the moon being within 1 degree of the degree of the lunar node in the sign that that the lunar node is in and every other sign after that one brings the value of the EUR/USD down. Since the moon being within this 1 degree of the degree of the lunar node would have taken place in Libra and Libra is on the path of every other sign from the sign that the lunar node is in(lunar node is in Aquarius), the conditions of the parameter 4 are fulfilled, HOWEVER, the prediction from parameter 4 turns out to be incorrect as the Eur/Usd was up on this day. It can be justified that another parameter could be involved, such as parameter 6, which says the moon within 3 degrees of the sun in an earth or water sign brings the value of Eur/usd down, however, even that would be incorrect.

Nov 25, 2008 + 1.12%

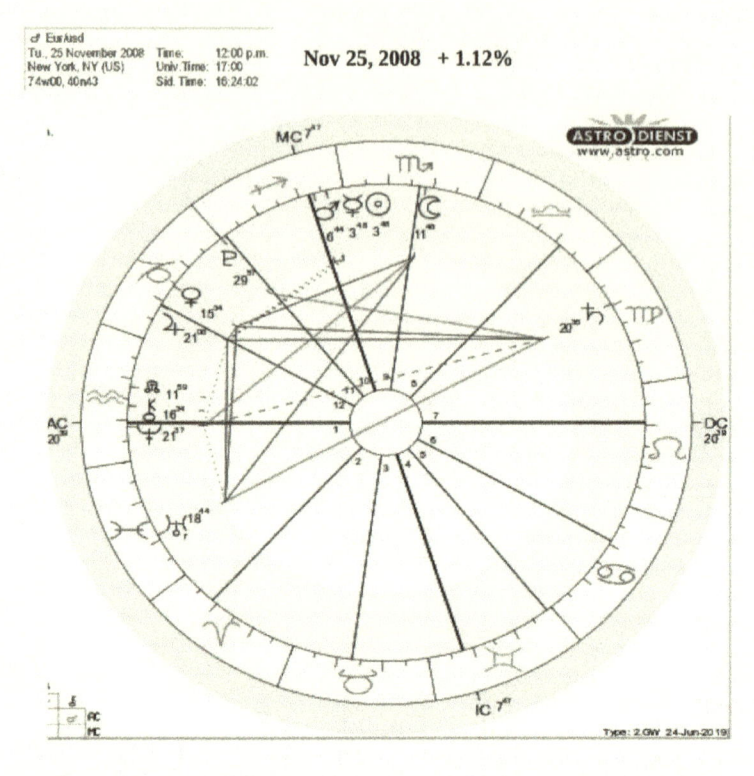

For November 25, 2008, the moon is at 11 degrees in Scorpio. The last parameter that would have applied here would be parameter 5 in **Figure 1a** which states the moon being within 1 degree of the degree of the lunar node in the sign next to the sign that the lunar node is in and every other sign from that point makes the Eur/Usd rise. The moon at 11 degrees scorpio would have last passed within 1 degree of the 11th degree in scorpio, which would be the degree of the lunar node. Scorpio is on the path relative to every other sign from the sign that's next to the sign that the lunar node is in. With the lunar node in Aquarius, the sign next to it would be Pisces and every other sign from Pisces eventually takes us to Scorpio. Therefore, the conditions for that parameter are fulfilled and the prediction of the Eur/Usd going up is correct. The Eur/Usd was up +1.12% this day.

Nov 26, 2008 -1.26%

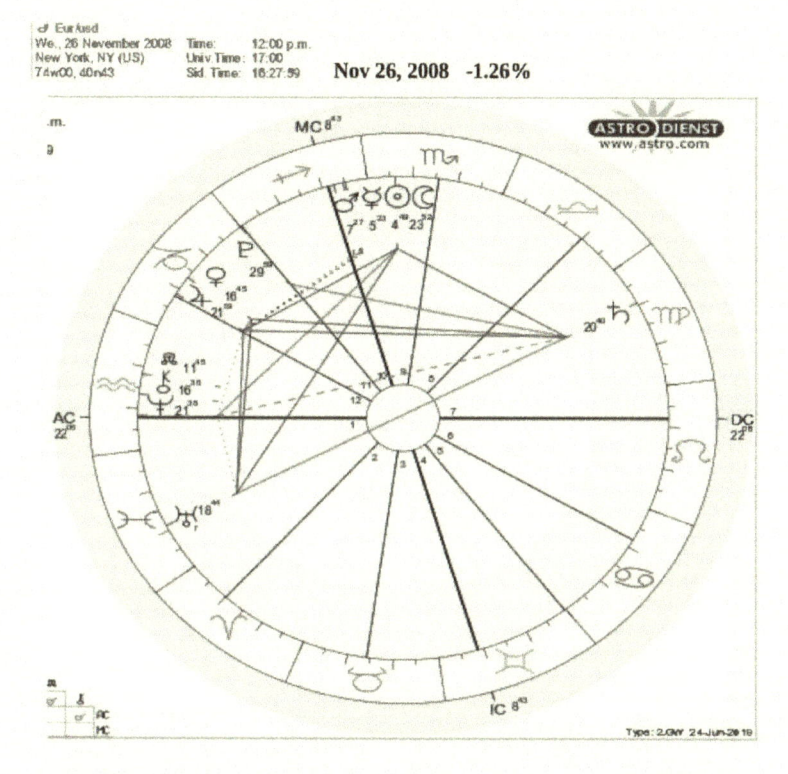

For November 26, 2008, the moon is at 23 degrees in Scorpio. The last parameter that would have applied here would be parameter 5 in **Figure 1a**. It would have applied exactly as it did the previous day on November 25th. However, in this case, the prediction for Parameter 5, which says the Eur/usd goes up, would be incorrect. The Eur/usd was actually down on this day. -1.26%

Nov 28, 2008 -1.51%

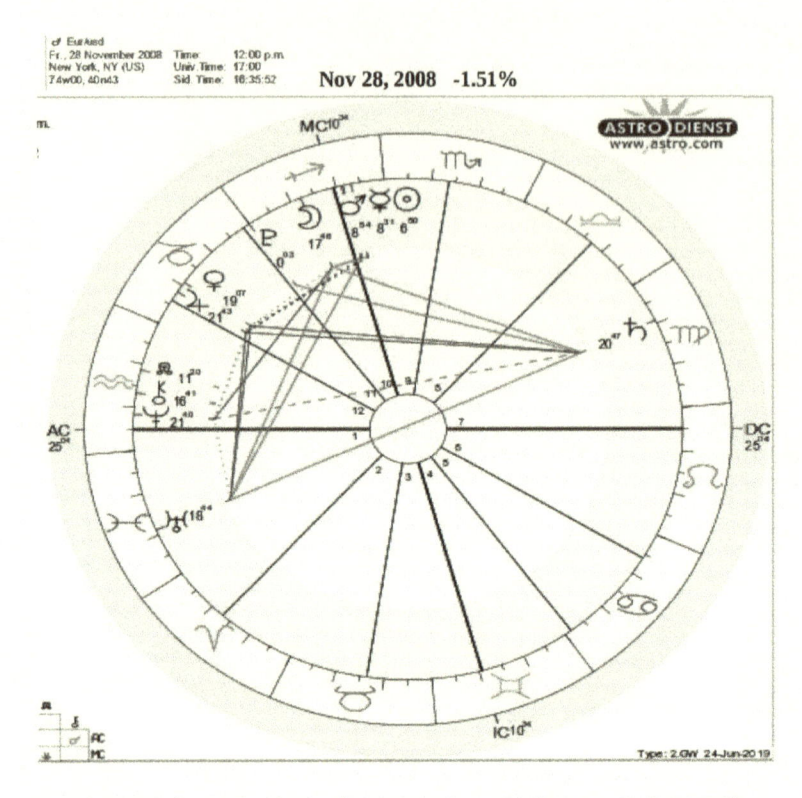

For November 28, 2008, the moon is at 17 degrees in Sagittarius. The last parameter that would have applied here would be parameter 4 in **Figure 1a** which says the moon being within 1 degree of the degree of the lunar node in the sign that the lunar node is in and every other sign after that brings the value of the Eur/usd down. Since the moon being within this 1 degree of the degree of the lunar node would have taken place in Sagittarius and Sagittarius is on the path of every other sign from the sign that the lunar node is in(lunar node is in Aquarius), the conditions of the parameter 4, as a result, are fulfilled and the prediction is correct. The Eur/usd was down -1.51%

After demonstrating November with the same algorithm that we used in October, we regain confidence that the fixed algorithm containing the 9 parameters in **Figure 1a** applies to the movements of the Eur/usd. In November, and in just the days used in this demonstration, the algorithm applied in all but 2 of the days. Back in October, the algorithm also applied most days. So even with an error here and there for predictions in October and November, its not enough to discount the fixed parameters as applicable due to the fact that it actually applied for most days where the price change was significant. Of course these particular examples relate to predictions for the Eur/usd in terms of what would be the final outcome at the end of the day relative to the previous day. Meaning, as stated before, the calculated chart for 12pm New York and its layout of the positions of the moon, lunar node, and mercury and how they are defined by the parameters in terms of prediction, is what is used to predict where the value of the Eur/usd would finish that day relative to where it was the day before. Of course, the parameters can also be used in real time. Meaning, the time that the actual parameter takes place can be applied to a prediction for the Eur/usd at that very time. For example, if the chart for 4am ET New York shows the moon meeting the condition of a parameter right at that time, then the parameter's prediction for what the price will do can be applied at that very time. If 3 hours later, the moon meets the conditions of another parameter then the prediction for that parameter can be applied. Anyone familiar with forex trading would understand this as signals.

Note: Historically, I find the lunar node's degree can be held constant in the fire/air signs and used to predict a subsequent EUR/USD downturn when the moon is within one degree of the lunar node's degree in any fire/air sign. It can also be used to predict a subsequent EUR/USD upswing when the moon is within one degree of the lunar node's degree in any earth/water sign. Just simply replace the 4th and 5th parameters from Figure 1a with this one in order to test it with the algorithm.

Volume II:

Stock Market Prediction Algorithm

The previous examples of market prediction techniques were only examples of stock market prediction at the micro level. This official economic engineering mandate will explain the nature of the market in both a macro and micro sense. It will also present a working model for predicting recessions successfully. The parameters for this algorithm are straightforward and simple. It outlines the basic factor for a market upswing, market downswing, boom, and recession.

Previously, we discussed the lunar nodes and their effect on the market in tandem with the sun, moon, and mercury. This one, however, is a basic economic plan that revolves simply around the lunar node and the sun. The parameters go as follows:

Figure C – Keep this page referenced for the upcoming examples. There are 4 parameters below

1. When the degree of the sun is lower than the degree of the lunar node, there is a market downturn,

2. When the degree of the sun is higher than the degree of the lunar node, there is a market upswing.

3. when the lunar node is between the 8th degree and the 24 degree as it travels backward(8, 7, 6, 5, 4 , 3 ,2, 1, 0, 29, 28, 27, 26, 25, 24), the market is in a boom.

4. when the lunar node is between the 23rd degree and the 9th degree as it travels backwards(23, 22, 21, 20, 19, 18, 17, 16, 15, 14, 13, 12, 11, 10, 9) the market is in recession.

*Reminder: new sign starts at the 24th degree, and the lunar nodes travel backward through the zodiac. Make sure to keep this page referenced for Figure C parameters.

These next 4 diagrams are examples of when and how each parameter applies.

Here is an example of how parameter 1 from Figure C applies, which says when the sun's degree is lower than the lunar node's degree, the market drops.

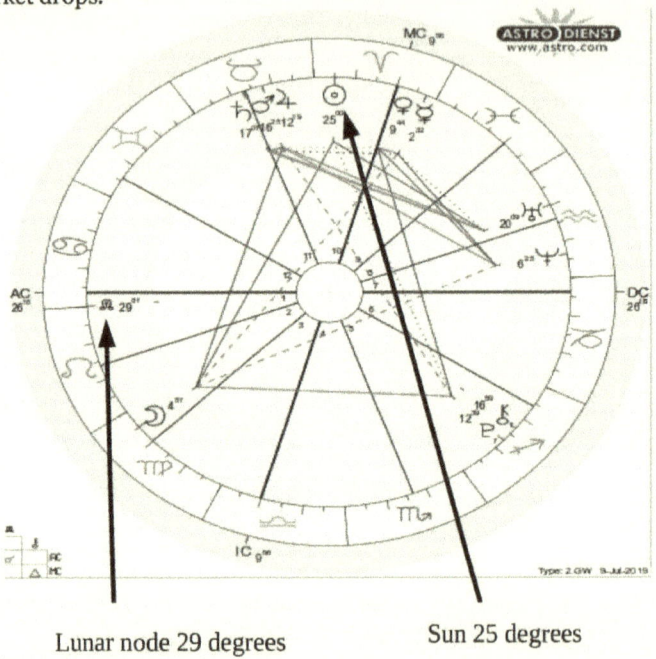

Lunar node 29 degrees   Sun 25 degrees

We can see that the sun's degree at 25 is lower than the lunar node's degree at 29. Therefore over the next few days before the sun's degree goes higher than the lunar node's, which it would do in 5 days from that 25th degree point, the market would be predicted to average lower. That would fulfill parameter 1. When the sun would reach the 30th or 0th degree mark of the sign its in, the market would be predicted to average higher because then it would be higher than the degree of the lunar node, which is at 29. That would fulfill parameter 2. With the lunar node at 29 degrees, the market would be considered in a boom phase since parameter 3 states that when the lunar node is between the 8th degree and the 24th degree as it travels backwards, the market is in a boom. When the lunar nodes would reach the 23rd degree mark, the phase of the market in a macro sense would change to recession as parameter 4 says when the lunar node is between the 23rd degree and the 9th degree as it travels backwards, the market phase is recession. Important to remember the lunar node travels backwards through the zodiac. We will start with the year 2000. Here are the prices of the S&P futures for January 2000. The total drop was – 5.61%

Date	Open	High	Low	Close	Volume	Change
Jan 31, 2000	1,401.00	1,365.25	1,403.00	1,357.00	64.07K	2.52%
Jan 28, 2000	1,366.50	1,411.00	1,420.00	1,361.25	70.01K	-3.07%
Jan 27, 2000	1,409.75	1,412.50	1,428.50	1,388.00	71.79K	-0.37%
Jan 26, 2000	1,415.00	1,417.50	1,422.75	1,408.25	58.34K	-0.18%
Jan 25, 2000	1,417.50	1,411.00	1,424.75	1,397.50	76.34K	0.41%
Jan 24, 2000	1,411.75	1,454.00	1,468.50	1,403.25	71.54K	-2.89%
Jan 21, 2000	1,453.75	1,455.25	1,463.25	1,449.25	58.52K	-0.22%
Jan 20, 2000	1,457.00	1,472.75	1,485.00	1,448.00	77.21K	-1.05%
Jan 19, 2000	1,472.50	1,468.75	1,474.00	1,450.25	57.79K	0.20%
Jan 18, 2000	1,469.50	1,478.00	1,480.25	1,462.00	65.45K	-0.58%
Jan 14, 2000	1,478.00	1,461.50	1,485.00	1,455.50	57.41K	1.34%
Jan 13, 2000	1,458.50	1,441.50	1,466.75	1,441.25	57.55K	1.14%
Jan 12, 2000	1,442.00	1,453.50	1,459.50	1,438.75	62.51K	-0.84%
Jan 11, 2000	1,454.25	1,473.75	1,475.00	1,447.00	70.10K	-1.41%
Jan 10, 2000	1,475.00	1,459.75	1,481.00	1,454.25	59.34K	0.99%
Jan 07, 2000	1,460.50	1,403.75	1,461.50	1,397.50	60.55K	4.02%
Jan 06, 2000	1,404.00	1,411.00	1,426.25	1,395.75	67.88K	-0.67%
Jan 05, 2000	1,413.50	1,411.50	1,427.25	1,385.00	73.12K	0.12%
Jan 04, 2000	1,411.75	1,467.00	1,468.75	1,409.50	64.05K	-3.75%
Jan 03, 2000	1,466.75	1,489.00	1,496.00	1,452.25	61.94K	-1.18%

Change %: -5.61

*all astro charts calculated using 12am ET time, New York, New york

Here is the chart layout for January 3rd. We see the sun's degree(12) is higher than the lunar node's(3). In Figure C, this means that parameter 2 applies and the market will upswing while the sun is in this position relative to the lunar node.

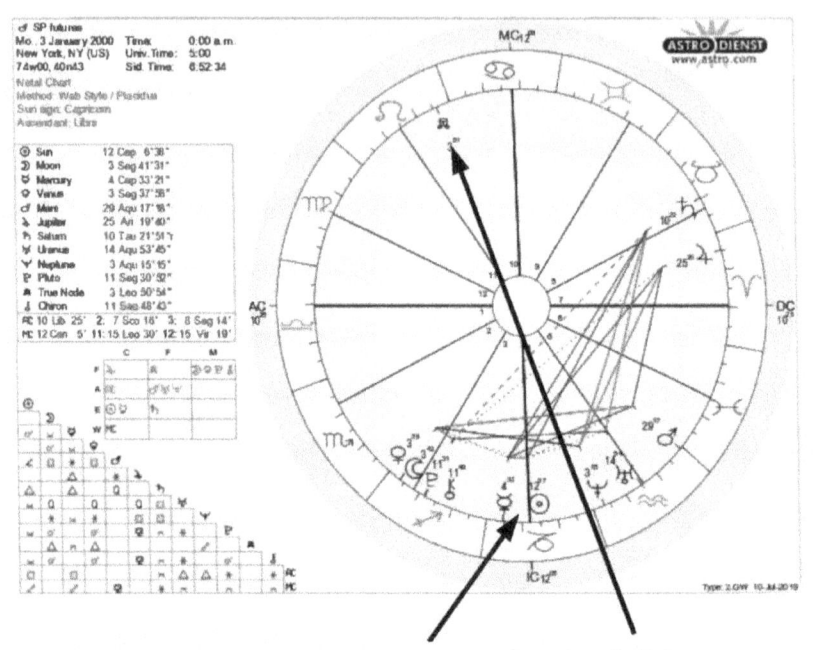

Sun 12 degrees   Lunar node 3 degrees

The sun will remain in this position relative to the lunar node from January 3 until January 14. So, during that time there should be a market upswing. From January 3rd to January 14th, the S&P futures didn't go up. They actually dropped slightly 0.42%.

On January 15th a new parameter applies as the sun enters a new sign at the 24th degree mark and is now less than the degree of the lunar node. It will stay in that position relative to the lunar node until January 24. Therefore, a downswing is predicted to occur during that time.

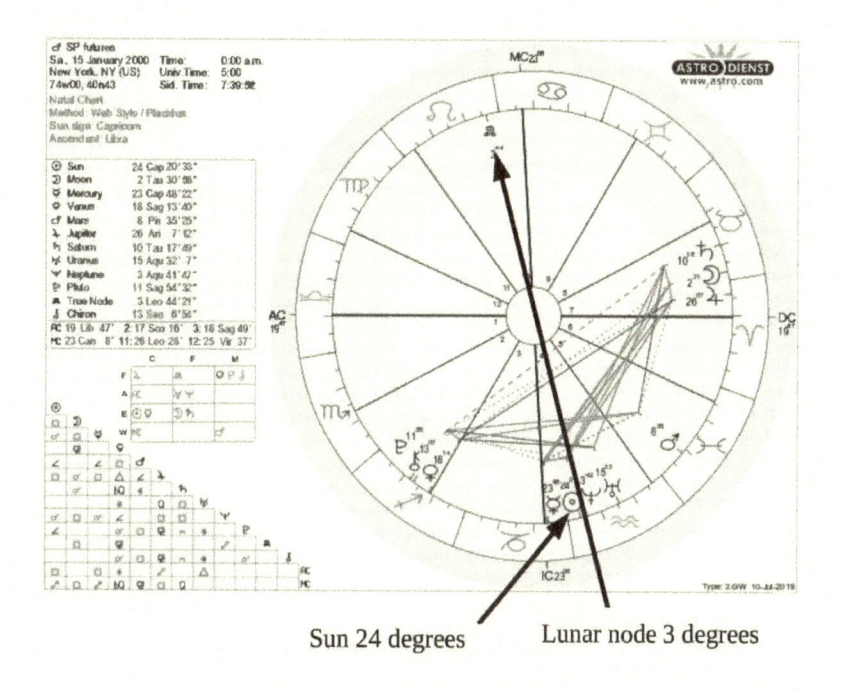

Sun 24 degrees   Lunar node 3 degrees

We can see in the chart above, the sun at 24 degrees(new sign starts at 24 degrees) is the less than the lunar node at 3 degrees. This position of the sun relative to lunar node will last until the 24th. This means parameter 1 from Figure C is in effect, which implies a market drop. From January 15th – January 24th, the s&p 500 futures dropped -4.48% during that time, which gives us a correct prediction.

On January 25th, when sun's degree becomes higher than the lunar nodes, parameter 2 from Figure C is then applied and a market upswing is expected to occur during that time. The sun in that position relative to the lunar node will stay that way through the end of the month of January.

Lunar node 3 degree   Sun 4 degrees

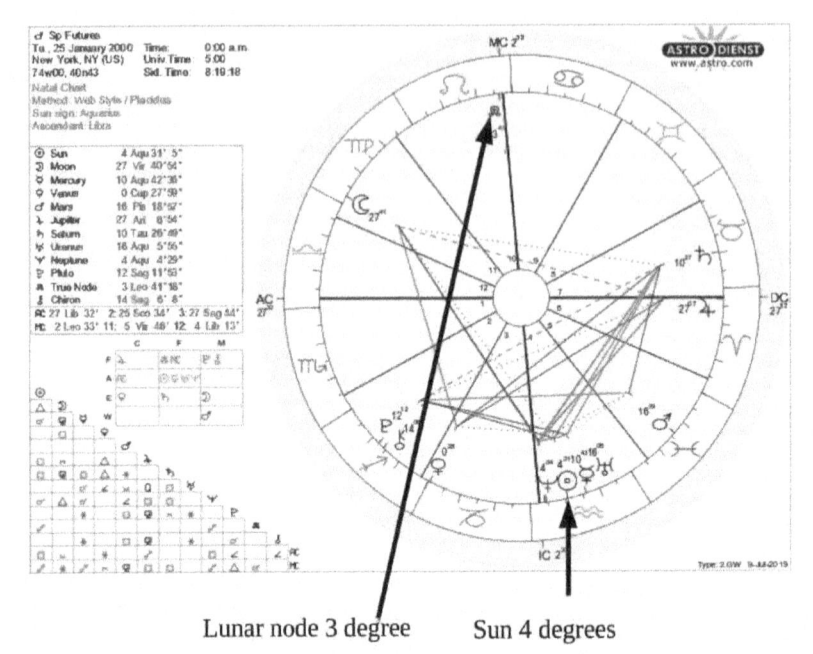

From January 25 until the end of the month, the S&P 500 futures didn't go up as predicted by parameter 2 in Figure C, but only dropped slightly -0.76%.

Using the parameters in Figure C has resulted us with just a -1.18% drop in January compared to the actual market drop of -5.61%.

We can move on to February and continue with the parameters in Figure C. On the next page are the S&P futures prices for February, 2000.

Feb 29, 2000	1,372.00	1,349.25	1,374.00	1,348.00	66.80K	1.80%
Feb 28, 2000	1,347.75	1,337.50	1,366.00	1,327.50	82.74K	0.73%
Feb 25, 2000	1,338.00	1,355.75	1,366.50	1,331.00	73.99K	-1.13%
Feb 24, 2000	1,353.25	1,365.00	1,370.00	1,331.00	81.16K	-0.88%
Feb 23, 2000	1,365.25	1,349.25	1,374.25	1,344.50	69.61K	1.20%
Feb 22, 2000	1,349.00	1,352.50	1,363.75	1,336.50	79.20K	-0.31%
Feb 18, 2000	1,353.25	1,386.75	1,393.50	1,349.00	63.49K	-2.33%
Feb 17, 2000	1,385.50	1,392.75	1,407.00	1,384.25	65.71K	-0.52%
Feb 16, 2000	1,392.75	1,410.00	1,413.50	1,390.25	70.14K	-1.22%
Feb 15, 2000	1,410.00	1,399.00	1,414.75	1,381.00	79.71K	0.80%
Feb 14, 2000	1,398.75	1,396.25	1,403.50	1,386.75	66.87K	0.14%
Feb 11, 2000	1,396.75	1,418.50	1,426.50	1,384.25	72.33K	-1.59%
Feb 10, 2000	1,419.25	1,418.75	1,429.25	1,412.25	68.75K	0.07%
Feb 09, 2000	1,418.25	1,448.00	1,454.75	1,417.00	77.38K	-1.94%
Feb 08, 2000	1,446.25	1,427.25	1,449.50	1,425.50	62.72K	1.33%
Feb 07, 2000	1,427.25	1,429.50	1,433.25	1,419.00	60.55K	-0.30%
Feb 04, 2000	1,431.50	1,436.50	1,449.50	1,426.50	60.84K	-0.35%
Feb 03, 2000	1,436.50	1,415.75	1,438.25	1,405.25	75.19K	1.48%
Feb 02, 2000	1,415.50	1,416.75	1,429.50	1,410.00	52.67K	-0.09%
Feb 01, 2000	1,416.75	1,402.75	1,421.75	1,391.25	58.19K	1.12%

Change %: -2.07

So far using just our parameters from Figure C, we are only down -1.18%, while the actual market is down -5.61% as of the end of January. During this month of February, the S&P futures dropped -2.07%. Here is the chart for Feb 1, 2000.

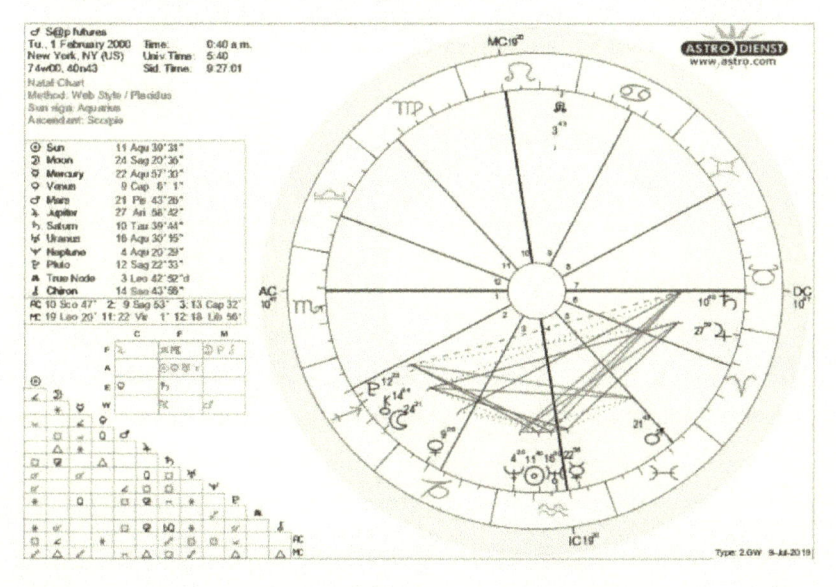

In February, we pick up where left off in January. The chart for Feb 1 on previous page shows that parameter 2 from Figure C would still apply, which predicts a market upswing during the time the sun's degree is higher than the lunar node's. This position of the sun's degree relative to the lunar node's remains in place until February 14, when the sun enters a new sign. From February 1st to February 13th, the S&P futures didn't go up as predicted, but only dropped -0.30%.

On February 14th, a new parameter is applied

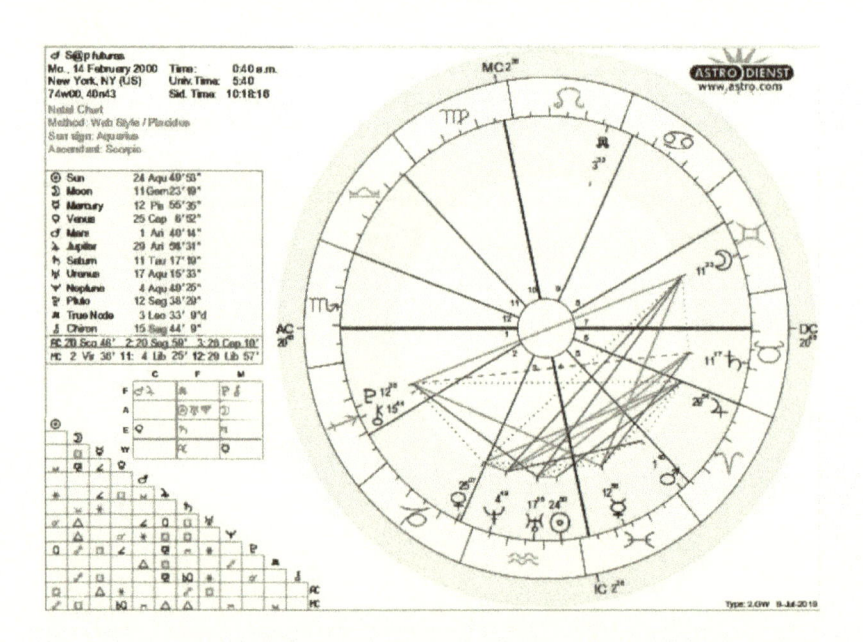

At 24 degrees, the sun's degree is now lower than the lunar node's degree. This means that parameter 1 from Figure C applies, which predicts a market downturn throughout the time the sun's degree is lower than the lunar node's. Its not until February 23rd that this position of the sun's degree relative to the lunar node changes. So from February 14th to February 22nd, if we check to see if the average for S&P futures was lower during that time, we find out that the market does drop during that time: -3.42%. This makes our prediction correct. So now we go to February 23rd, when the sun's degree relative to the Lunar node's changes.

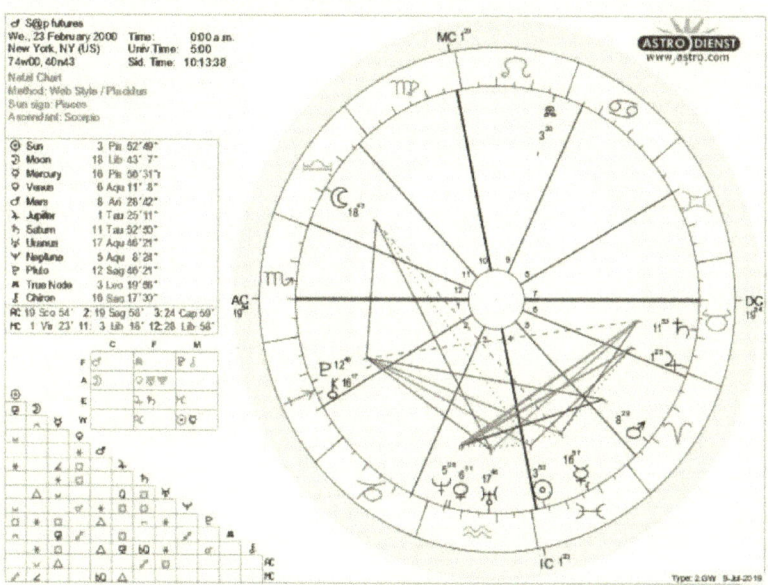

We can see in the chart of Feb 23rd that the Sun's degree(3) is now higher than the lunar node's degree(3). This means that parameter 2 from Figure C applies and a market upswing is predicted. Since the sun's degree remains in this position relative to the lunar node's through the end of the month, we can just check to see what the S&P does between February 23 and the end of the month on February 29th. During that time, the S&P did rise. It went up +1.70%. The prediction was correct. So now with February completed, its safe to say we beat the market with Figure C parameters, as they resulted in a +1.40% uptick, while the actual market dropped -2.07% in February. It would also be a good time to interject that since the lunar node is between the 24th degree, and the 8th degree, the current macro phase would be boom.

Here are the prices for the month of March, 2000

Date						
Mar 31, 2000	1,515.25	1,505.25	1,538.75	1,501.00	58.52K	0.73%
Mar 30, 2000	1,504.25	1,529.50	1,535.00	1,493.50	67.21K	-1.72%
Mar 29, 2000	1,530.50	1,529.25	1,541.25	1,515.00	60.10K	0.02%
Mar 28, 2000	1,530.25	1,540.00	1,549.50	1,523.00	61.00K	-0.54%
Mar 27, 2000	1,538.50	1,552.25	1,554.50	1,536.00	48.06K	-1.09%
Mar 24, 2000	1,555.50	1,542.75	1,574.25	1,535.25	67.50K	0.74%
Mar 23, 2000	1,544.00	1,517.25	1,553.00	1,510.00	68.60K	1.75%
Mar 22, 2000	1,517.50	1,508.00	1,525.25	1,504.00	63.80K	0.66%
Mar 21, 2000	1,507.50	1,477.50	1,514.25	1,463.25	69.38K	2.00%
Mar 20, 2000	1,478.00	1,486.00	1,490.50	1,466.75	58.30K	1.83%
Mar 17, 2000	1,451.48	1,461.75	1,465.00	1,454.50	0.30K	-0.52%
Mar 16, 2000	1,459.00	1,396.00	1,469.00	1,395.75	1.13K	4.57%
Mar 15, 2000	1,395.25	1,361.75	1,398.75	1,356.75	1.38K	2.42%
Mar 14, 2000	1,362.25	1,380.25	1,395.75	1,359.50	1.21K	-1.54%
Mar 13, 2000	1,383.50	1,398.00	1,415.75	1,364.75	2.03K	-1.14%
Mar 10, 2000	1,399.50	1,403.25	1,415.50	1,394.25	3.19K	-0.34%
Mar 09, 2000	1,404.25	1,367.00	1,405.00	1,357.50	7.15K	2.78%
Mar 08, 2000	1,366.25	1,352.75	1,376.00	1,348.50	73.91K	1.07%
Mar 07, 2000	1,351.75	1,394.50	1,404.50	1,351.00	85.26K	-3.10%
Mar 06, 2000	1,395.00	1,411.00	1,412.75	1,386.25	59.86K	-1.12%
Mar 03, 2000	1,410.75	1,384.75	1,414.50	1,383.50	65.43K	1.86%
Mar 02, 2000	1,385.00	1,384.25	1,390.50	1,372.50	62.49K	0.00%
Mar 01, 2000	1,385.00	1,372.25	1,388.75	1,371.00	60.89K	0.95%

Change %: 10.44

In March, the S&P future rose 10.44%. Lets see how the parameter from Figure C held up this month.

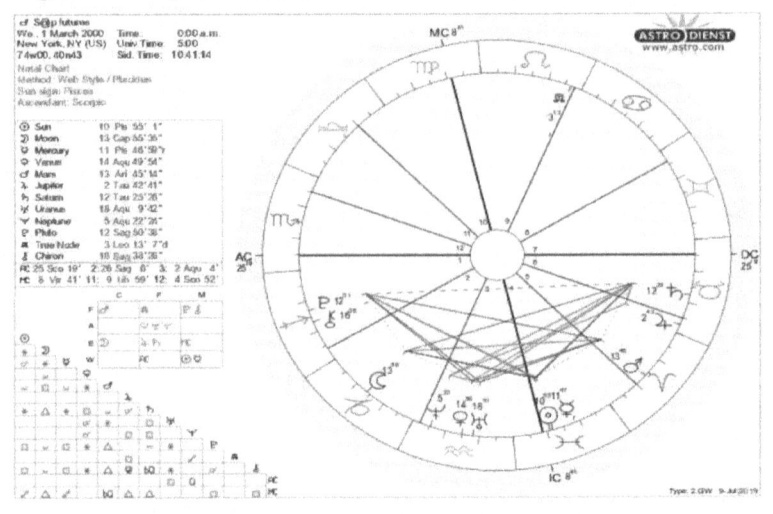

In the beginning of March, we pick up where we left off in February. We can see in the chart on the previous page that the sun's degree is higher than the lunar node's. This means parameter 2 from Figure C applies along with the prediction of a market upswing. The position of the sun's degree relative to the lunar node's remains in place through March 13th. So from March 1st to March 13th, we check to see if the prediction was accurate. During that time, the S&P futures rose 0.84%. So the prediction was accurate. On March 14th(chart below) the position of the sun's degree changes relative to the Lunar node's.

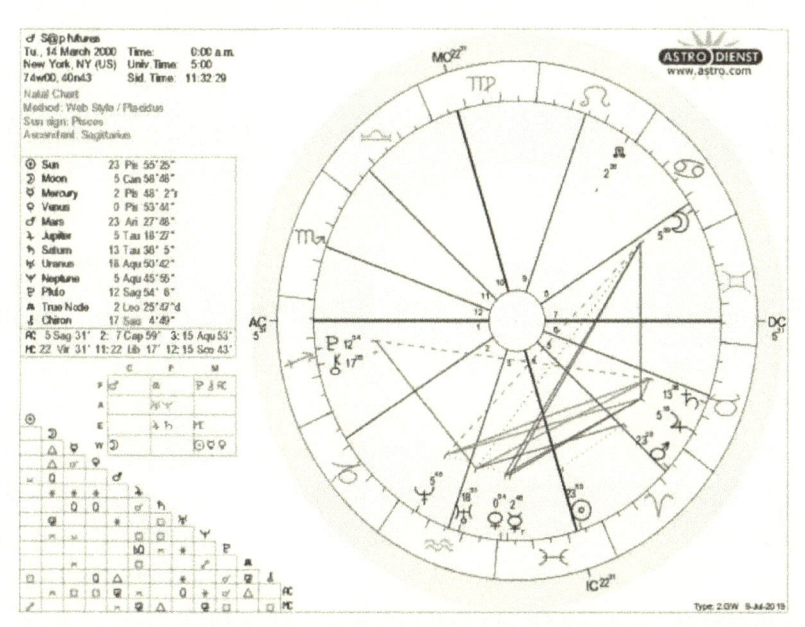

So now with the sun's degree lower than the lunar node's, parameter 1 is applied and the prediction of a market downturn is made. This position of the sun's degree relative to the lunar node's stays in place until March 21st. From March 14th to March 21st, the S&P futures actually rose considerably +8.96%. So our prediction was a bit off here.

The next position of the sun's degree relative to the lunar node takes place on March 22nd as shown below

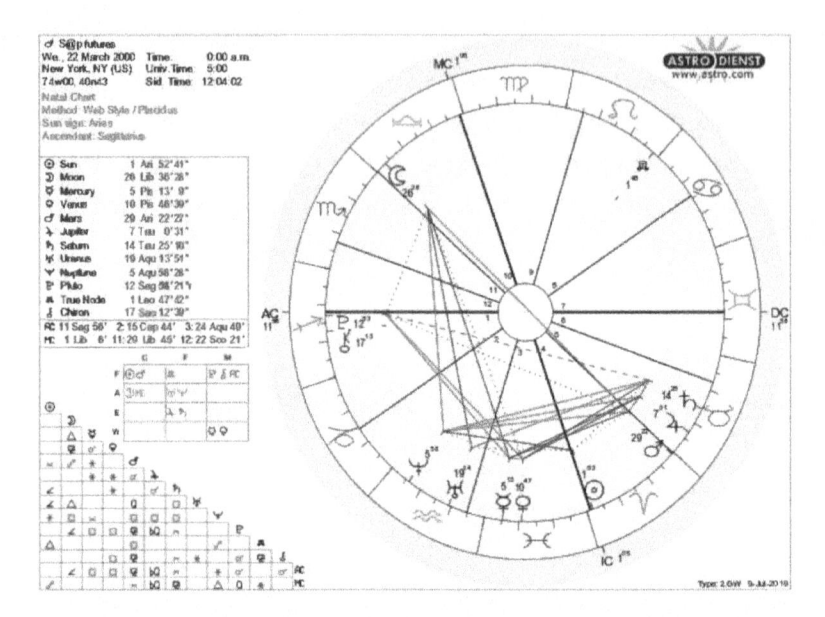

With the sun's degree(1) moving higher than the lunar node's(1), we apply parameter 2 from March 22nd until the end of the month. Parameter 2 says the market goes up during that time when sun's degree is higher than the lunar node's. From March 22nd until the end of the month, the S&P futures rose only slightly +0.51%. So the prediction is correct, but the actual market beat out the parameters in Figure C for the month of March. The actual market was up 10% and our applied parameters were only up 1%. While this is discouraging, we still have our macro assessment of the economy at boom, which is being fulfilled with the degree of the lunar node currently at 2 degrees, which is between the 8th degree and the 24th degree as it goes backwards(8, 7, 6, 5, 4, 3, 2, 1, 0, 29, 28, 27, 26, 25, 24). This means that parameter 3 in Figure C is in effect which assesses that position as a boom phase for the market.

*The monthly results below under the "Figure C parameters(1&2)" are measured in terms of theoretically only investing during times in which the applicable parameter from Figure C predicts a market upswing, while not investing in times when the applicable parameter from Figure C predicts a market downturn. The monthly results under "

Actual Market" are how the S&P really performed that month. Figure C parameters are calculated using astrocharts calculated for New York, New York, 12am ET and applied to the month according to the applicable parameters

S&P futures year:2000

	Figure C parameters(1 & 2)	Actual Market
April	-2.04%	-3.65%
May	-5.09%	-2.59%
June	+3.24 %	+3.22%
July	-1.98 %	-1.98%
August	+5.51%	+5.72%
September	+0.00%	-4.44%
October	+3.48%	-0.93%
November	-0.41%	-8.45%
December	+0.43%	+1.02%

On August 30, 2000, the lunar node went backwards into the next sign at the 23rd degree mark. This invoked Parameter 4 in Figure C, which says that when the degree of the lunar node is between the 9th degree and the 23rd degree, the market is in recession. From August 30 all the way until the end of the year, the market dropped -12%. So basically from August 30th to the end of the year, our parameters in Figure C allowed us to correctly assess the market in a macro sense and also outperform the actual market in a micro sense. Before that, from January 2000 to August 30, 2000, the overall market phase was up 1.30%. Using Figure C parameters during that time, we were able to accurately assess the market in a macro sense, but not very well in a micro sense.

We will do the same for 2001 and just post the statistics using Figure C Parameters.

*The monthly results below under the "Figure C parameters(1&2)" are measured in terms of theoretically only investing during times in which the applicable parameter from Figure C predicts a market upswing, while not investing in times when the applicable parameter from Figure C predicts a market downturn. The monthly results under "Actual Market" are how the S&P really performed that month. Figure C parameters are calculated using astrocharts calculated for New York, New York, 12am ET and applied to the month according to the applicable parameters

S&P futures year:2001

	Figure C parameters(1 & 2)	Actual Market
January	+1.97 %	+2.85%
February	-2.35 %	-9.54%
March	-3.04	-5.86
April	+1.97	+7.27
May	-1.78%	+0.26%
June	-2.46	-2.05%
July	-0.08%	-1.34
August	-6.69	-6.60
September	+7.63	-8.04
October	+4.24	+1.63
November	+7.97	+7.47
December	-0.86	+0.81

On April 20, 2001, the lunar node went backwards into the 8th degree mark, which implies parameter 3 from Figure C, which predicts a market boom phase. The previous recession phase which started on August 20th 2000 and ended April 20, 2001 did as predicted. The market dropped 17% during that time. The new boom phase is not going as predicted so far from April 20, 2001 until the end of the year. Market actually dropped overall -8%. However, our micro predictions did well compared to actual S&P results on a monthly basis in 2001 particularly in September/October.

*The monthly results below under the "Figure C parameters(1&2)" are measured in terms of theoretically only investing during times in which the applicable parameter from Figure C predicts a market upswing, while not investing in times when the applicable parameter from Figure C predicts a market downturn. The monthly results under "Actual Market" are how the S&P really performed that month. Figure C parameters are calculated using astrocharts calculated for New York, New York, 12am ET and applied to the month according to the applicable parameters

S&P futures year:2002

	Figure C parameters(1 & 2)	Actual Market
January	+0.52 %	-1.64%
February	-2.66%	-2.07%
March	-0.13%	+3.82%
April	-0.76%	-6.26%
May	+1.10%	-0.91%
June	-1.87%	-7.26%
July	-5.32%	-7.93%
August	+2.46%	+0.49%
September	+1.10%	-11.03%
October	+7.13%	+8.65%
November	+1.17%	+5.70%
December	-5.01 %	-6.19

On February 28, 2002, the lunar node went backwards into the 23rd degree mark, which starts a new recession phase according to parameter 4 from Figure C. The previous predicted boom phase from April 20th 2001 – February 28, 2002 was wrong as the market did not result in a rise, but actually dropped -12.30% during that time. However, the predicted recession phase according to Parameter 4 in Figure C which started on February 28, 2002 and ended on November 1st 2002 did as predicted as the market dropped 20% during that time. At the micro level for 2002, Figure C parameters do well on a month to month basis and outperforms the actual market in a critical months like September, while keeping up with the rare upswings during that time.

So far, we can see that the parameters from Figure C are a viable metric for predicting the market at a micro and macro level. There are times when the predictions are wrong, however, when looking at the big picture at least from our examples from the year 2000 – 2002 when the market dropped, we can asses that the predictions were correct enough to warn about a significant drop during a recession phase, even if the boom phase predictions were off. We can also see the various times when the parameters from Figure C were able to outperform the market significantly at a micro level. In the month of September for 2001 and 2002, when the marked dropped significantly...-8% for 2001, and -11% for 2002, the parameters applied from Figure C accordingly during that month of September resulted in a +7% jump for sept 2001, and a +1% jump for September of 2002.

We left off in 2002 with the market predicted to be in a boom phase starting in November 2nd of 2002 when the lunar node went to the 8th degree mark, which invokes parameter 3 from Figure C. So far from that point till the end of the year, market is down 2.17%...not necessarily a boom, but also not that bad. However, the predicted boom phase still has some time to go . On the next page we will pick up from 2003.

*The monthly results below under the "Figure C parameters(1&2)" are measured in terms of theoretically only investing during times in which the applicable parameter from Figure C predicts a market upswing, while not investing in times when the applicable parameter from Figure C predicts a market downturn. The monthly results under "Actual Market" are how the S&P really performed that month. Figure C parameters are calculated using astrocharts calculated for New York, New York, 12am ET and applied to the month according to the applicable parameters

S&P futures year:2003

	Figure C parameters(1 & 2)	Actual Market
January	+6.29 %	-2.76%
February	-5.19%	1.61%
March	-5.44%	+0.71%
April	+7.18%	+8.15%
May	+8.09%	+4.79%
June	-0.08%	+1.04%
July	+2.10%	+1.64%
August	-0.23%	+1.87%
September	-0.22%	-1.36%
October	-0.93 %	+5.58%
November	-0.85%	+0.79%
December	+0.09	+4.49%

Our boom phase did as predicted by the parameter 3 in Figure C. Between November 2, 2002, when the lunar node went to the 8th degree mark, all the way until August 27, 2003 when it went to the 24th degree mark, the market was up 10% during that time. From that point of August 27, 2003, the market is predicted for recession. So far at the end of 2003 from that August 27th point, the market is up 10 percent, which is not according to the prediction, but there is still some time to go. Figure C parameters in Micro month-to-month had some issues keeping up with some of the upswings.

*The monthly results below under the "Figure C parameters(1&2)" are measured in terms of theoretically only investing during times in which the applicable parameter from Figure C predicts a market upswing, while not investing in times when the applicable parameter from Figure C predicts a market downturn. The monthly results under "Actual Market" are how the S&P really performed that month. Figure C parameters are calculated using astrocharts calculated for New York, New York, 12am ET and applied to the month according to the applicable parameters

S&P futures year:2004

	Figure C parameters(1 & 2)	Actual Market
January	+1.00%	+1.76%
February	+1.71%	+1.28%
March	-2.74%	-1.70%
April	+0.29%	-1.69%
May	-1.02%	+1.29%
June	+0.47%	+1.81%
July	-3.17%	-3.46%
August	-2.18%	+0.21%
September	+2.12%	+1.00%
October	+2.59%	+1.37%
November	+4.48%	+3.87%
December	+3.10%	+3.39%

From August 27, 2003, at the beginning of the predicted recession (as indicated in Figure C with parameter 4) until July 4th 2004, at the end of the predicted recession, the market actually jumped 12%. So the prediction was inaccurate. However, the predicted boom from July 4th 2004 through the end of the year is showing itself accurate as the market is up 7%. At the micro level, month to month, the parameters from Figure C are roughly tied with the actual market.

*The monthly results below under the "Figure C parameters(1&2)" are measured in terms of theoretically only investing during times in which the applicable parameter from Figure C predicts a market upswing, while not investing in times when the applicable parameter from Figure C predicts a market downturn. The monthly results under "Actual Market" are how the S&P really performed that month. Figure C parameters are calculated using astrocharts calculated for New York, New York, 12am ET and applied to the month according to the applicable parameters

S&P futures year:2005

	Figure C parameters(1 & 2)	Actual Market
January	-2.64%	-2.64%
February	+1.73%	+1.88%
March	+0.56%	-1.66%
April	-1.18%	-2.15%
May	-0.22%	+2.91%
June	+0.50%	+0.27%
July	+1.21%	+3.45%
August	-0.67 %	-1.23%
September	+1.07 %	+1.01%
October	-0.23%	-1.99%
November	+1.04%	+3.41%
December	+0.28%	+0.30%

From July 4, 2004, the market is predicted to be in a boom by parameter 3 in Figure C, which applies when the lunar node is between the 24th degree and the 8th degree. This phase of the lunar node lasted from July 4, 2004, till February 22, 2005. The market was up 5% during that time so our boom assessment can be considered accurate. The predicted recession phase starting from February 23, 2005 and ending December 28 2005 is off. The market actually went up during that time. Month-to month predictions for Figure C parameters were neck and neck with Actual Market results in the year 2005.

*The monthly results below under the "Figure C parameters(1&2)" are measured in terms of theoretically only investing during times in which the applicable parameter from Figure C predicts a market upswing, while not investing in times when the applicable parameter from Figure C predicts a market downturn. The monthly results under "Actual Market" are how the S&P really performed that month. Figure C parameters are calculated using astrocharts calculated for New York, New York, 12am ET and applied to the month according to the applicable parameters

S&P futures year:2006

	Figure C parameters(1 & 2)	Actual Market
January	+3.48%	+2.29%
February	-1.79	-0.08%
March	+0.53%	+1.62%
April	-0.58%	+0.98%
May	-0.09%	-3.34%
June	+0.33%	+0.59%
July	-0.79%	+0.18%
August	+1.24%	+1.85%
September	+2.19%	+3.06%
October	+2.74%	+2.81%
November	+1.57%	+1.43%
December	+1.13%	+1.82

From January 1 2006, a predicted boom phase applied as the lunar node went to the 8th degree, which invokes parameter 3 from Figure C parameters. That phase lasted until November 8th 2006 when the lunar node's degree hit the 24th degree. During that time, the market rose 10%, which makes our prediction from parameter 3 in Figure C correct. So, now starting from November 9 2006, we can apply parameter 4 from Figure C as the lunar node would now be at the 23rd degree mark, which invokes the parameter. Month to month comparison between Figure C parameters and actual market results show that Figure C parameters were able to keep up with the upswings during 2006.

*The monthly results below under the "Figure C parameters(1&2)" are measured in terms of theoretically only investing during times in which the applicable parameter from Figure C predicts a market upswing, while not investing in times when the applicable parameter from Figure C predicts a market downturn. The monthly results under "Actual Market" are how the S&P really performed that month. Figure C parameters are calculated using astrocharts calculated for New York, New York, 12am ET and applied to the month according to the applicable parameters

S&P futures year:2007

	Figure C parameters(1 & 2)	Actual Market
January	+1.28%	+1.02%
February	-1.08%	-2.36%
March	-0.43%	+1.58%
April	+0.59%	+4.00%
May	-0.36%	+2.99%
June	-0.40%	-1.14%
July	+1.65%	-3.53%
August	+0.26%	+1.01%
September	+0.02%	+4.15%
October	+1.74%	+1.10%
November	-3.19%	-4.58%
December	-0.90%	-0.44%

From November 9 2006, when the lunar node went to the 23rd degree mark, all the way until June 29 2007, when the lunar hit the 9th degree, the market was predicted by parameter 4 from Figure C for recession during that time frame. The market actually rose 4 percent. So there was no recession; the prediction was inaccurate. The micro level month to month comparison between Figure C parameters and the actual market results show that the Figure C parameters had trouble keeping up with the upswings, but managed to avoid some damage during major downturns.

*The monthly results below under the "Figure C parameters(1&2)" are measured in terms of theoretically only investing during times in which the applicable parameter from Figure C predicts a market upswing, while not investing in times when the applicable parameter from Figure C predicts a market downturn. The monthly results under "Actual Market" are how the S&P really performed that month. Figure C parameters are calculated using astrocharts calculated for New York, New York, 12am ET and applied to the month according to the applicable parameters

S&P futures year:2008

	Figure C parameters(1 & 2)	Actual Market
January	+0.23%	-6.62%
February	-2.62%	-3.50%
March	+0.57%	-0.54%
April	+4.61%	+4.68%
May	+1.82%	+1.05%
June	+0.09%	-8.53%
July	-3.43%	-1.09%
August	+0.58%	+1.22%
September	-1.54%	-8.85%
October	+3.12%	-17.26%
November	-10.07%	-7.44%
December	+ 2.86%	+0.53%

On June 30, 2007, when the lunar node hit the 8th degree mark, parameter 3 was invoked and thus a prediction for an market boom phase. This phase of the lunar node from the 8th degree to the 24th degree going backwards lasted from June 30 2007 all the way till May 5 2008. During that time the market dropped 7 percent, so there was no boom. However the next applied parameter for the prediction of a recession after May 5th 2008 is turning out very accurate. From May 6th 2008 till the end of that year, the market dropped 36%. That recession prediction phase from parameter 4 in Figure C wont end until early 2009. At the micro month to month level in 2008, the Figure C parameters avoided major catastrophe in January, June, September and October and actually averaged up for those months.

*The monthly results below under the "Figure C parameters(1&2)" are measured in terms of theoretically only investing during times in which the applicable parameter from Figure C predicts a market upswing, while not investing in times when the applicable parameter from Figure C predicts a market downturn. The monthly results under "Actual Market" are how the S&P really performed that month. Figure C parameters are calculated using astrocharts calculated for New York, New York, 12am ET and applied to the month according to the applicable parameters

S&P futures year:2009

	Figure C parameters(1 & 2)	Actual Market
January	-9.12%	-8.61%
February	+1.58	-10.73%
March	+0.60	+8.24%
April	+7.86	+9.47
May	+5.97	+5.52
June	+1.76	-0.27
July	+5.90	+7.54
August	+1.62	+3.58
September	+3.00	+3.26
October	-1.78	-1.90
November	+1.93	+5.98
December	+0.07	+1.46

From May 6 2008, the market was predicted to enter recession by the applied parameter 4 from Figure C, when the lunar node hit the 23rd degree mark. From that point all the way until the lunar node hit the 9th degree (as it goes backwards) on February 27, 2009, the market tanked 47%. So the recession prediction was accurate. The next parameter to apply would have been parameter 3 from Figure C on March 1st as the lunar node hit the 8th degree mark. This would call for a market boom prediction. From that point, March 1st 2009, until the lunar node hit the 24th degree mark(goes backwards) on November 3 2009, the market jumped 41%. So, this market boom prediction turns out correct. We can also see that at a micro month to month level how Figure C parameters successfully evaded the major downturns during the recession phase of 2008/2009, and also climbed with the major upswings during the boom phase of 2009.

By using the time between 2000 and 2009 to asses how the market correlated with the sun and the lunar nodes, we get a better picture of how a system can be formed. As a working model for macro economics, even though some predictions were not perfect, the timeframe between lunar node points are a viable solution to deciding whether not to raise or lower interest rates. We saw in the examples how the predictions for a recession or a boom were correct when it truly mattered and were incorrect when it wouldn't have mattered all that much. We also saw how the parameters that cover predictions in a micro sense still managed to accurately asses the up and downs during both recession periods and boom periods.

In terms of macro economics, the basic standard for a global economy would be for a central bank to predict a market recession during the time starting from when the lunar node reaches the 23rd degree mark-- traveling backwards(23, 22, 21, 20, etc.)-- and ending when it gets to the 9th degree mark. The prediction for a boom economy would start from when the lunar node reaches the 8th degree mark—traveling backwards(8, 7, 6, 5, 4, 3, 2, 1, 0, 29, 28, 27)--- and end when the lunar node hits the 24th degree mark.

In terms of micro economics, a basic standard for the global economy would be for the individual investor to expect a market upswing during the time when the sun's degree is higher than the lunar node's degree, and a downswing when the sun's degree is lower than the lunar node's degree...while keeping in mind that the 24th degree is the first degree of a sign and therefore the lowest. One can also delineate and apply an entry point a few days after the sun's degree would move higher than the lunar node's degree in order to further validate a historical perspective that this algorithm avoids major crashes

In terms of volatility, Mars 360 would influence that part of the economy by allowing Mars to asses when volatility would take place. This would be 666 having influence on the economic system. The predictive algorithm using the lunar nodes will not try to asses how bad a recession will be or how good a boom will be in terms of intensity. The economy under Mars 360, with Mars integrated as a factor, will asses how volatile a recession or boom will be. This means the highs and lows could take on a significant effect no matter which phase the market is in, whether that be boom or recession. When Mars gets to within 30 degrees of the sun(not just the degree of the sun, but the actual position of the sun), a prediction of increased volatility would apply during that time frame no matter if the market is in a boom phase or recession phase as indicated by the lunar node's degree. For instance if the Sun is at 20 degrees Cancer, Mars would gets to within 30 degrees of that at 20 degrees Gemini. When that happens, a prediction for increased volatility will apply until Mars leaves from within 30 degrees of the sun. It has to be within 30 degrees of the actual position of the Sun. The Market could be in a boom phase as indicated by the position of lunar node, and could suffer dramatic losses and major market bounces if Mars goes to with 30 degrees of the position of the sun. The same would happen if Mars goes to within 30 degrees of the position of Sun during a recession phase....... dramatic losses and major market bounces also.

Here is a demonstration of Mars's effect on the market. On the next page are the 12 worst months in history for the Dow Jones. I will show how Mars was within 30 degrees of the sun in nearly every single month within this ranking of worst months for the Dow Jones.

These are the top 12 worst months in Dow Jones History. This is taken from www.davemanuel.com

September, 1931 (-30.7%)

April, 1932 (-23.68%)

March, 1938 (-23.67%)

October, 1987 (-23.22%)

May, 1940 (-21.70%)

October, 1929 (-20.36%)

May, 1932 (-20.01%)

June, 1930 (-17.72%)

December, 1931 (-17.01%)

February, 1933 (-15.62%)

August, 1998 (-15.13%)

October, 2008 (-14.06%)

All the astro charts for each month will calculated using New York, New York, 12am ET for any day of the month that Mars was within 30 degrees. This would allow us to say that the month in which Mars is within 30 degrees of the sun is the month that will be affected. For instance, if Mars goes to within 30 degrees of the sun late in the month, we can still say it applies to affecting the entire month. See the next page.

Market Prediction Algorithms for the US Dollar, the Stock Market and Bitcoin

September, 1931 (-30.7%)

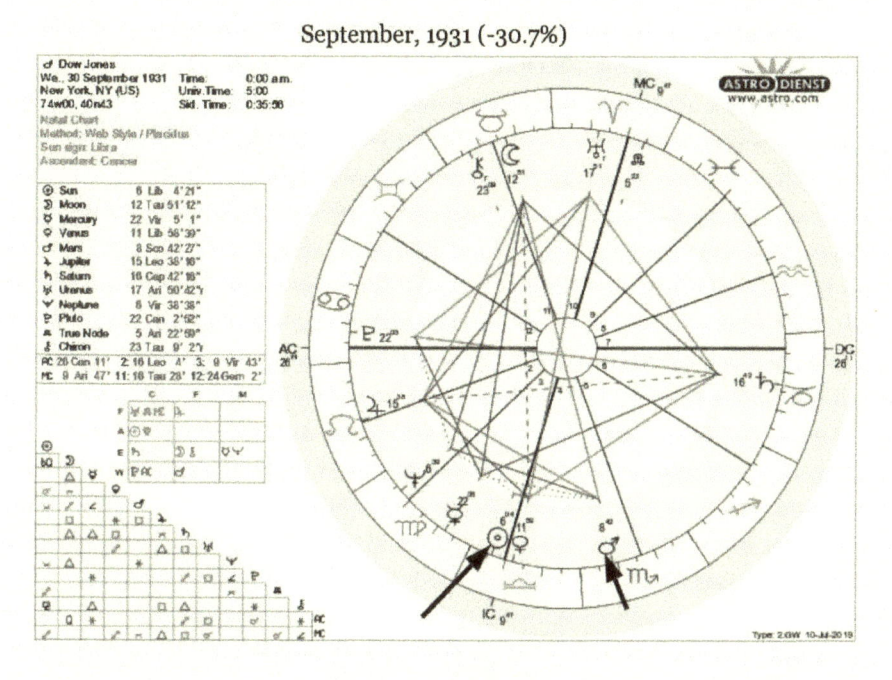

April, 1932 (-23.68%)

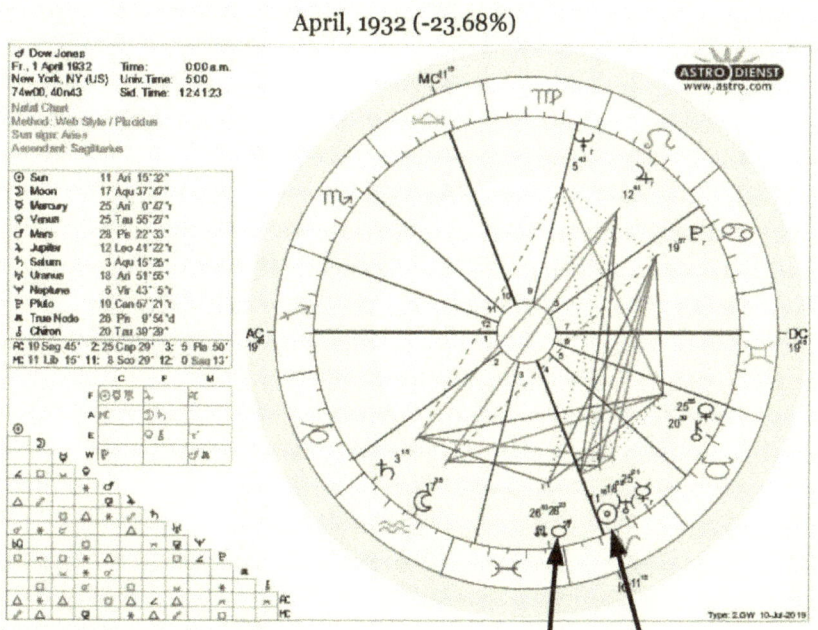

Market Prediction Algorithms for the US Dollar, the Stock Market and Bitcoin

March, 1938 (-23.67%)

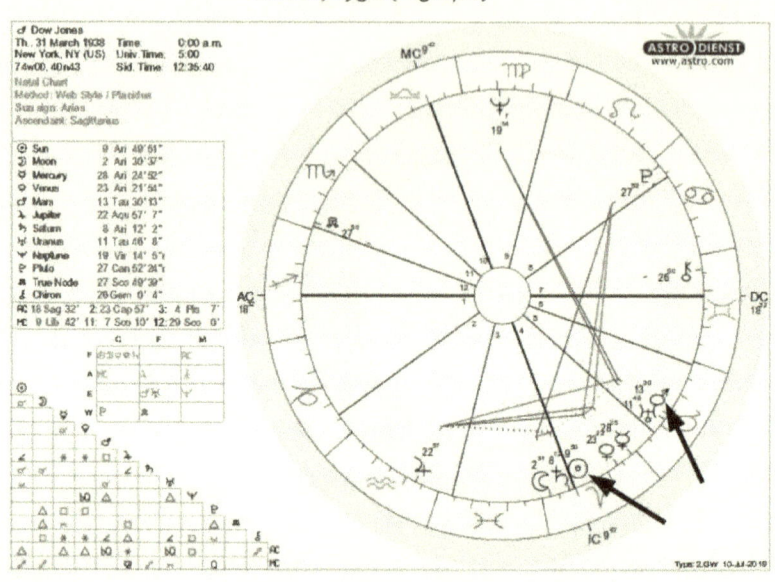

October, 1987 (-23.22%)

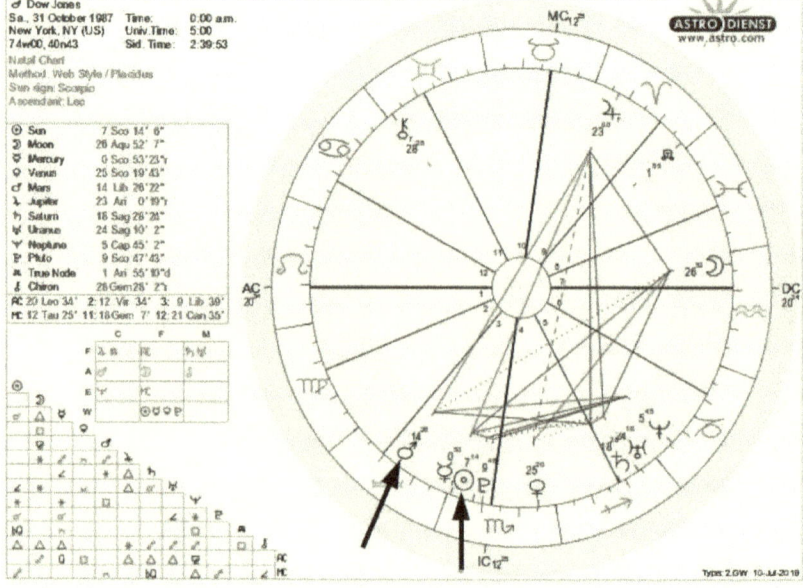

Market Prediction Algorithms for the US Dollar, the Stock Market and Bitcoin

May, 1940 (-21.70%)

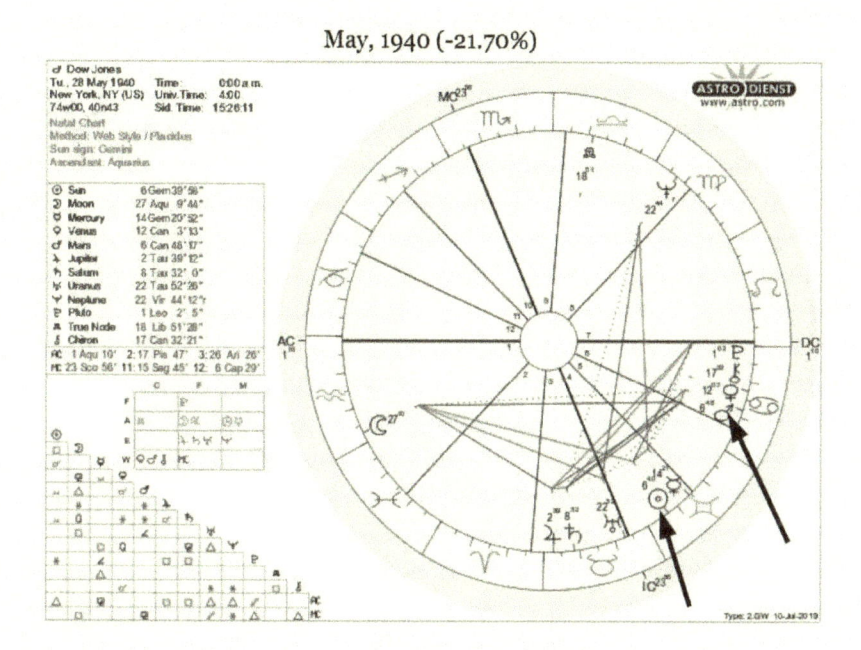

October, 1929 (-20.36%)

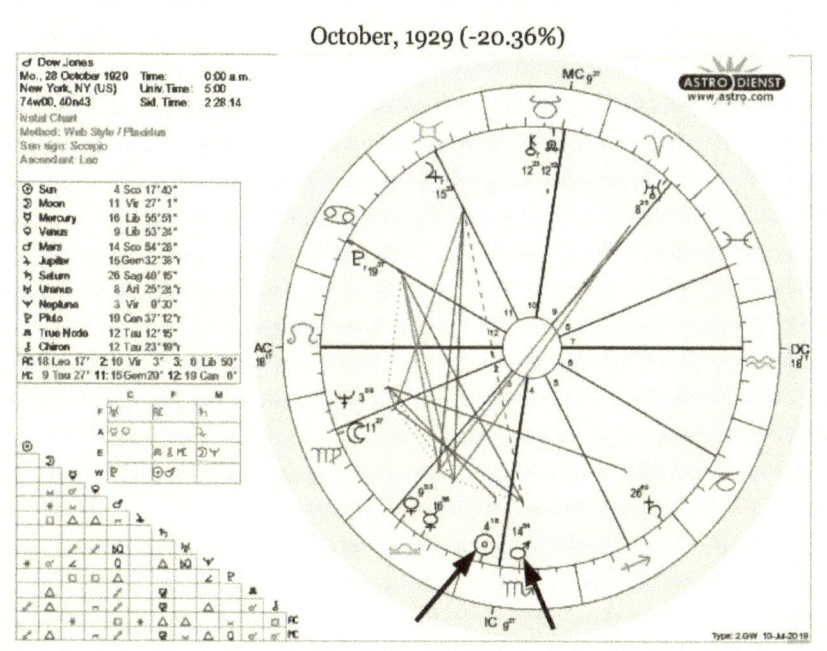

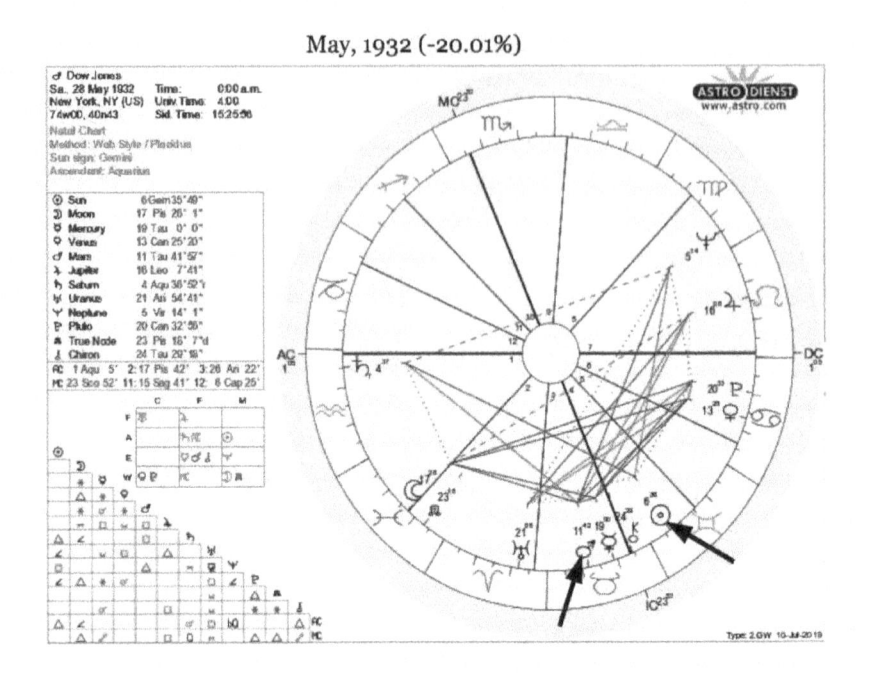

Market Prediction Algorithms for the US Dollar, the Stock Market and Bitcoin

May, 1932 (-20.01%)

June, 1930 (-17.72%)

Market Prediction Algorithms for the US Dollar, the Stock Market and Bitcoin

December, 1931 (-17.01%)

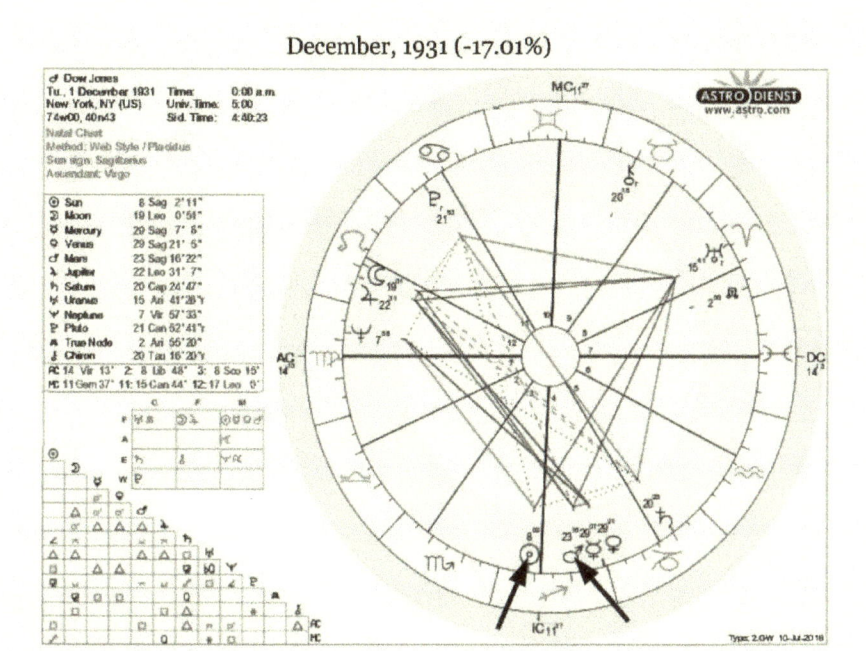

♂ Dow Jones
Tu, 1 December 1931   Time: 0:00 a.m.
New York, NY (US)   Univ. Time: 5:00
74w00, 40n43   Sid. Time: 4:40:23
Natal Chart
Method: Web Style / Placidus
Sun sign: Sagittarius
Ascendant: Virgo

⊙ Sun	8 Sag 2' 11"
☾ Moon	19 Leo 0' 54"
☿ Mercury	29 Sag 7' 6"
♀ Venus	29 Sag 21' 5"
♂ Mars	23 Sag 16' 22"
♃ Jupiter	22 Leo 31' 7" r
♄ Saturn	20 Cap 24' 47"
♅ Uranus	15 Ari 41' 28" r
♆ Neptune	7 Vir 57' 33" r
♇ Pluto	21 Can 52' 41" r
☊ True Node	2 Ari 55' 20"
⚷ Chiron	20 Tau 16' 20" r

AC 14 Vir 13'   2: 8 Lib 48'   3: 8 Sco 15'
MC 11 Gem 37'   11: 15 Can 44'   12: 17 Leo 0'

February, 1933 (-15.62%)

♂ Dow Jones
Sa, 25 February 1933   Time: 0:00 a.m.
New York, NY (US)   Univ. Time: 5:00
74w00, 40n43   Sid. Time: 10:22:26
Natal Chart
Method: Web Style / Placidus
Sun sign: Pisces
Ascendant: Scorpio

⊙ Sun	6 Pis 9' 25"
☾ Moon	14 Pis 27' 52"
☿ Mercury	20 Pis 9' 9"
♀ Venus	22 Aqu 11' 2"
♂ Mars	12 Vir 38' 54" r
♃ Jupiter	19 Vir 53' 41" r
♄ Saturn	10 Aqu 30' 2"
♅ Uranus	20 Ari 50' 0"
♆ Neptune	8 Vir 53' 24" r
♇ Pluto	21 Can 31' 27" r
☊ True Node	7 Pis 45' 5" d
⚷ Chiron	23 Tau 53' 21"

AC 21 Sco 37'   2: 21 Sag 54'   3: 27 Cap 13'
MC 3 Vir 42'   11: 5 Lib 26'   12: 0 Sco 51'

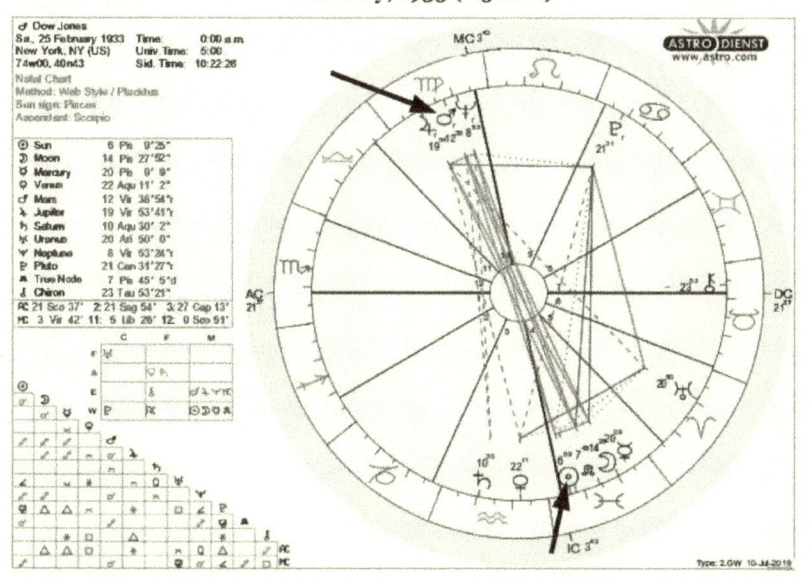

Market Prediction Algorithms for the US Dollar, the Stock Market and Bitcoin

August, 1998 (-15.13%)

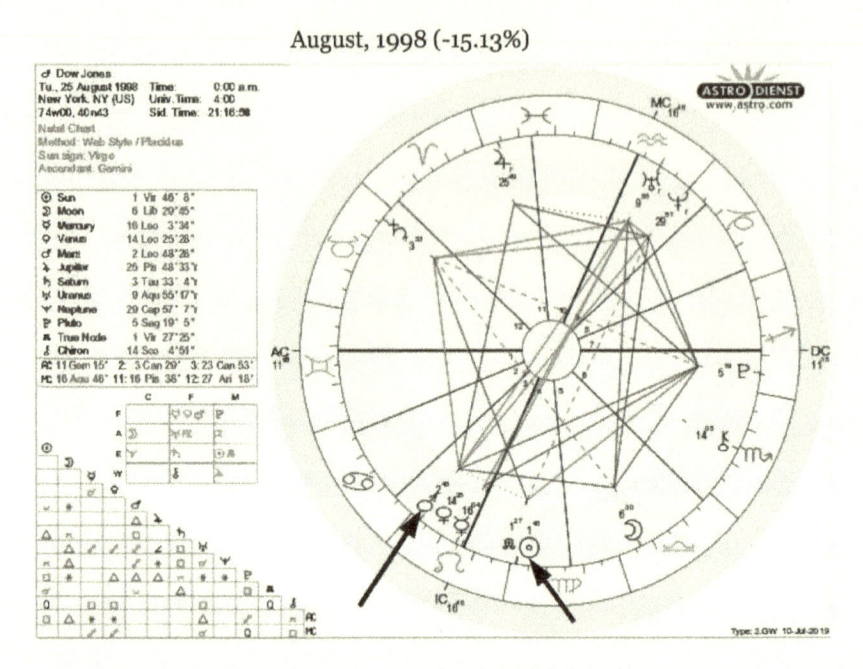

October, 2008 (-14.06%)

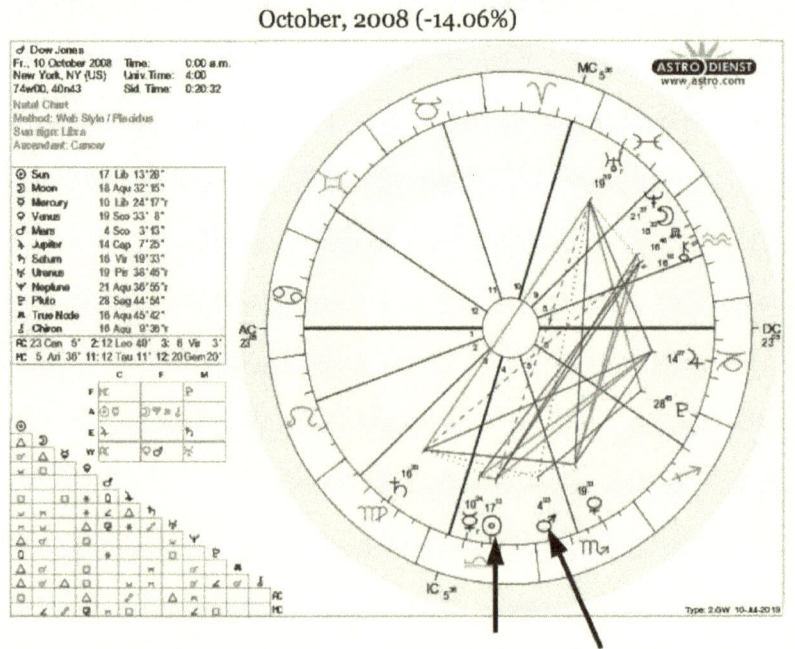

In 9 of the 12 examples, Mars and the Sun were within 30 degrees of each other. Its likely that within those months, there would have also been significant market bounces. That is how Mars can be related to volatility.

Overall, in this chapter, we're presented with a working model of an economy influenced by Mars that can be applied at the macro economist level and the micro individual level.

We can add a slight improvisation to Figure C that would improve the accuracy of the algorithm

Here is the algorithm from Figure C

1. When the degree of the sun is lower than the degree of the lunar node, there is a market downturn,

2. When the degree of the sun is higher than the degree of the lunar node, there is a market upswing.

3. when the lunar node is between the 8th degree and the 24 degree as it travels backward(8, 7, 6, 5, 4 , 3 ,2, 1, o, 29, 28, 27, 26, 25, 24), the market is in a boom.

4. when the lunar node is between the 23rd degree and the 9th degree as it travels backwards(23, 22, 21, 20, 19, 18, 17, 16, 15, 14, 13, 12, 11, 10, 9) the market is in recession.

*Reminder: new sign starts at the 24th degree, and the lunar nodes travel backward through the zodiac. Make sure to keep this page referenced for Figure C parameters.

If we simply change parameter 2 to:

2. When the degree of the sun is higher than the degree of the lunar node **by 3 degrees or more**, there is a market upswing

Now we have an algorithm that looks like this:

1. When the degree of the sun is lower than the degree of the lunar node, there is a market downturn,

2. When the degree of the sun is higher than the degree of the lunar node **by 3 degrees or more**, there is a market upswing.

3. when the lunar node is between the 8th degree and the 24 degree as it travels backward(8, 7, 6, 5, 4 , 3 ,2, 1, o, 29, 28, 27, 26, 25, 24), the market is in a boom.

4. when the lunar node is between the 23rd degree and the 9th degree as it travels backwards(23, 22, 21, 20, 19, 18, 17, 16, 15, 14, 13, 12, 11, 10, 9) the market is in recession.

*Reminder: new sign starts at the 24th degree, and the lunar nodes travel backward through the zodiac. Make sure to keep this page referenced for Figure C parameters.

Market Prediction Algorithms for the US Dollar, the Stock Market and Bitcoin

If we apply this slightly improvised algorithm historically to dates in which the market dropped significantly, we theoretically would have been able to avoid all the major market drops. These dates below were taken from wikipedia and are the dates for 20 largest percentage drops for the Dow Jones. Each astrology chart is calculated for the day of the drop. Out of the 20 dates, the algorithm only missed 2 dates: **March 14 1907 and October 15 2008**

−22.61%

−12.82%

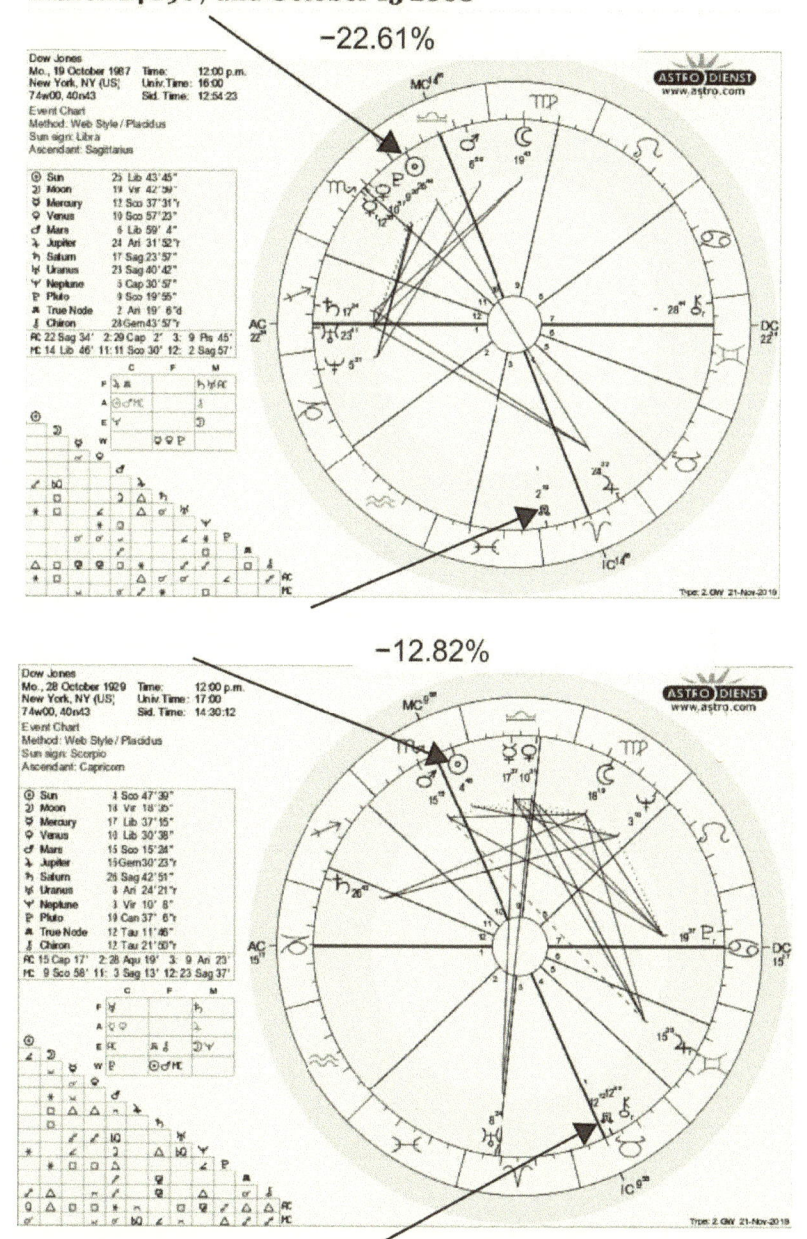

72

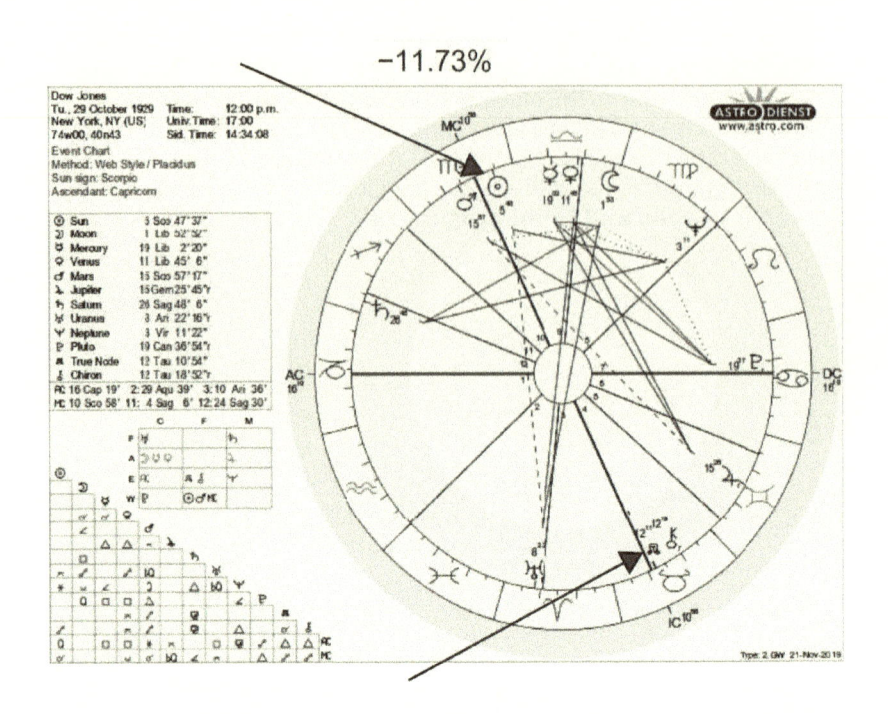

Market Prediction Algorithms for the US Dollar, the Stock Market and Bitcoin

−11.73%

Dow Jones
Tu., 29 October 1929 Time: 12:00 p.m.
New York, NY (US) Univ. Time: 17:00
74w00, 40n43 Sid. Time: 14:34:08
Event Chart
Method: Web Style / Placidus
Sun sign: Scorpio
Ascendant: Capricorn

☉ Sun	5 Sco 47'37"
☽ Moon	1 Lib 52'52"
☿ Mercury	19 Lib 2'20"
♀ Venus	11 Lib 45' 6"
♂ Mars	15 Sco 57'17"
♃ Jupiter	16 Gem 25'45"ɼ
♄ Saturn	26 Sag 48' 6"
♅ Uranus	3 Ari 22'16"ɼ
♆ Neptune	3 Vir 11'22"
♇ Pluto	19 Can 36'54"ɼ
⚸ True Node	12 Tau 10'54"
⚷ Chiron	12 Tau 18'52"ɼ

AC 16 Cap 19' 2:29 Aqu 39' 3:10 Ari 36'
MC 10 Sco 58' 11: 4 Sag 6' 12:24 Sag 30'

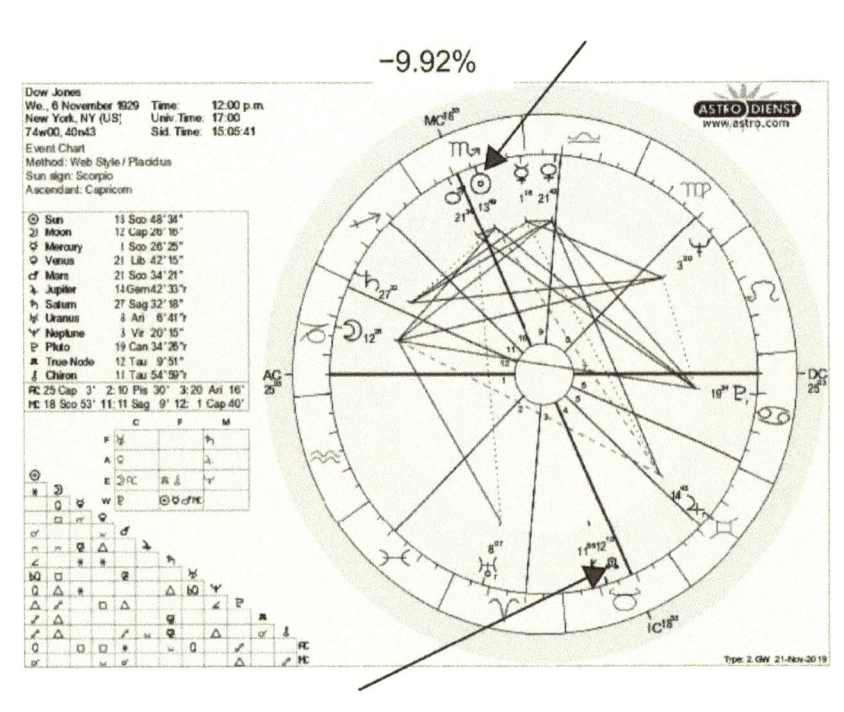

−9.92%

Dow Jones
We., 6 November 1929 Time: 12:00 p.m.
New York, NY (US) Univ. Time: 17:00
74w00, 40n43 Sid. Time: 15:05:41
Event Chart
Method: Web Style / Placidus
Sun sign: Scorpio
Ascendant: Capricorn

☉ Sun	13 Sco 48'34"
☽ Moon	12 Cap 26'16"
☿ Mercury	1 Sco 26'25"
♀ Venus	21 Lib 42'15"
♂ Mars	21 Sco 34'21"
♃ Jupiter	14 Gem 42'33"ɼ
♄ Saturn	27 Sag 32'18"
♅ Uranus	3 Ari 6'41"ɼ
♆ Neptune	3 Vir 20'15"
♇ Pluto	19 Can 34'26"ɼ
⚸ True Node	12 Tau 9'51"
⚷ Chiron	11 Tau 54'59"ɼ

AC 25 Cap 3' 2:10 Pis 30' 3:20 Ari 16'
MC 18 Sco 53' 11:11 Sag 9' 12: 1 Cap 40'

Market Prediction Algorithms for the US Dollar, the Stock Market and Bitcoin

−8.72 %

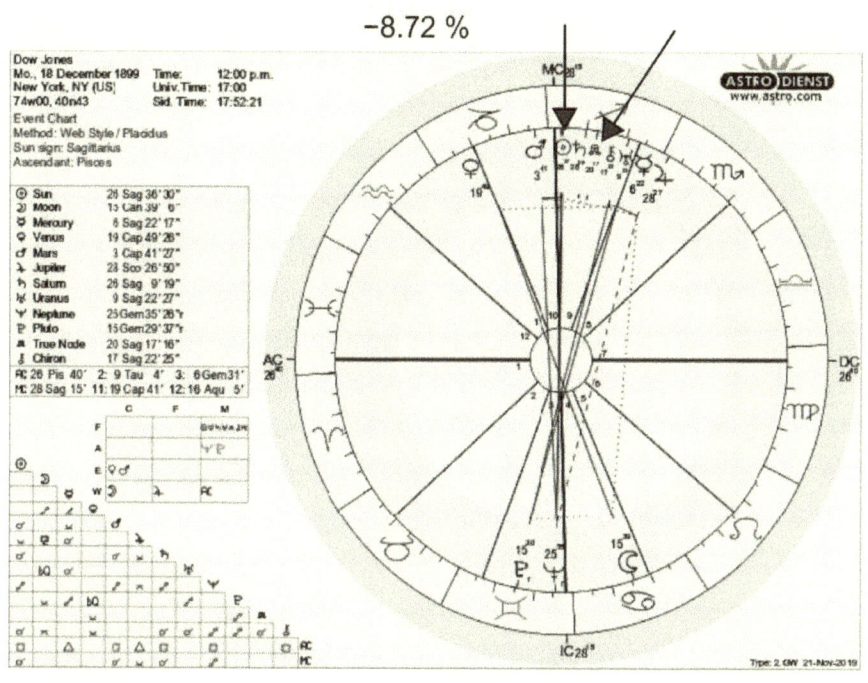

Dow Jones
Mo., 18 December 1899 Time: 12:00 p.m.
New York, NY (US) Univ.Time: 17:00
74w00, 40n43 Sid. Time: 17:52:21
Event Chart
Method: Web Style / Placidus
Sun sign: Sagittarius
Ascendant: Pisces

☉ Sun	26 Sag 36' 30"
☽ Moon	13 Can 39' 6"
☿ Mercury	6 Sag 22' 17"
♀ Venus	19 Cap 49' 28"
♂ Mars	3 Cap 41' 27"
♃ Jupiter	23 Sco 26' 50"
♄ Saturn	26 Sag 9' 19"
♅ Uranus	9 Sag 22' 27"
♆ Neptune	25 Gem 35' 26" ℞
♇ Pluto	15 Gem 29' 37" ℞
☊ True Node	20 Sag 17' 16"
⚷ Chiron	17 Sag 22' 25"

AC 26 Pis 40' 2: 9 Tau 4' 3: 6 Gem 31'
MC 28 Sag 15' 11: 19 Cap 41' 12: 16 Aqu 5'

−8.40 %

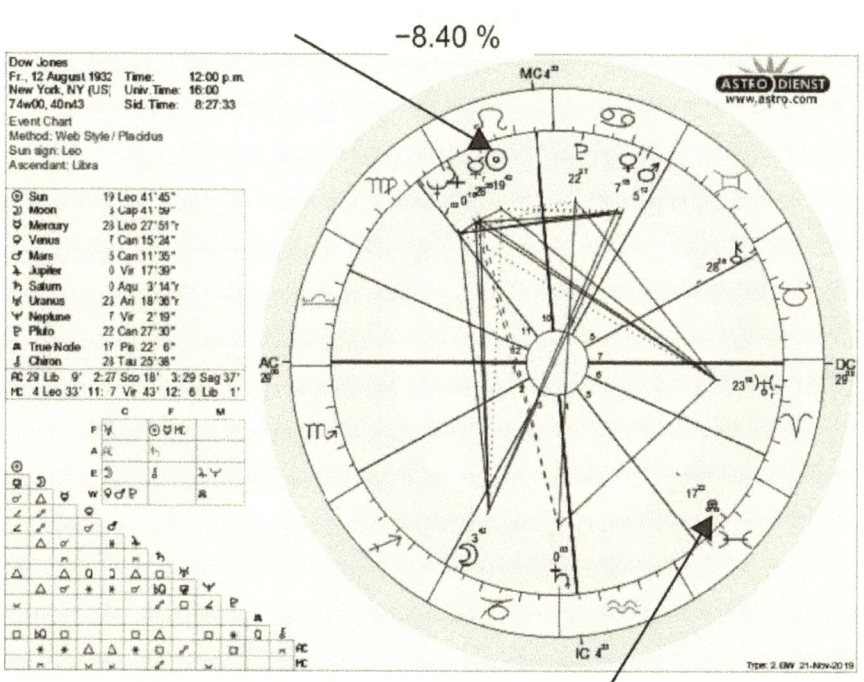

Dow Jones
Fr., 12 August 1932 Time: 12:00 p.m.
New York, NY (US) Univ.Time: 16:00
74w00, 40n43 Sid. Time: 8:27:33
Event Chart
Method: Web Style / Placidus
Sun sign: Leo
Ascendant: Libra

☉ Sun	19 Leo 41' 45"
☽ Moon	3 Cap 41' 59"
☿ Mercury	23 Leo 27' 51" ℞
♀ Venus	7 Can 15' 24"
♂ Mars	5 Can 11' 35"
♃ Jupiter	0 Vir 17' 39"
♄ Saturn	0 Aqu 3' 14" ℞
♅ Uranus	23 Ari 18' 36" ℞
♆ Neptune	7 Vir 2' 19"
♇ Pluto	22 Can 27' 30"
☊ True Node	17 Pis 22' 6"
⚷ Chiron	28 Tau 25' 38"

AC 29 Lib 9' 2: 27 Sco 18' 3: 29 Sag 37'
MC 4 Leo 33' 11: 7 Vir 43' 12: 6 Lib 1'

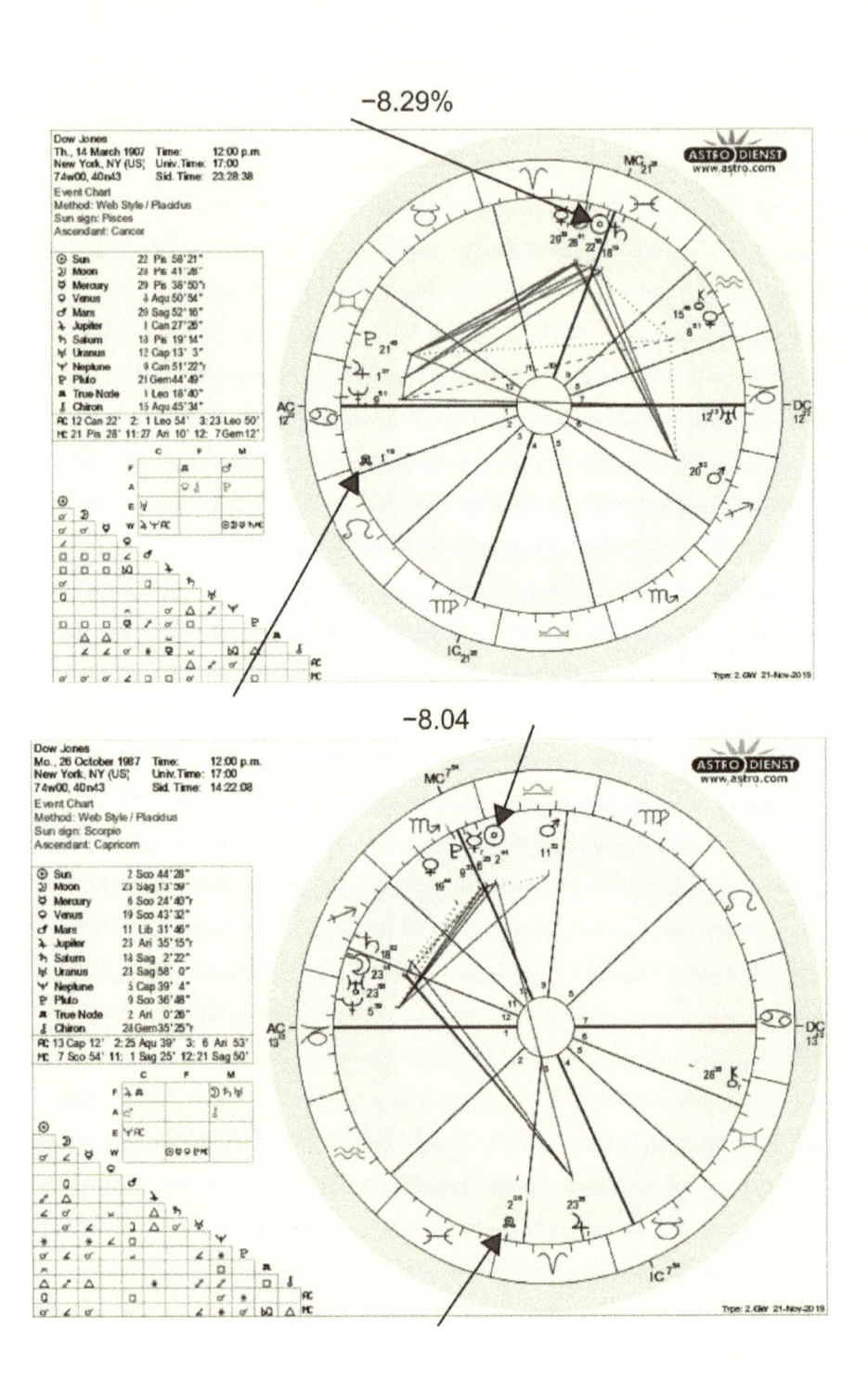

Market Prediction Algorithms for the US Dollar, the Stock Market and Bitcoin

−8.29%

Dow Jones
Th., 14 March 1907
New York, NY (US)
74w00, 40n43
Time: 12:00 p.m.
Univ. Time: 17:00
Sid. Time: 23:28:38

Event Chart
Method: Web Style / Placidus
Sun sign: Pisces
Ascendant: Cancer

- ☉ Sun 22 Pis 58'21"
- ☽ Moon 24 Pis 41'26"
- ☿ Mercury 29 Pis 38'50" ℞
- ♀ Venus 3 Aqu 50'54"
- ♂ Mars 20 Sag 52'18"
- ♃ Jupiter 1 Can 27'26"
- ♄ Saturn 18 Pis 19'14"
- ♅ Uranus 12 Cap 13' 3"
- ♆ Neptune 9 Can 51'22" ℞
- ♇ Pluto 21 Gem 44'49"
- ☊ True Node 1 Leo 18'40"
- ⚷ Chiron 15 Aqu 45'34"

AC 12 Can 22' 2: 1 Leo 54' 3: 23 Leo 50'
MC 21 Pis 28' 11: 27 Ari 10' 12: 7 Gem 12'

−8.04

Dow Jones
Mo., 26 October 1987
New York, NY (US)
74w00, 40n43
Time: 12:00 p.m.
Univ. Time: 17:00
Sid. Time: 14:22:08

Event Chart
Method: Web Style / Placidus
Sun sign: Scorpio
Ascendant: Capricorn

- ☉ Sun 2 Sco 44'28"
- ☽ Moon 23 Sag 13'39"
- ☿ Mercury 6 Sco 24'40" ℞
- ♀ Venus 19 Sco 43'32"
- ♂ Mars 11 Lib 31'46"
- ♃ Jupiter 23 Ari 35'15" ℞
- ♄ Saturn 14 Sag 2'22"
- ♅ Uranus 23 Sag 58' 0"
- ♆ Neptune 5 Cap 39' 4"
- ♇ Pluto 9 Sco 36'48"
- ☊ True Node 2 Ari 0'26" ℞
- ⚷ Chiron 24 Gem 35'25" ℞

AC 13 Cap 12' 2: 25 Aqu 39' 3: 6 Ari 53'
MC 7 Sco 54' 11: 1 Sag 25' 12: 21 Sag 50'

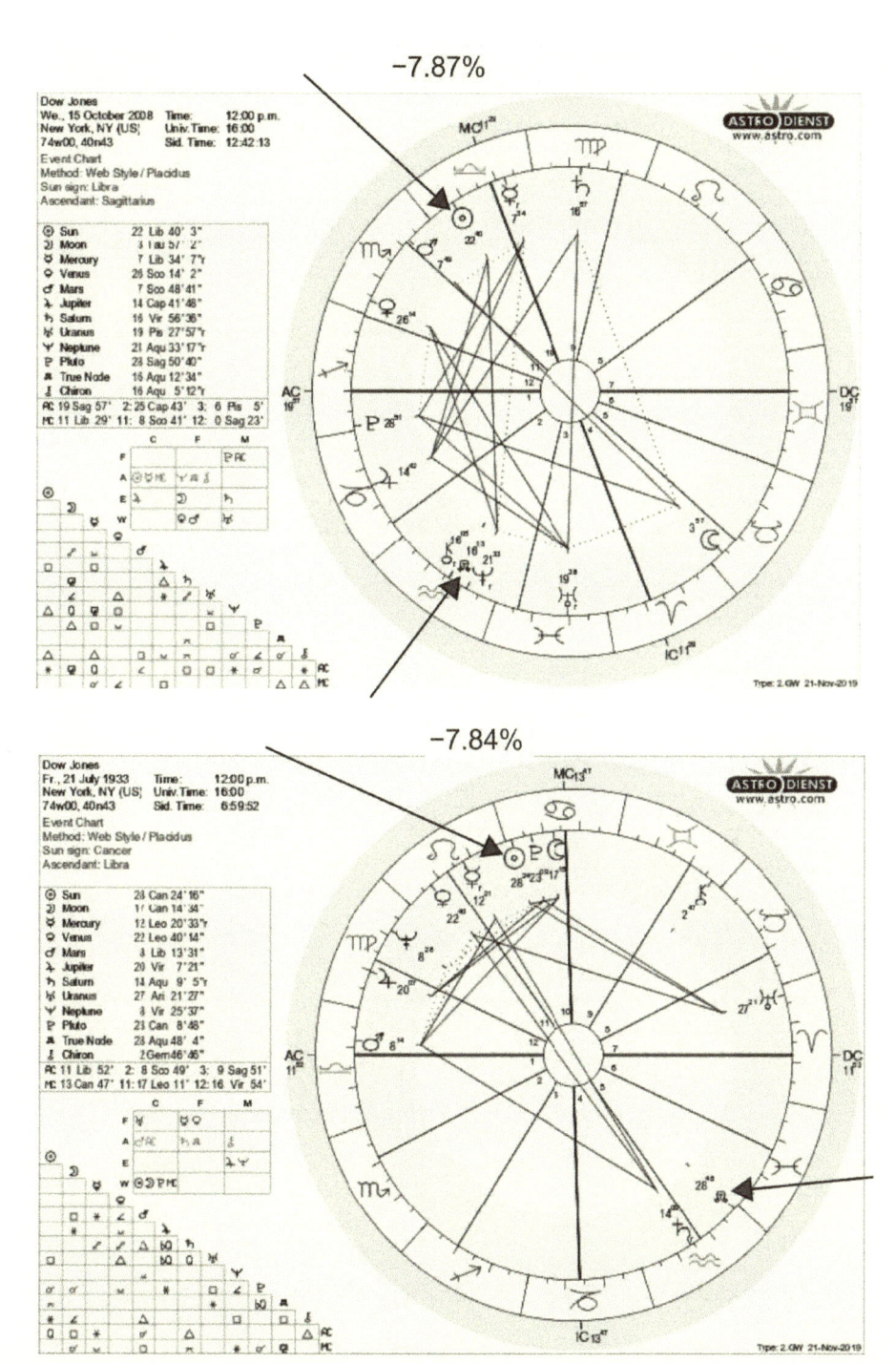

Market Prediction Algorithms for the US Dollar, the Stock Market and Bitcoin

−7.87%

Dow Jones
We., 15 October 2008 Time: 12:00 p.m.
New York, NY (US) Univ. Time: 16:00
74w00, 40n43 Sid. Time: 12:42:13
Event Chart
Method: Web Style / Placidus
Sun sign: Libra
Ascendant: Sagittarius

☉ Sun	22 Lib 40' 3"
🌙 Moon	3 Tau 57' 2"
☿ Mercury	7 Lib 34' 7"r
♀ Venus	26 Sco 14' 2"
♂ Mars	7 Sco 48' 41"
♃ Jupiter	14 Cap 41' 48"
♄ Saturn	16 Vir 56' 36"
♅ Uranus	19 Pis 27' 57"r
♆ Neptune	21 Aqu 33' 17"r
♇ Pluto	28 Sag 50' 40"
☊ True Node	16 Aqu 12' 34"
⚷ Chiron	16 Aqu 5' 12"r

AC 19 Sag 57' 2: 25 Cap 43' 3: 6 Pis 5'
MC 11 Lib 29' 11: 8 Sco 41' 12: 0 Sag 23'

−7.84%

Dow Jones
Fr., 21 July 1933 Time: 12:00 p.m.
New York, NY (US) Univ. Time: 16:00
74w00, 40n43 Sid. Time: 6:59:52
Event Chart
Method: Web Style / Placidus
Sun sign: Cancer
Ascendant: Libra

☉ Sun	28 Can 24' 16"
🌙 Moon	1 Can 14' 34"
☿ Mercury	12 Leo 20' 33"r
♀ Venus	22 Leo 40' 14"
♂ Mars	3 Lib 13' 31"
♃ Jupiter	20 Vir 7' 21"
♄ Saturn	14 Aqu 9' 5"r
♅ Uranus	27 Ari 21' 27"
♆ Neptune	8 Vir 25' 37"
♇ Pluto	21 Can 8' 48"
☊ True Node	28 Aqu 48' 4"
⚷ Chiron	2 Gem 46' 46"

AC 11 Lib 52' 2: 8 Sco 49' 3: 9 Sag 51'
MC 13 Can 47' 11: 17 Leo 11' 12: 16 Vir 54'

Market Prediction Algorithms for the US Dollar, the Stock Market and Bitcoin

−7.75%

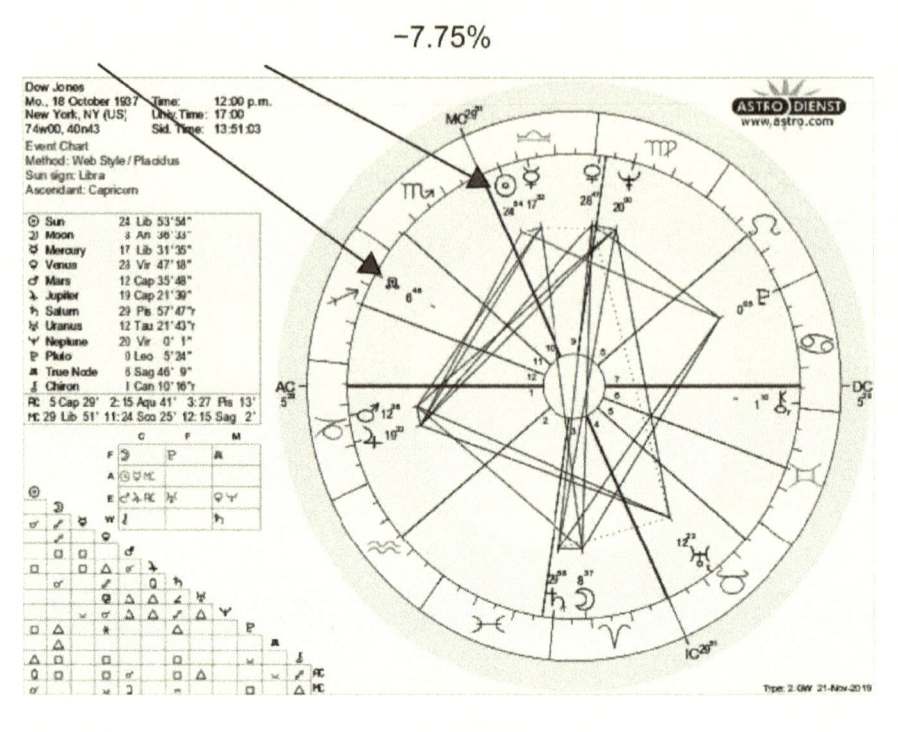

Dow Jones
Mo., 18 October 1987 Time: 12:00 p.m.
New York, NY (US) Univ. Time: 17:00
74w00, 40n43 Sid. Time: 13:51:03
Event Chart
Method: Web Style / Placidus
Sun sign: Libra
Ascendant: Capricorn

☉ Sun	24 Lib 53'54"
☽ Moon	8 Ari 36'33"
☿ Mercury	17 Lib 31'35"
♀ Venus	23 Vir 47'18"
♂ Mars	12 Cap 35'48"
♃ Jupiter	19 Cap 21'39"
♄ Saturn	29 Pis 57'47"r
⛢ Uranus	12 Tau 21'43"r
♆ Neptune	26 Vir 0' 1"
♇ Pluto	0 Leo 5'24"
☊ True Node	6 Sag 46' 9"
⚷ Chiron	1 Can 10'16"r

AC: 5 Cap 29' 2:15 Aqu 41' 3:27 Pis 13'
MC: 29 Lib 51' 11:24 Sco 25' 12:15 Sag 2'

−7.70%

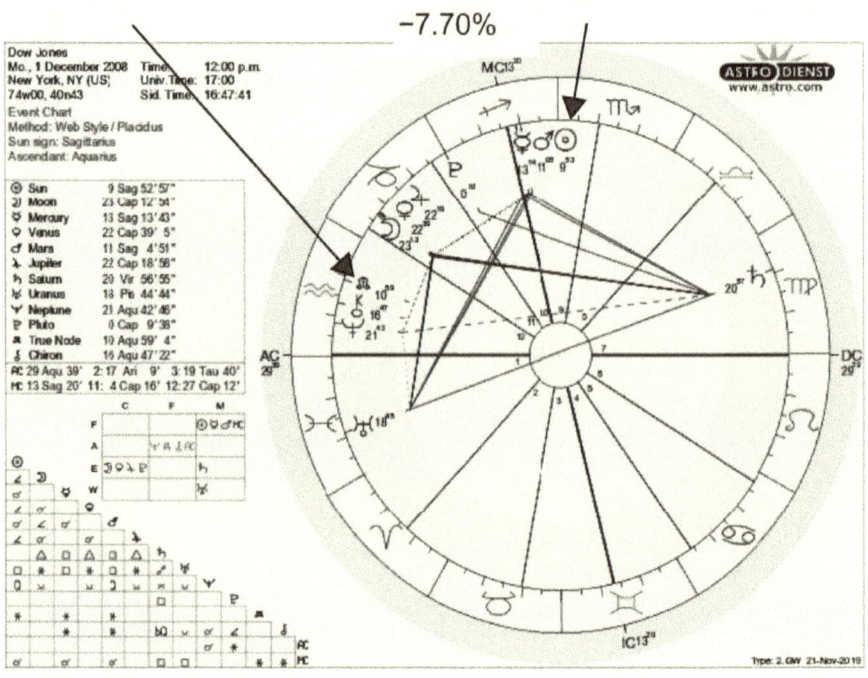

Dow Jones
Mo., 1 December 2008 Time: 12:00 p.m.
New York, NY (US) Univ. Time: 17:00
74w00, 40n43 Sid. Time: 16:47:41
Event Chart
Method: Web Style / Placidus
Sun sign: Sagittarius
Ascendant: Aquarius

☉ Sun	9 Sag 52'57"
☽ Moon	23 Cap 12'54"
☿ Mercury	13 Sag 13'43"
♀ Venus	22 Cap 39' 5"
♂ Mars	11 Sag 4'51"
♃ Jupiter	22 Cap 18'56"
♄ Saturn	20 Vir 56'55"
⛢ Uranus	18 Pis 44'44"
♆ Neptune	21 Aqu 42'46"
♇ Pluto	0 Cap 9'38"
☊ True Node	19 Aqu 59' 4"
⚷ Chiron	16 Aqu 47'22"

AC: 29 Aqu 39' 2:17 Ari 9' 3:19 Tau 40'
MC: 13 Sag 20' 11: 4 Cap 16' 12:27 Cap 12'

Market Prediction Algorithms for the US Dollar, the Stock Market and Bitcoin

−7.33 %

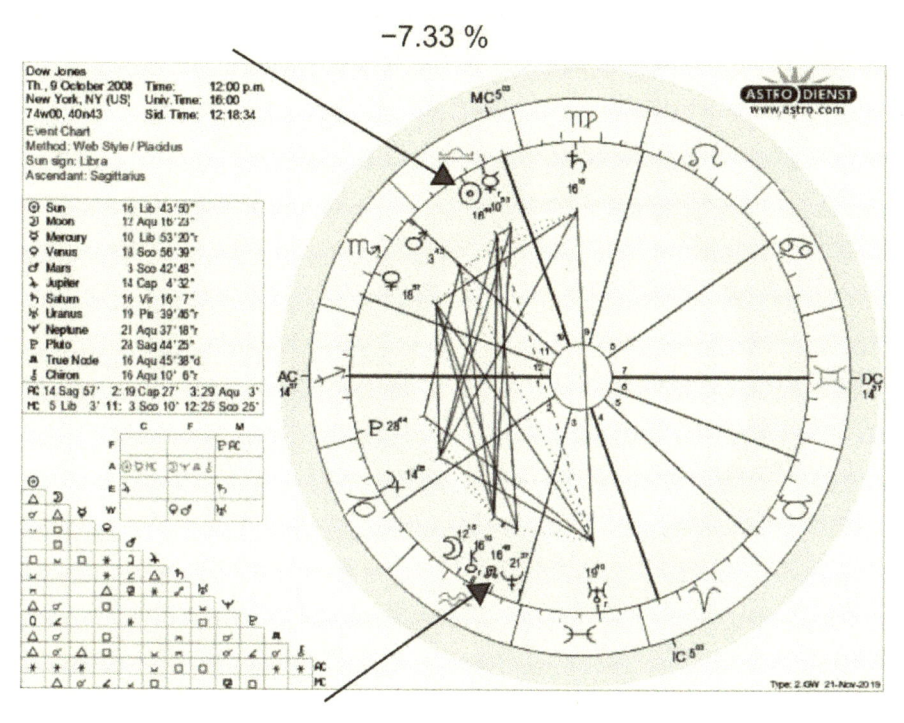

Dow Jones
Th., 9 October 2008
New York, NY (US)
74w00, 40n43
Time: 12:00 p.m.
Univ. Time: 16:00
Sid. Time: 12:18:34
Event Chart
Method: Web Style / Placidus
Sun sign: Libra
Ascendant: Sagittarius

☉ Sun	16 Lib 43' 50"	
☽ Moon	17 Aqu 16' 23"	
☿ Mercury	10 Lib 53' 20"r	
♀ Venus	18 Sco 56' 39"	
♂ Mars	3 Sco 42' 48"	
♃ Jupiter	14 Cap 4' 32"	
♄ Saturn	16 Vir 16' 7"	
♅ Uranus	19 Pis 39' 45"r	
♆ Neptune	21 Aqu 37' 18"r	
♇ Pluto	28 Sag 44' 25"	
⚷ True Node	16 Aqu 45' 38"d	
⚸ Chiron	16 Aqu 10' 6"r	

AC 14 Sag 57' 2: 19 Cap 27' 3: 29 Aqu 3'
MC 5 Lib 3' 11: 3 Sco 10' 12: 25 Sco 25'

−7.24 %

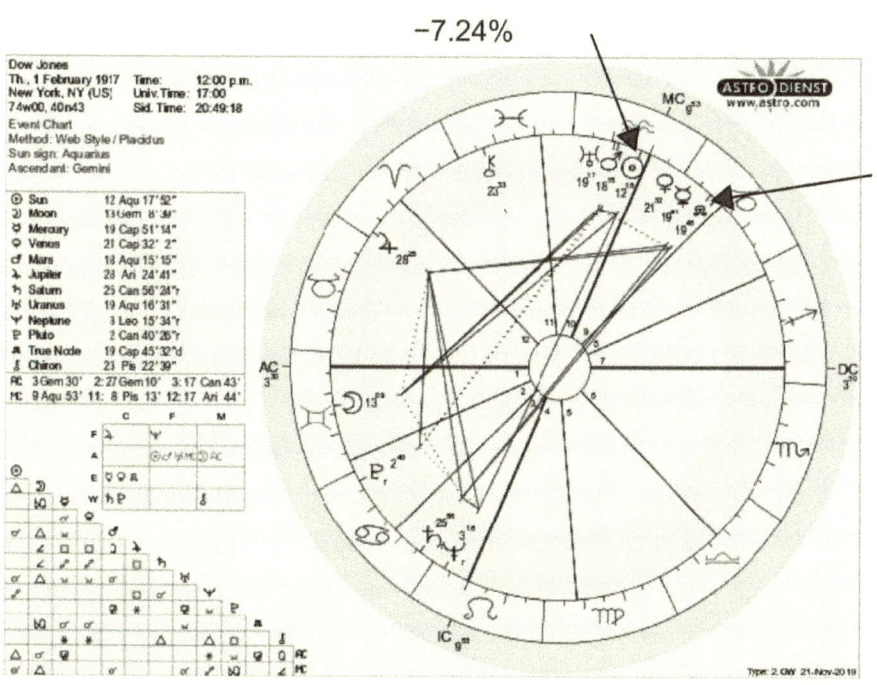

Dow Jones
Th., 1 February 1917
New York, NY (US)
74w00, 40n43
Time: 12:00 p.m.
Univ. Time: 17:00
Sid. Time: 20:49:18
Event Chart
Method: Web Style / Placidus
Sun sign: Aquarius
Ascendant: Gemini

☉ Sun	12 Aqu 17' 52"	
☽ Moon	13 Gem 8' 39"	
☿ Mercury	19 Cap 51' 14"	
♀ Venus	21 Cap 32' 2"	
♂ Mars	18 Aqu 15' 15"	
♃ Jupiter	28 Ari 24' 41"	
♄ Saturn	25 Can 56' 24"r	
♅ Uranus	19 Aqu 16' 31"	
♆ Neptune	3 Leo 15' 34"r	
♇ Pluto	2 Can 40' 26"r	
⚷ True Node	12 Cap 45' 32"d	
⚸ Chiron	23 Pis 22' 39"	

AC 3 Gem 30' 2: 27 Gem 10' 3: 17 Can 43'
MC 9 Aqu 53' 11: 8 Pis 13' 12: 17 Ari 44'

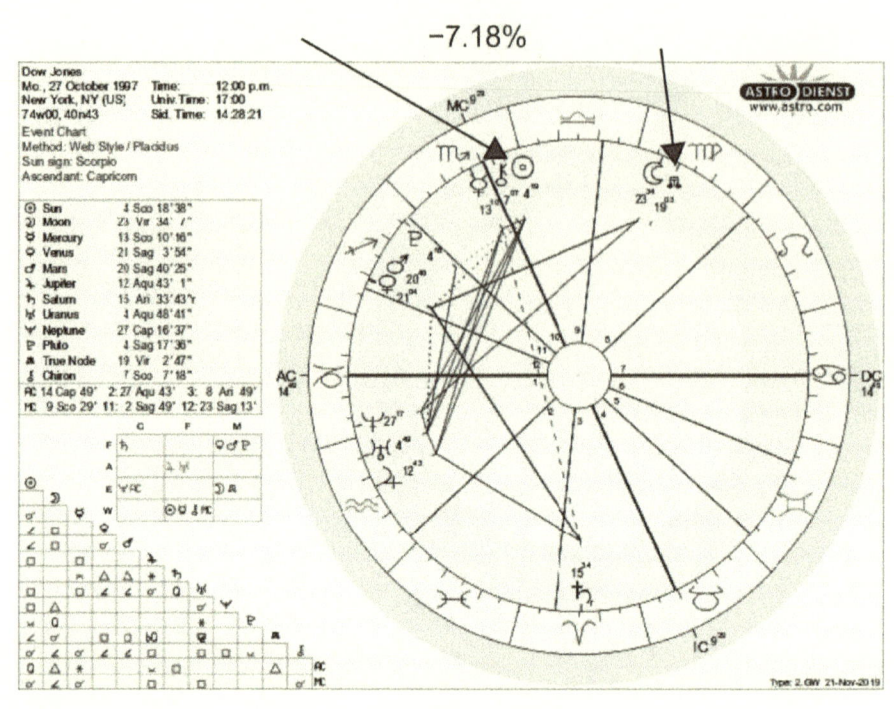

Market Prediction Algorithms for the US Dollar, the Stock Market and Bitcoin

−7.18%

Dow Jones
Mo., 27 October 1997 Time: 12:00 p.m.
New York, NY (US) Univ.Time: 17:00
74w00, 40n43 Sid. Time: 14:28:21
Event Chart
Method: Web Style / Placidus
Sun sign: Scorpio
Ascendant: Capricorn

- ☉ Sun   4 Sco 18'38"
- ☽ Moon   23 Vir 34' 1"r
- ☿ Mercury   13 Sco 10'16"
- ♀ Venus   21 Sag 3'54"
- ♂ Mars   29 Sag 40'25"
- ♃ Jupiter   12 Aqu 43' 1"
- ♄ Saturn   15 Ari 33'43"r
- ♅ Uranus   4 Aqu 48'41"
- ♆ Neptune   27 Cap 16'37"
- ♇ Pluto   4 Sag 17'36"
- ⚷ True Node 19 Vir 2'47"
- ⚹ Chiron   7 Sco 7'18"

AC 14 Cap 49' 2: 27 Aqu 43' 3: 8 Ari 49'
MC 9 Sco 29' 11: 2 Sag 49' 12: 23 Sag 13'

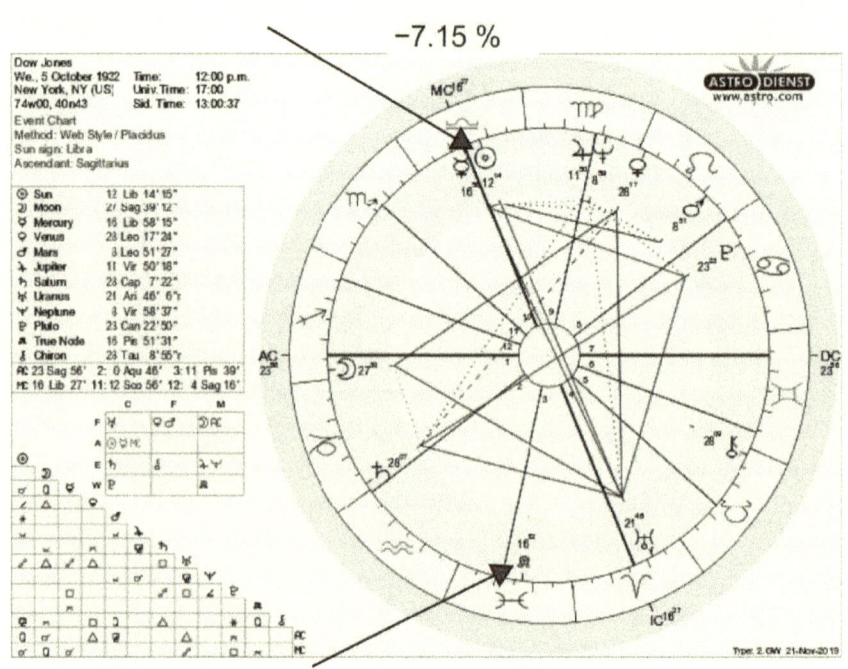

−7.15 %

Dow Jones
We., 5 October 1922 Time: 12:00 p.m.
New York, NY (US) Univ.Time: 17:00
74w00, 40n43 Sid. Time: 13:00:37
Event Chart
Method: Web Style / Placidus
Sun sign: Libra
Ascendant: Sagittarius

- ☉ Sun   12 Lib 14'15"
- ☽ Moon   27 Sag 39'12"
- ☿ Mercury   16 Lib 58'15"
- ♀ Venus   28 Leo 17'24"
- ♂ Mars   8 Leo 51'27"
- ♃ Jupiter   11 Vir 50'18"
- ♄ Saturn   28 Cap 7'22"
- ♅ Uranus   21 Ari 46' 6"r
- ♆ Neptune   8 Vir 58'37"
- ♇ Pluto   23 Can 22'50"
- ⚷ True Node 16 Pis 51'31"
- ⚹ Chiron   28 Tau 8'55"r

AC 23 Sag 56' 2: 0 Aqu 46' 3: 11 Pis 39'
MC 16 Lib 27' 11: 12 Sco 56' 12: 4 Sag 16'

79

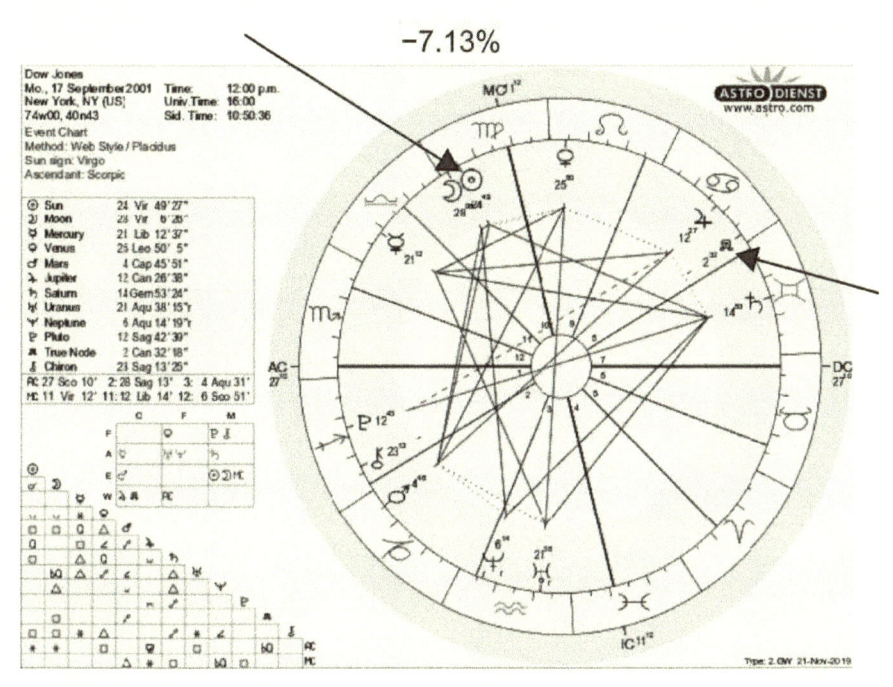

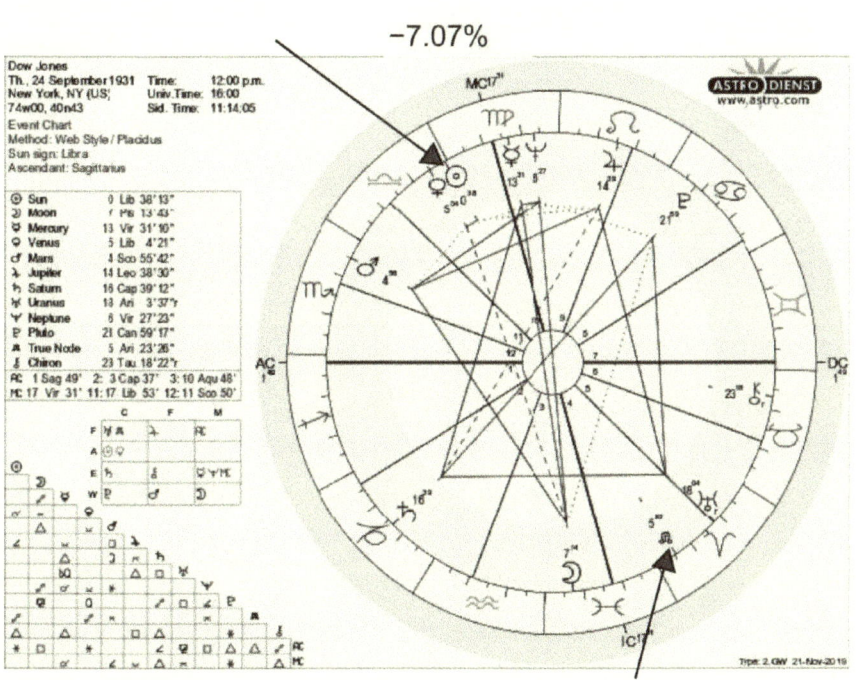

Market Prediction Algorithms for the US Dollar, the Stock Market and Bitcoin

−7.13%

−7.07%

Market Prediction Algorithms for the US Dollar, the Stock Market and Bitcoin

−7.07%

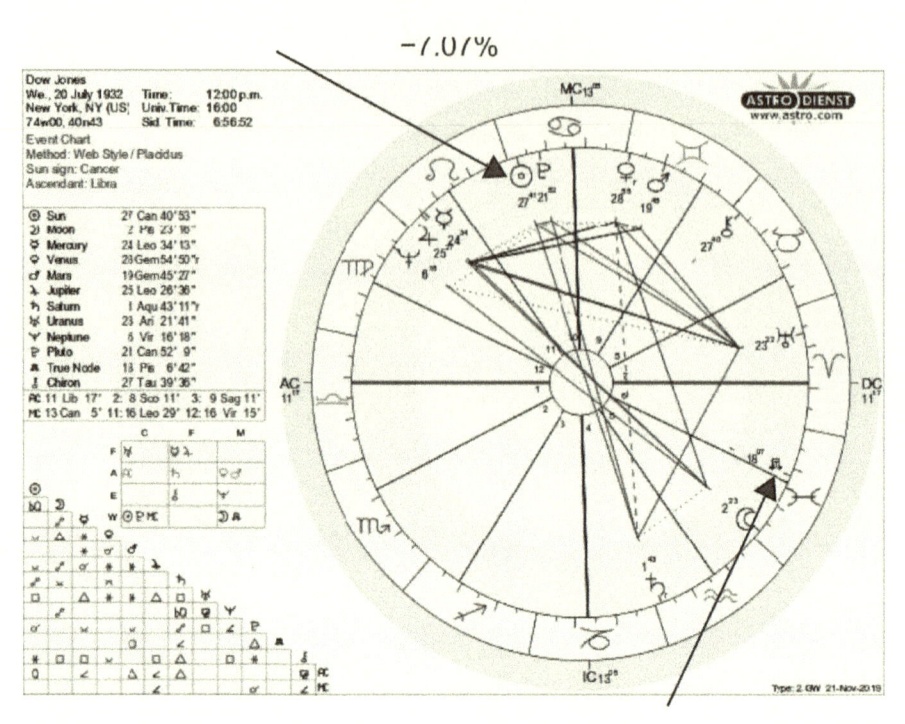

Dow Jones
We., 20 July 1932 Time: 12:00 p.m.
New York, NY (US) Univ. Time: 16:00
74w00, 40n43 Sid. Time: 6:56:52
Event Chart
Method: Web Style / Placidus
Sun sign: Cancer
Ascendant: Libra

☉ Sun	27 Can 40'53"	
☽ Moon	2 Pis 23'16"	
☿ Mercury	24 Leo 34'13"	
♀ Venus	28 Gem 54'50" ʳ	
♂ Mars	19 Gem 45'27"	
♃ Jupiter	25 Leo 26'36"	
♄ Saturn	1 Aqu 43'11" ʳ	
♅ Uranus	23 Ari 21'41"	
♆ Neptune	6 Vir 16'18"	
♇ Pluto	21 Can 52' 9"	
☊ True Node	13 Pis 6'42"	
⚷ Chiron	27 Tau 39'36"	

AC 11 Lib 17' 2: 8 Sco 19' 3: 9 Sag 11'
MC 13 Can 5' 11: 16 Leo 29' 12: 16 Vir 15'

−6.91%

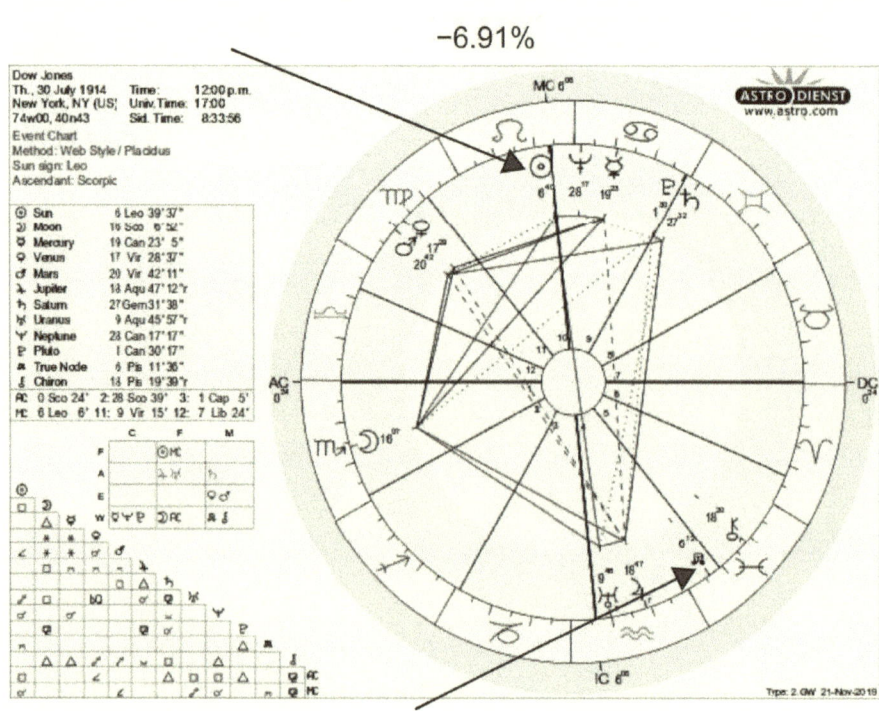

Dow Jones
Th., 30 July 1914 Time: 12:00 p.m.
New York, NY (US) Univ. Time: 17:00
74w00, 40n43 Sid. Time: 8:33:56
Event Chart
Method: Web Style / Placidus
Sun sign: Leo
Ascendant: Scorpio

☉ Sun	6 Leo 39'37"	
☽ Moon	19 Sco 6'52"	
☿ Mercury	19 Can 23' 5"	
♀ Venus	17 Vir 28'37"	
♂ Mars	20 Vir 42'11"	
♃ Jupiter	18 Aqu 47'12" ʳ	
♄ Saturn	27 Gem 31'38"	
♅ Uranus	9 Aqu 45'57" ʳ	
♆ Neptune	28 Can 17'17"	
♇ Pluto	1 Can 30'17"	
☊ True Node	6 Pis 11'36"	
⚷ Chiron	18 Pis 19'39" ʳ	

AC 0 Sco 24' 2: 28 Sco 39' 3: 1 Cap 5'
MC 6 Leo 6' 11: 9 Vir 15' 12: 7 Lib 24'

Market Prediction Algorithms for the US Dollar, the Stock Market and Bitcoin

This slight improvisation to the parameter 2 in the Figure C algorithm from Chapter 25 would provide a historical perspective to the algorithm that would deem its application as being safer in terms of avoiding crashes. While the Chapter 25 explanation of the Sun's degree in relation to the lunar node's degree avoids major crashes, a delineation around the point when the Sun's degree crosses the lunar node's...to which one would apply an entry point anticipating a market upswing when the Sun's degree is at least 3 degrees higher than the lunar node's degree..... provides an even greater sense of security.

To Reaffirm:

The basic gist of this improvised algorithm decrees that from the point when the degree of the sun is 3 degrees past(or higher than) the degree of the lunar node(in any sign) all the way until the degree of the sun enters a new sign at the 24th degree mark(using western astrology), a prediction of a market upswing should be applied. From the point when the degree of the sun enters a new sign at the 24th degree mark all the way until the degree of the sun goes 3 degrees past the degree of the lunar node(in any sign), the prediction of a market downswing should be applied.

Jan 31, 2020(2am) - Feb 13, 2020(2am)
Dow Jones Upswing Prediction
RESULT - Dow +2.3%

Feb 13, 2020(2am) - Feb 28, 2020(1am)
Dow Jones Downswing Prediction
RESULT - Dow -12.83%

Feb 28, 2020(1am) - Mar 13, 2020(11pm)
Dow Jones Upswing Prediction
RESULT - Dow -10.01%

Mar 13, 2020(11pm) - Mar 26, 2020(7am)
Dow Jones Downswing Prediction
RESULT - Dow -8.64%

Mar 26, 2020(7am) - Apr 13 2020 (8am)
Dow Jones Upswing Prediction
RESULT - Dow +11.88%

April 13, 2020(8am) - April 23, 2020(8am)
Dow Jones Downswing Prediction
RESULT - Dow -1.05%

April 23, 2020(8am) - May 14, 2020(5am)
Dow Jones Upswing Prediction
RESULT - Dow -0.57%

May 14, 2020(5am) - May 22 2020 (7pm)
Dow Jones Downswing Prediction
RESULT - Dow +5.24%

May 22, 2020(7pm) - Jun 14 2020 (11am)
Dow Jones Upswing Prediction
RESULT - Dow +4.90%

Jun 14, 2020(11am) - Jun 23, 2020(12am)
Dow Jones Downswing Prediction
RESULT - Dow +1.64%

Jun 23, 2020(12am) - Jul 16, 2020(12am)
Dow Jones Upswing Prediction
RESULT - Dow +3.25%

Jul 16, 2020(12am) - Jul 24, 2020(12am)
Dow Jones Downswing Prediction
RESULT - Dow -0.81%

Jul 24, 2020(12am) - Aug 16 2020(8am)
Dow Jones Upswing Prediction
RESULT - Dow +4.80%

Aug 16 2020(8am) - Aug 22 2020(10am)
Dow Jones Downswing Prediction
RESULT - Dow -0.00%

Aug 22 2020(10am) - Sep 16 2020(8am)
Dow Jones Upswing Prediction
RESULT - Dow +0.20%

Sep 16 2020(8am) - Sep 19 2020(11am)
Dow Jones Downswing Prediction
RESULT - Dow -1.21%

Sep 19 2020(11am) - Sep 20 2020(9pm)
Dow Jones Upswing Prediction
RESULT - Dow 0.00%

Sep 20 2020(9pm) - Nov 14 2020(6pm)
Dow Jones Downswing Prediction
RESULT - Dow +6.59%

Nov 14 2020(6pm) - Nov 15 2020(5pm)
Dow Jones Upswing Prediction
RESULT - Dow -0.00%

Nov 15 2020(5pm) - Dec 14 2020(4am)
Dow Jones Downswing Prediction
RESULT - Dow -1.29%

Dec 14 2020(4am) - Dec 15 2020(8am)
Dow Jones Upswing Prediction
RESULT - Dow +0.51%

Dec 15 2020(8am) - Jan 12 2021(11am)
Dow Jones Downswing Prediction
RESULT - Dow +4.04%

For the year 2020, this algorithm was accurate in 15 of 22 predictions

Volume III:

Bitcoin Research Prediction Algorithms

In the next example using Bitcoin(BTC/USD), we have a different algorithm with a different set of parameters and also 2 sets of parameter. Once again, the predictions apply to where the value of Bitcoin finishes relative to the day before.

In these examples we will have 2 sets of 9 parameters based on Eclipses360 to see how it correlates to the daily Bitcoin(BTC/USD) movements. This is a much more complicated algorithm and is likely a hint to the mark of the beast economy. In my studies there seems to be something taking place when the Sun and Mercury changes relationship to each other. It seems as though whatever is applied during the time when the degree of mercury is less than the degree of the sun in any sign is exactly the opposite of what happens when the degree of mercury is more than the degree of the sun in any sign. That change in the relationship between the sun and mercury seems to change the outcome of the applied algorithm.

The algorithm is made up 2 sets of parameters defined to predict the movements of the BTC/USD. See the next page for the first set of parameters.

These "**Figure Set 1**" parameters only apply when the degree of mercury is **less** than the degree of the sun.

Note: Keep these pages of "Figure Set 1" referenced to see how the parameters correlate to past Bitcoin prices in the upcoming examples

Figure Set 1

1. When the moon is within 1 degree of the degree of the sun in an Earth or Water sign, the value of Bitcoin(BTC/USD) tends to go up. For instance, the zodiac goes as follows: **aries, taurus, gemini, cancer, leo, virgo, libra, scorpio, sagittarius, capricorn, aquarius, and pisces**. The Earth and Water signs are Taurus, Cancer, Virgo, Scorpio, Capricorn, and Pisces. .

2. When the moon is within 1 degree of the degree of the sun in an Fire or Air sign, the value of Bitcoin(BTC/USD) tends to go down. For instance, the zodiac goes as follows: **aries, taurus, gemini, cancer, leo, virgo, libra, scorpio, sagittarius, capricorn, aquarius, and pisces**. The Fire and Air signs are Aries, Gemini, Leo, Libra, Sagittarius, Aquarius.

3. When the moon is within 3 degrees of the degree of the lunar node in any sign, the result is that the value of Bitcoin(BTC/USD) drops.

4. when the moon is within 1 degree of the degree of the lunar node after the moon has passed the degree of the sun in an Earth or Water sign, Bitcoin's(BTC/USD) value tends to drop.

5. when the moon is within 1 degree of the degree of the lunar node after the moon has passed the degree of the sun in a Fire or Air sign, Bitcoin's(BTC/USD) value tends to rise.

Figure Set 1 cont'd

6. When moon is within 3 degrees of the degree of the Sun in an Earth or Water sign, Bitcoin's(BTC/USD) value tends to drop.

7. When the moon is within 3 degrees of the degree of the Sun in a Fire or Air sign, Bitcoin(BTC/USD) tends to rise.

8. When the moon is within 1 degree of the degree of the Mercury after the moon has passed the degree of the sun in an Earth or Water sign, Bitcoin's(BTC/USD) value tends to drop.

9. When the moon is within 1 degree of the degree of Mercury after the moon has passed the degree of the sun in a Fire or Air sign, the Bitcoin's(BTC/USD) value tends to rise.

Figure Set 2 starts on the next page

Keep the pages of "Figure Set 2" referenced to see how the parameters correlate to past Bitcoin prices in the upcoming examples

These "**Figure Set 2**" parameters only apply when the degree of mercury is **greater** than the degree of the sun.

Figure Set 2

1. When the moon is within 1 degree of the degree of the sun in an Earth or Water sign, the value of Bitcoin(BTC/USD) tends to go down. For instance, the zodiac goes as follows: **aries, taurus, gemini, cancer, leo, virgo, libra, scorpio, sagittarius, capricorn, aquarius, and pisces**. The Earth and Water signs are Taurus, Cancer, Virgo, Scorpio, Capricorn, and Pisces. .

2. When the moon is within 1 degree of the degree of the sun in an Fire or Air sign, the value of Bitcoin(BTC/USD) tends to go up. For instance, the zodiac goes as follows: **aries, taurus, gemini, cancer, leo, virgo, libra, scorpio, sagittarius, capricorn, aquarius, and pisces**. The Fire and Air signs are Aries, Gemini, Leo, Libra, Sagittarius, Aquarius.

3. When the moon is within 3 degrees of the degree of the lunar node in any sign, the result is that the value of Bitcoin(BTC/USD) drops.

4. when the moon is within 1 degree of the degree of the lunar node after the moon has passed the degree of the sun in an Earth or Water sign, Bitcoin's(BTC/USD) value tends to rise.

5. when the moon is within 1 degree of the degree of the lunar node after the moon has passed the degree of the sun in a Fire or Air sign, Bitcoin's(BTC/USD) value tends to drop.

6. When moon is within 3 degrees of the degree of the Sun in an Earth or Water sign, Bitcoin's(BTC/USD) value tends to rise.

Figure Set 2 cont'd

7. When the moon is within 3 degrees of the degree of the Sun in a Fire or Air sign, Bitcoin(BTC/USD) tends to drop.

8. When the moon is within 1 degree of the degree of the Mercury after the moon has passed the degree of the sun in an Earth or Water sign, the Bitcoin's(BTC/USD) value tends to rise.

9. When the moon is within 1 degree of the degree of the Mercury after the moon has passed the degree of the sun in a Fire or Air sign, the Bitcoin's(BTC/USD) value tends to drop.

Go to the next page to see how these parameters apply to trading.

Bitcoin/USD

Date	Price	Open	High	Low	Vol.	Change %	
Jan 31, 2014	800.0	801.7	803.3	791.8	0.22K	-0.49%	
Jan 30, 2014	803.9	794.4	803.9	785.4	0.27K	0.49%	
Jan 29, 2014	800.0	789.0	800.0	783.6	0.13K	0.63%	
Jan 28, 2014	795.0	779.8	812.0	770.0	0.56K	4.57%	
Jan 27, 2014	760.3	810.9	810.9	757.0	0.74K	-6.10%	
Jan 26, 2014	809.7	804.2	823.9	731.0	0.15K	-0.04%	
Jan 25, 2014	810.0	795.8	810.0	789.4	0.23K	3.60%	
Jan 24, 2014	781.9	800.0	800.0	773.2	0.36K	-4.21%	
Jan 23, 2014	816.2	819.0	820.0	804.3	0.26K	1.14%	These are the
Jan 22, 2014	807.0	807.0	807.0	807.0	0.00K	-0.37%	prices for the
Jan 21, 2014	810.0	810.0	824.7	794.2	0.37K	-1.62%	BTC/USD
Jan 20, 2014	823.4	831.0	831.0	795.2	0.15K	-0.80%	for the month
Jan 19, 2014	830.0	819.0	830.0	814.2	0.14K	3.75%	of
Jan 18, 2014	800.0	810.0	815.0	799.0	0.15K	1.39%	January 2014
Jan 17, 2014	789.0	820.0	820.7	789.0	0.07K	-4.25%	
Jan 16, 2014	824.0	847.1	847.1	822.4	0.20K	-1.87%	
Jan 15, 2014	839.7	835.5	842.2	833.7	0.05K	1.56%	
Jan 14, 2014	826.9	827.8	833.4	815.1	0.14K	1.03%	
Jan 13, 2014	818.4	846.6	857.3	818.4	0.06K	-7.85%	
Jan 12, 2014	888.1	892.0	892.0	888.1	0.00K	-0.98%	
Jan 11, 2014	896.9	899.0	900.3	895.0	0.01K	7.44%	
Jan 10, 2014	834.7	833.0	834.7	833.0	0.00K	-1.79%	
Jan 09, 2014	850.0	833.7	850.0	794.9	0.29K	2.59%	
Jan 08, 2014	828.5	781.0	838.0	771.0	0.14K	4.75%	
Jan 07, 2014	791.0	928.7	928.7	791.0	0.10K	-15.36%	
Jan 06, 2014	934.5	910.0	950.0	900.0	0.10K	3.38%	
Jan 05, 2014	904.0	839.5	904.0	839.5	0.02K	12.74%	
Jan 04, 2014	801.8	806.5	806.5	801.8	0.01K	-1.26%	
Jan 03, 2014	812.1	801.0	812.1	801.0	-	4.78%	
Jan 02, 2014	775.0	746.2	775.0	740.2	0.13K	4.69%	
Jan 01, 2014	740.3	740.0	757.0	733.5	0.01K	1.73%	

Highest: 950.0   Lowest: 731.0   Difference: 219.0   Average: 819.4   Change %: 9.9

We will use January, February and early March of 2014 in our example for Bitcoin's value correlating with Eclipses. **Remember**: we have 2 sets of parameters for this Bitcoin algorithm: Figure Set 1 and Figure Set 2. Both are based on the relationship between the degree of the sun and the degree of mercury. **Figure Set 1** applies when the degree of mercury is less than the degree of the sun, while **Figure Set 2** applies when the degree of mercury is greater than the degree of the sun. So lets start with January. On January 1st, 2nd, and 3rd, BTC/USD's value rose all three days. See the chart on the next page. Please note: Figure Set 1 and Figure Set 2 are basically the opposite of each other, with the exception of parameter 3. That one is the same in both.

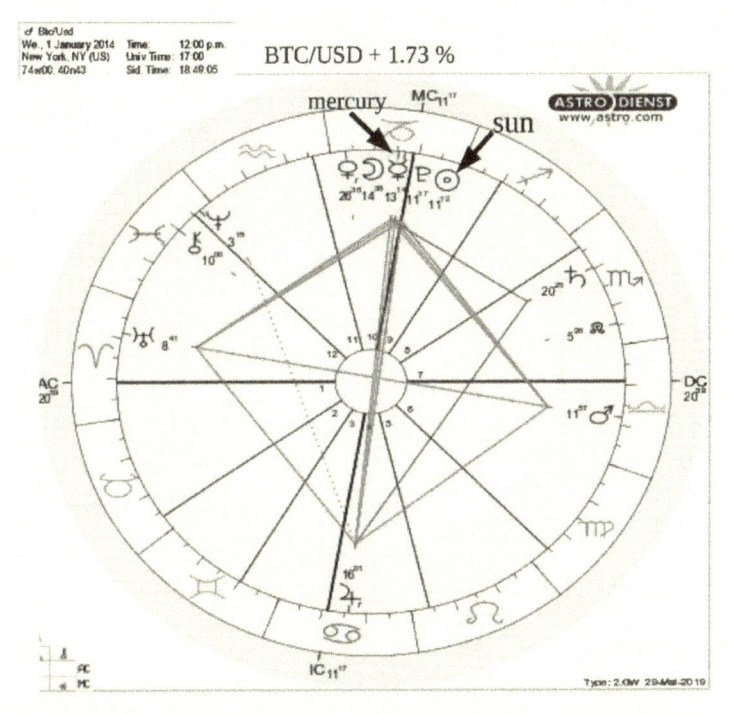

Since we have 2 sets of parameters for this algorithm, we have to see which set do we apply here. We do that by looking at the relationship between the degree of the sun and the degree of mercury. In this chart for January 1st 2014, mercury is at 13 degrees and the sun is at 11 degrees. Therefore, the degree of mercury is higher than the sun's degree. So that means we use "**Figure Set 2**" parameters to asses where BTC/USD would go this day. Just go back to the page where the **Figure Set 2** parameters are laid out. The last parameter that applies in this chart would be parameter 8 which says the moon being within 1 degree of the degree of the Mercury after the moon has passed the degree of the sun in an Earth or Water sign makes the value of BTC/USD to go up. The sun is in capricorn, so the moon having been within 1 degree of the degree of mercury becomes defined by the fact that the sun's degree is in an Earth sign. So the parameter's prediction is correct. BTC/USD was up + 1.73%

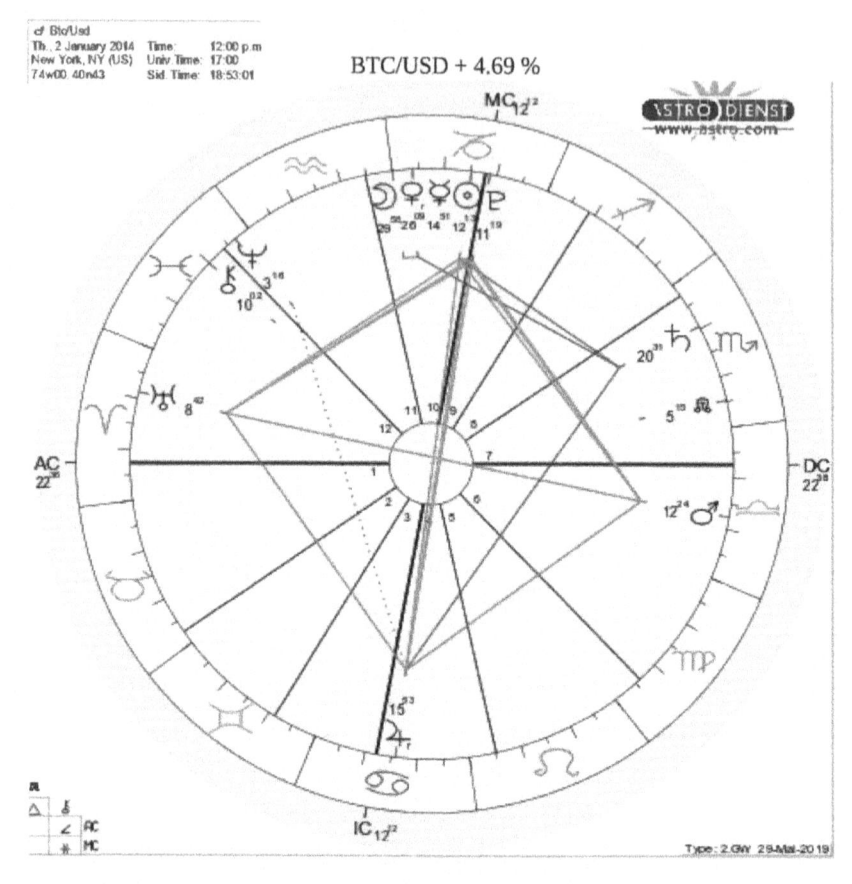

In this chart for Jan 2 2014, the degree of mercury is still higher than the sun's degree, so the **"Figure Set 2"** parameters still apply. When looking at the chart, the last parameter that would have applied from **"Figure Set 2"** would be parameter 8 again. The moon being within 1 degree of the degree of mercury with the degree of the sun being in an earth or water sign is defined to bring the value of BTC/USD up. The BTC/USD was up +4.69% that day.

BTC/USD + 4.78 %

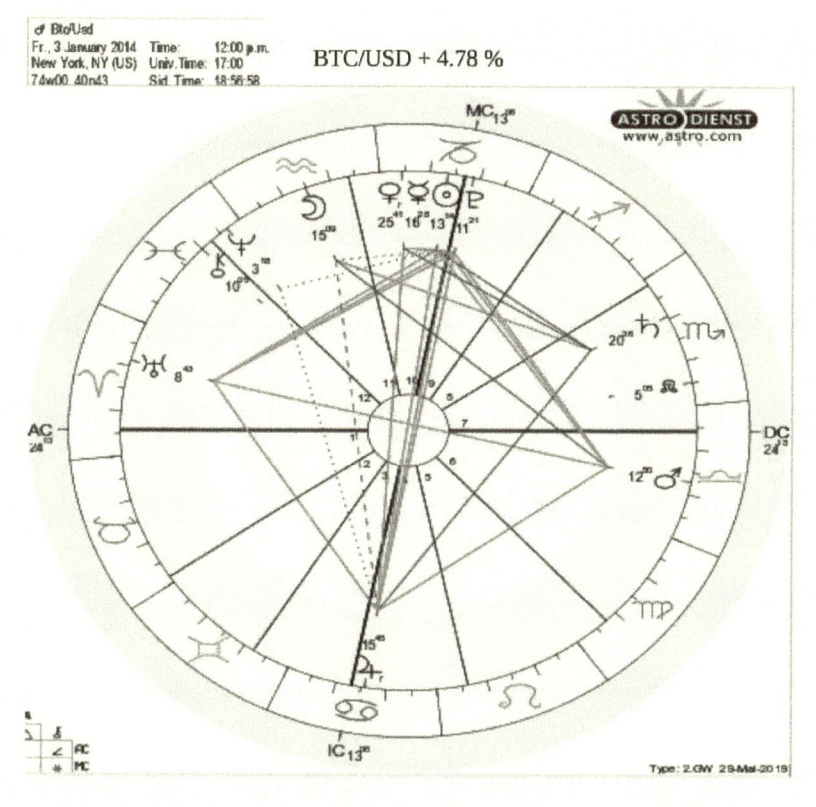

In this chart for Jan 3, 2014, the degree of mercury(16 degrees) is still higher than the sun's degree(13 degrees), so the **"Figure Set 2"** parameters still apply here. When looking at the chart, the last parameter that would have applied from **"Figure Set 2"** would be parameter 2, which says the moon being within 1 degree of the degree of the sun in a fire or air sign brings the value of BTC/USD up. That moon is in Aquarius and the parameter 2 would have occurred in Aquarius, an air sign. The BTC/USD was up +4.78% this day. Its important to notice that with the moon at 15^{09} degrees and almost exactly within 1 degree of the degree of mercury(which is 16^{28} degrees), its close to its next parameter that describes what happens when the moon is within 1 degree of the degree of mercury after the moon has passed the degree of the sun in an air or fire sign.

BTC/USD + 1.26 %

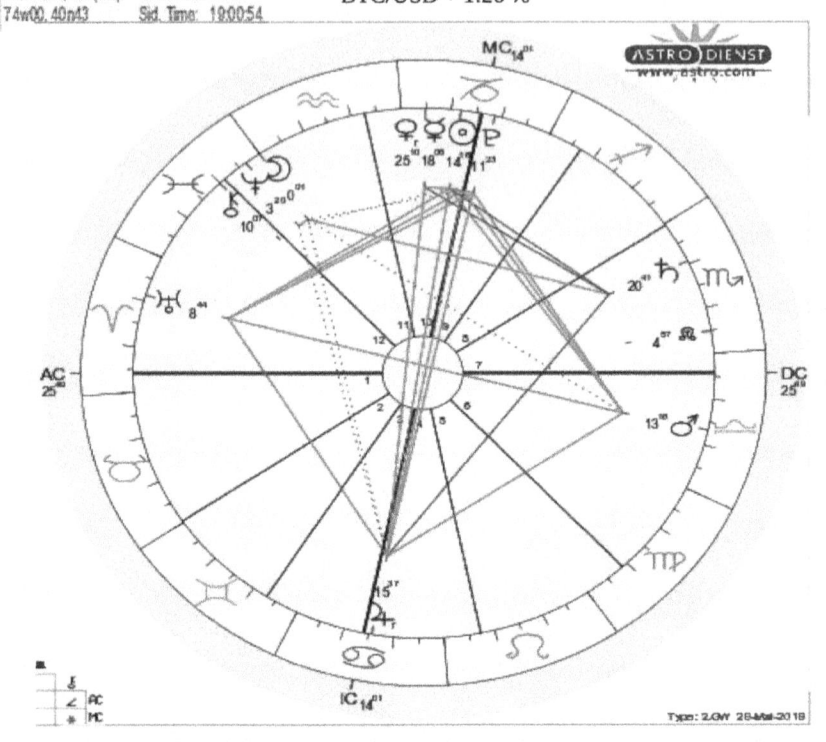

In this chart Jan 4 2014, the degree of mercury(18 degrees) is still higher than the sun's degree(14 degrees), so the **"Figure Set 2"** parameters still apply. When looking at the chart, the last parameter that would have applied from **"Figure Set 2"** would be parameter 9. When the moon was in aquarius and within 1 degree of the degree of mercury and after the moon passed the degree of the sun in an air or fire sign(aquarius is an air sign), the parameter defined the value of BTC/USD to drop. It was down -1.26% that day.

BTC/USD + 12.74%

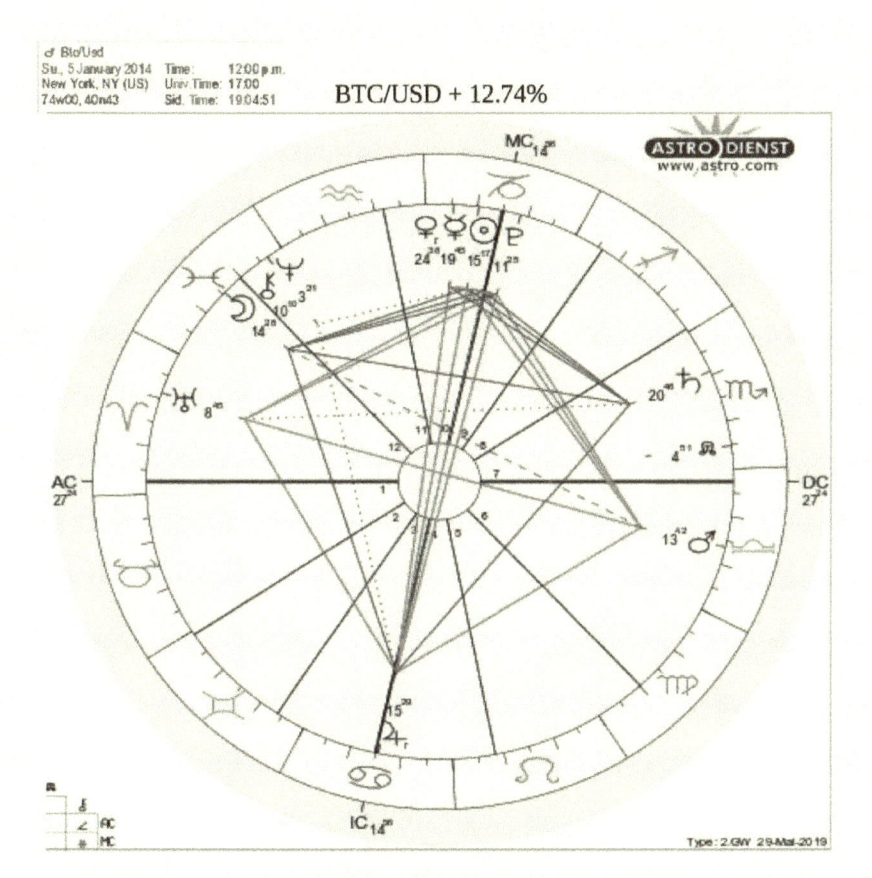

In this chart for Jan 5 2014, the degree of mercury(19 degrees) is still higher than the sun's degree(15 degrees), which means the "**Figure Set 2**" parameters still apply here. When looking at the chart, the last parameter that would have applied from "**Figure Set 2**" would be parameter 6, which says the moon being within 3 degrees of the degree of the sun in an earth or water sign brings the value of BTC/USD up. Pisces is a water sign. So, the parameter's prediction is correct. BTC/USD rose +12.74%.

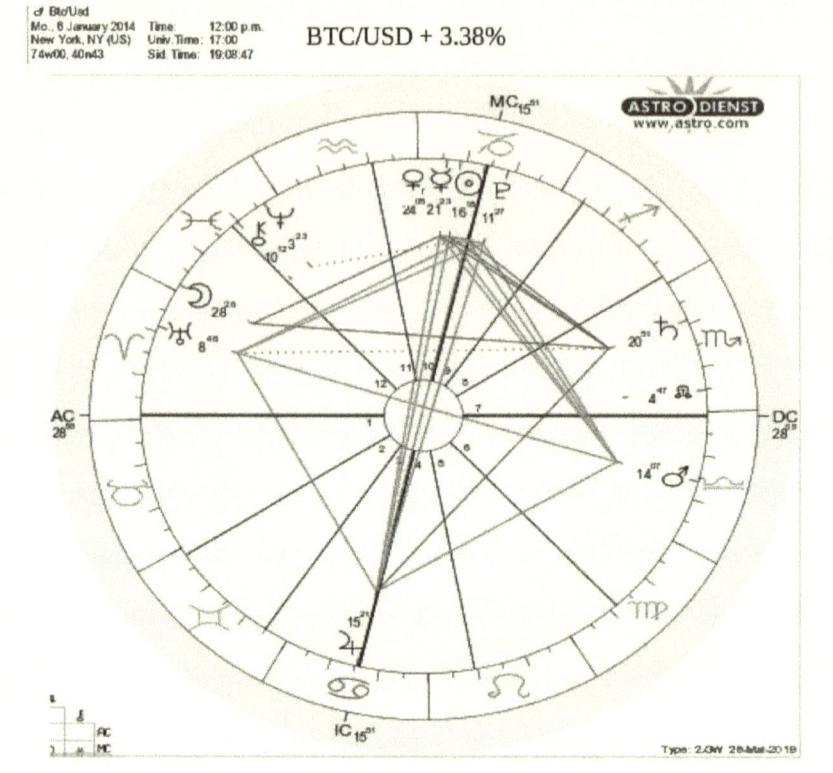

In this chart for Jan 6 2014, the degree of mercury(21 degrees) is still higher than the sun's degree(16 degrees), which means the **"Figure Set 2"** parameters still apply. When looking at the chart, the last parameter that would have applied from **"Figure Set 2"** would be parameter 8, which says the moon being within 1 degree of the degree of the mercury after the moon has passed the degree of the sun in an earth or water sign brings the value of BTC/USD up. Pisces is a water sign. Once again the prediction is correct. BTC/USD rose +3.38% that day.

BTC/USD - 15.36%

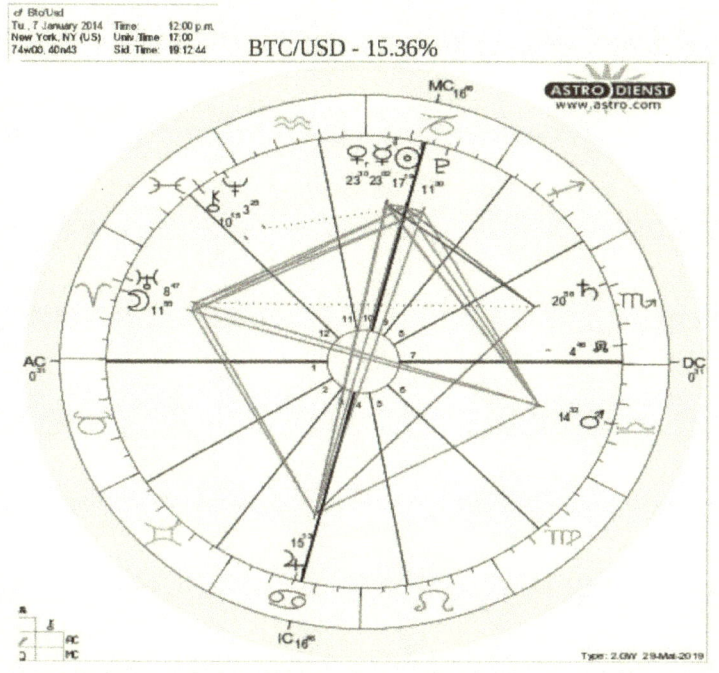

In this chart for Jan 7 2014, the degree of mercury(23 degrees) is still higher than the sun's degree(17 degrees), which means the **"Figure Set 2"** parameters still apply. When looking at the chart, the last parameter that would have applied from **"Figure Set 2"** would be parameter 4, which says the moon being within 1 degree of the degree of the lunar node after the moon passes the degree of the sun in an earth or water sign brings the value of BTC/USD up. The last degree of the sun that was passed by the moon was the 17th degree in pisces, so thus parameter 4 is invoked because Pisces is a water sign. However the prediction from that parameter would be wrong because BTC/USD dropped significantly that day. It was close because Mercury is at 23 degrees. One more degree to 24 degrees and the **"Figure Set 1"** parameters would have been effectuated and the parameter 4 from that set would be correct. Mercury goes into the next sign at 24 degrees which would be counted as a lesser degree than the 17th degree of the sun.

Market Prediction Algorithms for the US Dollar, the Stock Market and Bitcoin

BTC/USD +4.75%

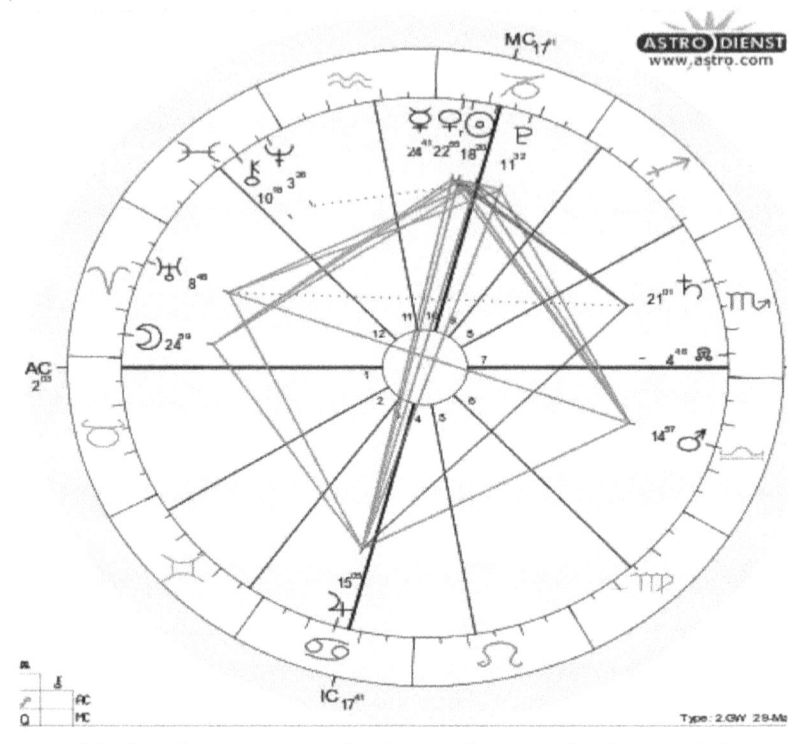

In this chart for Jan 8 2014, the degree of mercury(24 degrees) is lower than the sun's degree(18 degrees). Remember the 24th degree marks the beginning of a new sign. This now means that the "**Figure Set 2**" parameters that we have been using thus far no longer applies at the moment. The "**Figure Set 1**" parameters would now apply. When looking at the chart, the last parameter that would have applied from "Figure Set 1" would be parameter 9, which says the moon being within 1 degree of the degree of mercury after the moon passes the degree of the sun in a fire or air sign brings the value of BTC/USD up. The last degree being the degree of the sun that was passed by the moon was the 18th degree in Aries before it made its way to within 1 degree of the degree of mercury, so thus parameter 9 is invoked because Aries is a fire sign. The prediction was correct as BTC/USD rose +4.75% that day.

BTC/USD +2.59%

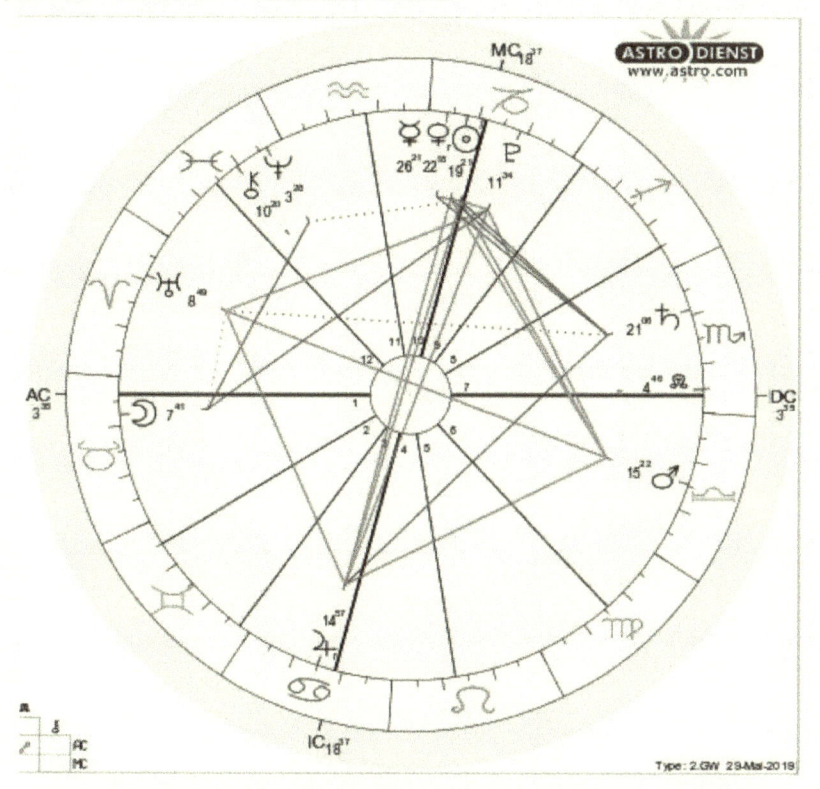

In this chart for Jan 9 2014, the degree of mercury(26 degrees) is lower than the sun's degree(19 degrees). Remember the 24th degree marks the beginning of a new sign. The **"Figure Set 1"** parameters would apply here. When looking at the chart, the last parameter that would have applied from **"Figure Set 1"** would be parameter 5, which says the moon being within 1 degree of the degree of lunar node after the moon passes the degree of the sun in a fire or air sign brings the value of BTC/USD up. The last degree being the degree of the sun that was passed by the moon was the 19th degree in Aries before it made its way to within 1 degree of the degree of lunar node, so thus parameter 5 is invoked because Aries is a fire sign. The prediction was correct as BTC/USD rose +2.59% that day.

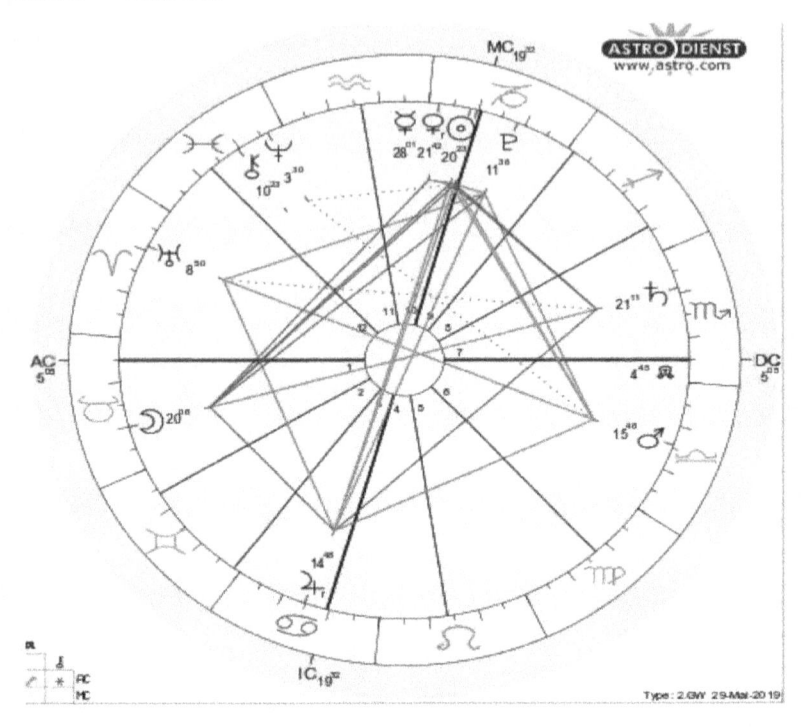

In this chart for Jan 10, 2014, the degree of mercury(28 degrees) is lower than the sun's degree(20 degrees). Remember the 24th degree marks the beginning of a new sign. The **"Figure Set 1"** parameters on would apply here. When looking at the chart, the last parameter that would have applied from **"Figure Set 1"** would be parameter 1, which says the moon being within 1 degree of the degree of the sun in an Earth or water sign brings the value of BTC/USD up. That didn't happen because BTC/USD was down this day. However, it would only be 2 hours before the time used to calculate this chart that parameter 6 would have applied, which states that the moon within 3 degrees of the degree of the sun in an earth or water sin brings the value of BTC/USD down.

BTC/USD +7.44%

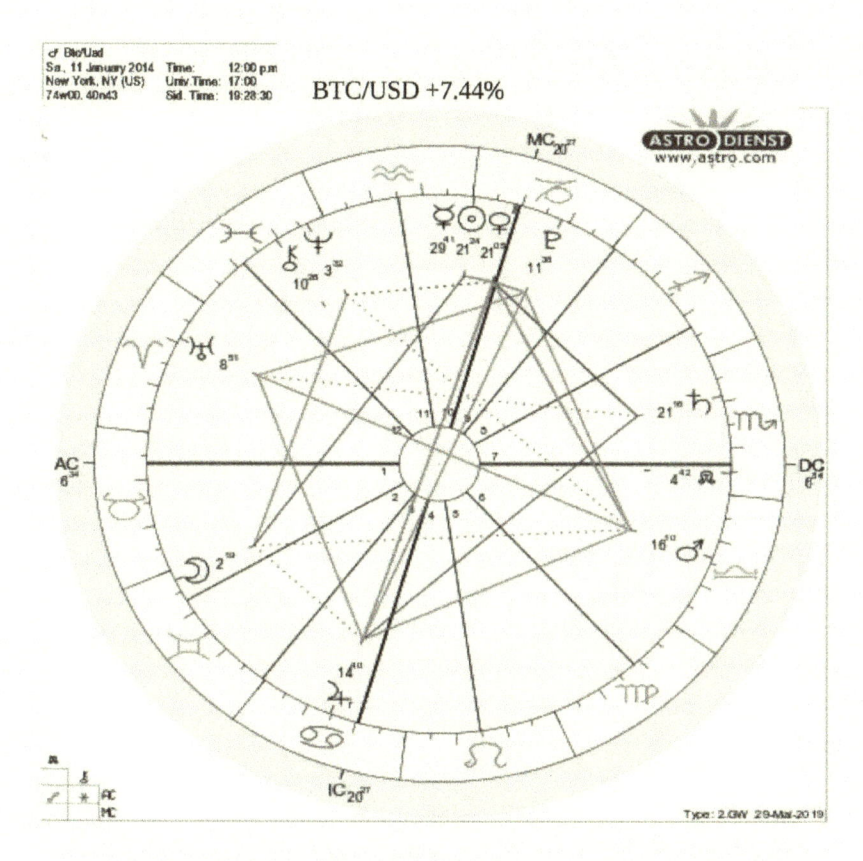

In this chart for Jan 11, 2014, the degree of mercury(29 degrees) is lower than the sun's degree(20 degrees). Remember the 24th degree marks the beginning of a new sign. The **"Figure Set 1"** parameters would apply here. When looking at the chart, the last parameter that would have applied from **"Figure Set 1"** would be parameter 8, which says the moon within 1 degree of the degree of the mercury after the moon has passed the degree of the sun in an Earth or water sign brings the value of BTC/ USD down. That didn't happen because BTC/USD was up significantly this day. So, we have another wrong prediction.

--Since Jan 12 2014 was break-even for BTC/USD, we'll skip to Jan 13th--

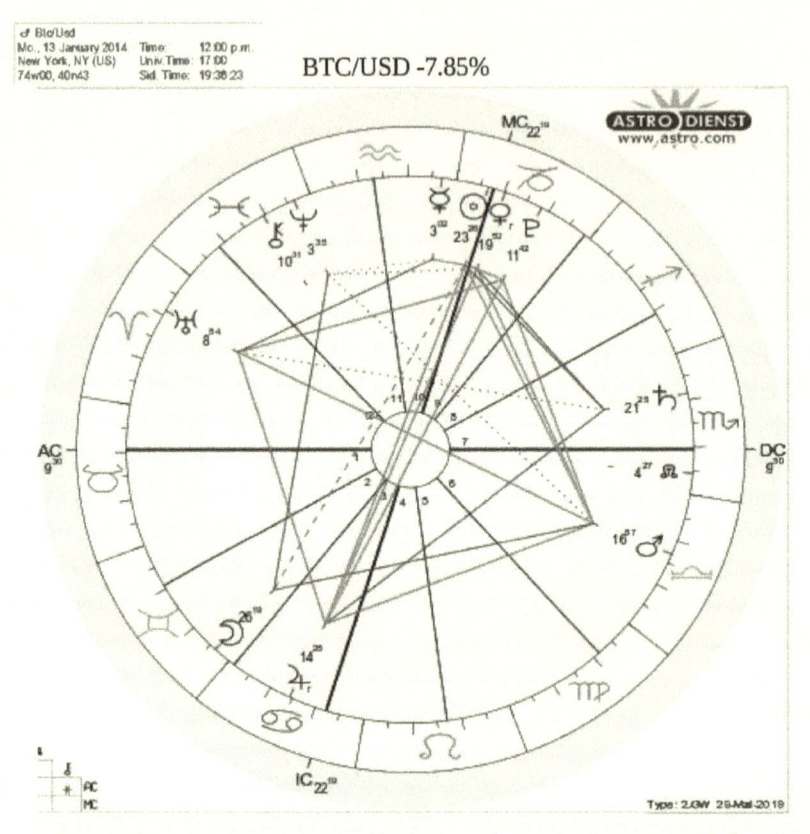

BTC/USD -7.85%

In this chart for Jan 13, 2014, the degree of mercury(3 degrees) is lower than the sun's degree(23 degrees). Remember the 24th degree marks the beginning of a new sign. The **"Figure Set 1"** parameters would apply here. When looking at the chart, the last parameter that would have applied from **"Figure Set 1"** would be parameter 2, which says the moon within 1 degree of the degree of the sun in a Fire or Air sign brings the value of BTC/USD down. The degree of the sun, in this case of the moon going to within 1 degree of the degree of the sun, would be the 23rd degree mark of gemini, which is an air sign. So from that standpoint, the prediction is correct as BTC/USD dropped that day.

BTC/USD +1.03%

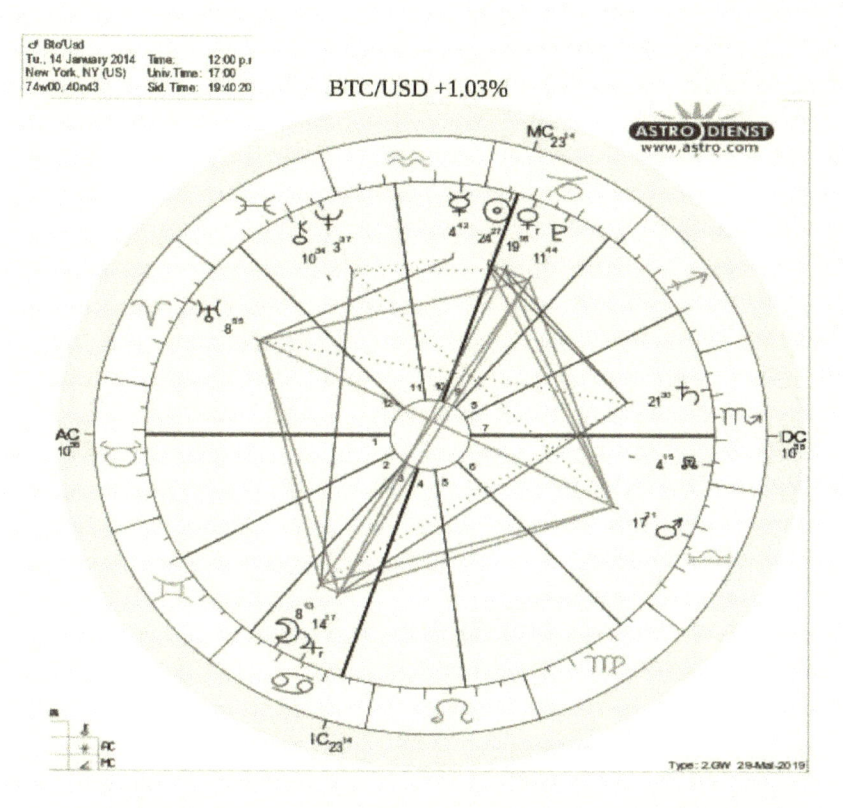

In this chart for Jan 14, 2014, the degree of mercury(4 degrees) is higher than the sun's degree(24 degrees). Remember the 24th degree marks the beginning of a new sign. Therefore, the **"Figure Set 1"** parameters that we have been using no longer apply for now. Because Mercury is at a higher degree than the degree of the sun, we go back to the **"Figure Set 2"** parameters which is invoked when that happens. When looking at the chart, the last parameter that would have applied from **"Figure Set 2"** on would be parameter 8, which says the moon within 1 degree of the degree of the Mercury after the moon has passed the sun's degree in an Earth or water sign brings the value of BTC/USD up. The degree of the sun is 24 degrees, and since the 24th degree marks the beginning of the next sign, the 24th degree mark in gemini is interpreted to the sign of Cancer, which is a water sign. The prediction would be correct as BTC/USD was up 1.03%.

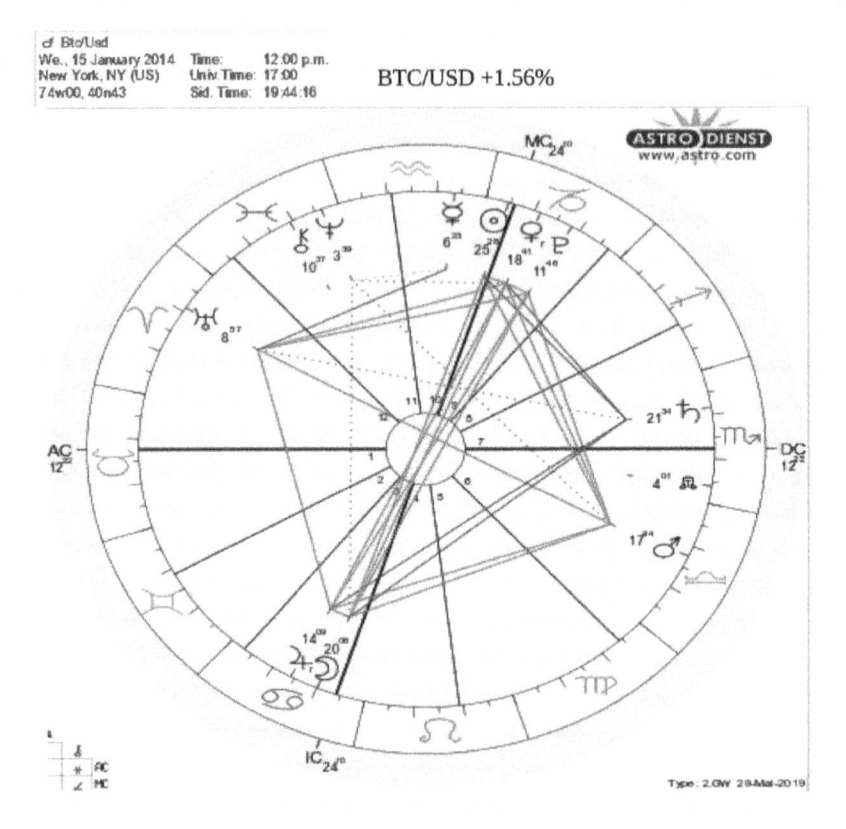

BTC/USD +1.56%

In this chart for Jan 15, 2014, the degree of mercury(6 degrees) is higher than the sun's degree(25 degrees). Remember the 24th degree marks the beginning of a new sign. Because Mercury's degree is at a higher degree than the degree of the sun, we use **"Figure Set 2"** parameters, which is invoked when that happens. When looking at the chart, the last parameter that would have applied from **"Figure Set 2"** would be parameter 8, which says the moon within 1 degree of the degree of Mercury after the moon has passed the sun's degree in an Earth or water sign brings the value of BTC/USD up. That prediction would be correct as BTC/USD was up 1.56% on this day.

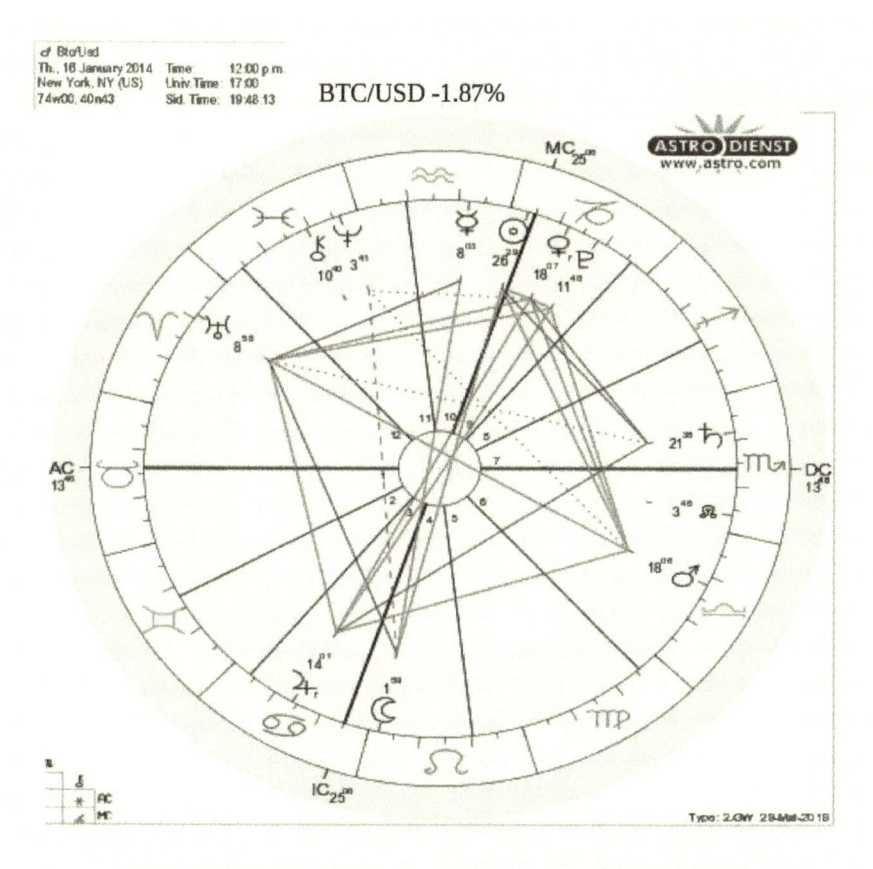

BTC/USD -1.87%

In this chart for Jan 16, 2014, the degree of mercury(8 degrees) is higher than the sun's degree(26 degrees). Remember the 24th degree marks the beginning of a new sign. In light of that, because Mercury's degree is at a higher degree than the degree of the sun, we use **"Figure Set 2"** parameters, which is invoked when that happens. When looking at the chart, the last parameter that would have applied from **"Figure Set 2"** would be parameter 3, which says the moon within 3 degrees of the degree of the Lunar node in any sign brings the value of BTC/USD down. That prediction would be correct as BTC/USD was down -1.87% on this day.

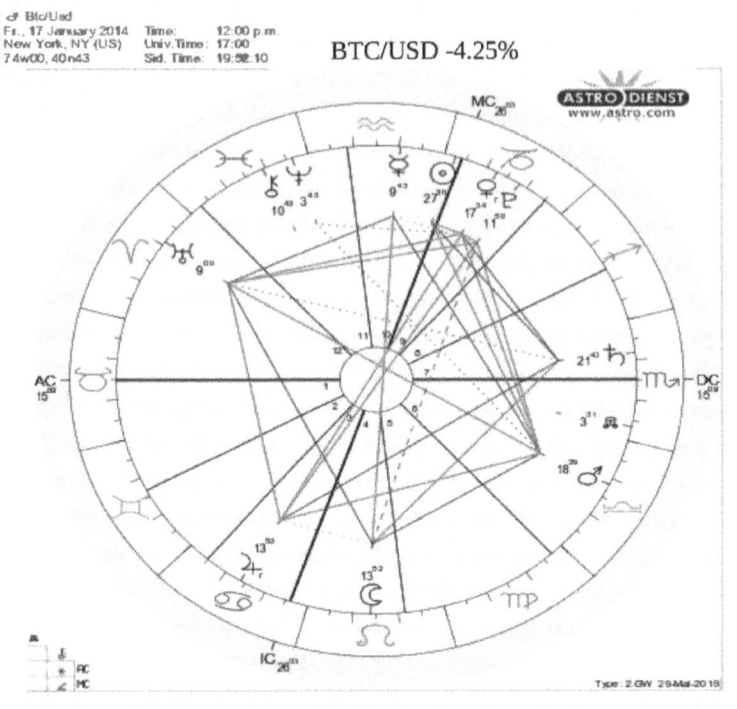

BTC/USD -4.25%

In this chart for Jan 17, 2014, the degree of mercury(9 degrees) is higher than the sun's degree(27 degrees). Remember the 24th degree marks the beginning of a new sign. In light of that, because Mercury's degree is at a higher degree than the degree of the sun, we use **"Figure Set 2"** parameters, which is invoked when that happens. When looking at the chart, the last parameter that would have applied from **"Figure Set 2"** would be parameter 9, which says the moon within 1 degree of the degree of Mercury after the moon has passed the sun's degree in an air or fire sign brings the value of BTC/USD down. The degree of the sun is 27 degrees, and that 27th degree mark for this parameter applied at the 27 degree mark of Cancer, which is interpreted to Leo because the 24th degree mark marks the beginning of the next sign, which in this case is Leo, which is also a fire sign. In that regard, parameter 9 is applied and the prediction would be correct as BTC/USD was down -4.25% on this day.

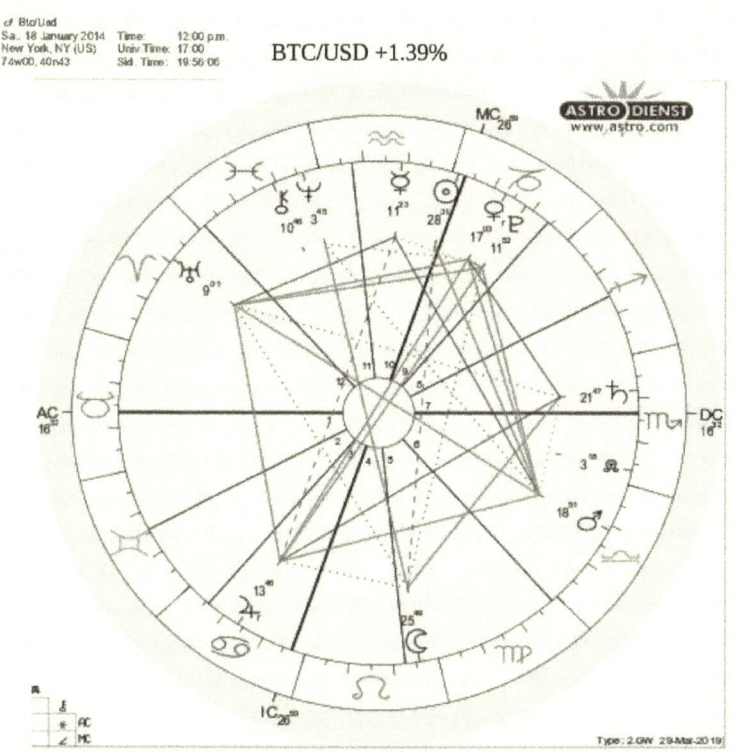

Market Prediction Algorithms for the US Dollar, the Stock Market and Bitcoin

BTC/USD +1.39%

In this chart for Jan 18, 2014, the degree of mercury(11 degrees) is higher than the sun's degree(28 degrees). Remember, the 24th degree marks the beginning of a new sign. So therefore, 11 degrees is later in the sign than 28 degrees, which thus makes the 11th degree higher than the 28th degree. In light of that, because Mercury's degree is at a higher degree than the degree of the sun, we use **"Figure Set 2"** parameters, which is invoked when that happens. When looking at the chart, the last parameter that would have applied from **"Figure Set 2"** would be parameter 6, which says the moon within 3 degrees of the degree of the sun in an earth or water sign brings the value of BTC/USD up. The moon at 25 degrees is 3 degrees from the 28 degree mark of Leo which is the degree of the sun. That 28th degree mark is interpreted to the next sign of Virgo, which is an Earth sign and thus a fulfilled requirement for parameter 6. This prediction would be correct as BTC/USD was up +1.39% for this day.

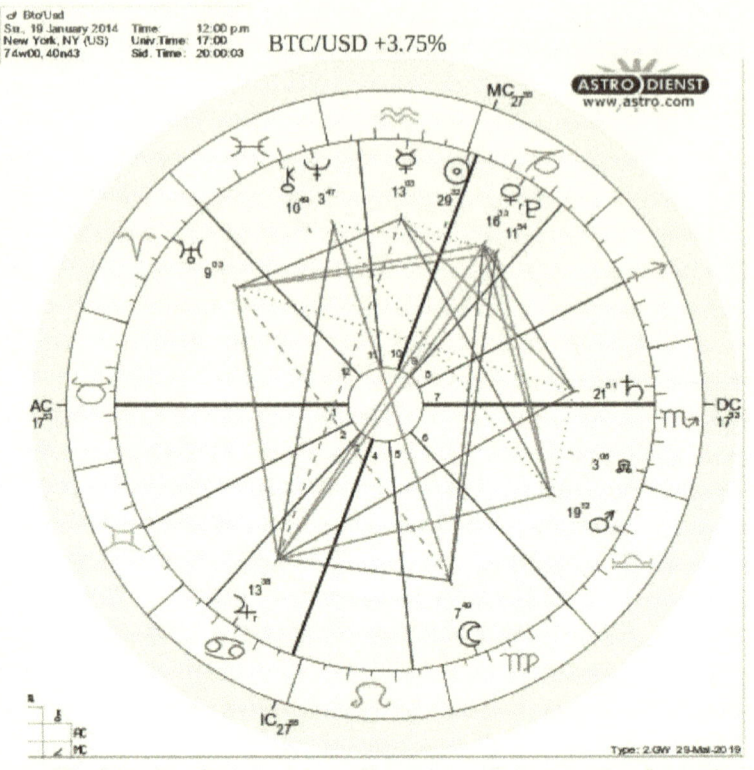

In this chart for Jan 19, 2014, the degree of mercury(13 degrees) is higher than the sun's degree(29 degrees). Remember, the 24th degree marks the beginning of a new sign. Therefore, the 13th degree would be considered higher than the 29th degree. In light of that, because Mercury's degree is at a higher degree than the degree of the sun, we use **"Figure Set 2"** parameters. When looking at the chart, the last parameter that would have applied from **"Figure Set 2"** would be parameter 4, which says the moon within 1 degree of the degree of the lunar node after the moon has passed the sun's degree in an earth of water sign brings the value of BTC/USD up. Because the sun is 29 degrees, the degree of sun for this parameter would have applied to the 29th degree of Leo, which is thus interpreted to the sign of Virgo, which is an earth sign. This prediction would be correct as BTC/USD was up +3.75% for this day.

We will skip to Jan 24, 2014 since that's the next significant price change

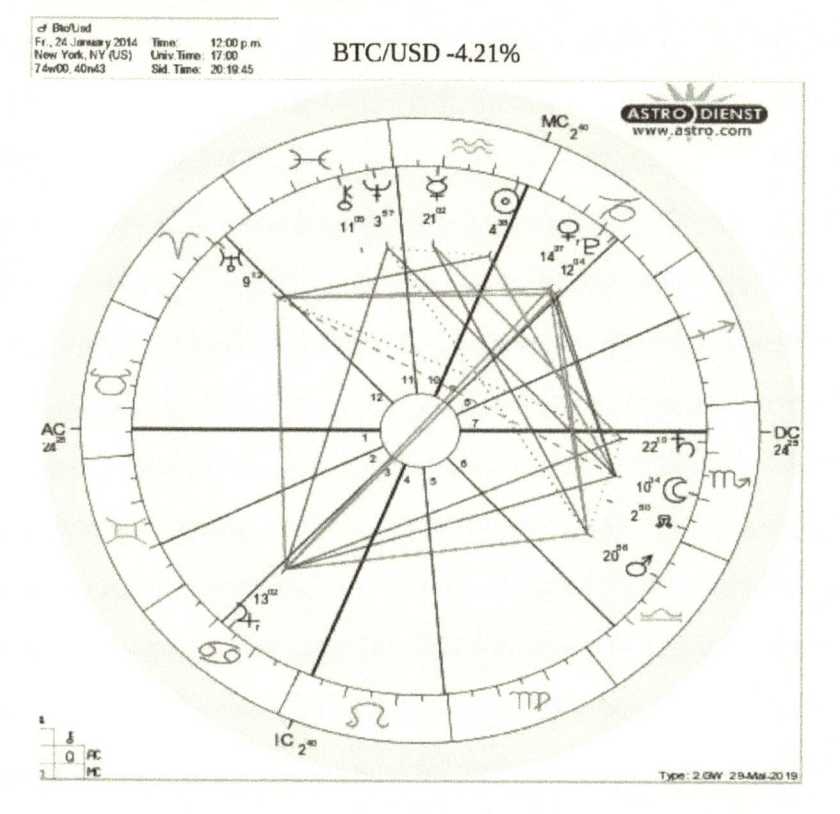

BTC/USD -4.21%

In this chart for Jan 24, 2014, the degree of mercury(21 degrees) is higher than the sun's degree(4 degrees). Therefore, we continue to use **"Figure Set 2"** parameters. When looking at the chart, the last parameter that would have applied from **"Figure Set 2"** would be parameter 1, which says the moon within 1 degree of the degree of the sun in an earth or water sign brings the value of BTC/USD down. Since the Sun is at 4 degrees, the degree of the sun referred to in this case is the 4th degree of Scorpio, which is a water sign. The prediction would be correct as BTC/USD was down -4.21% for this day.

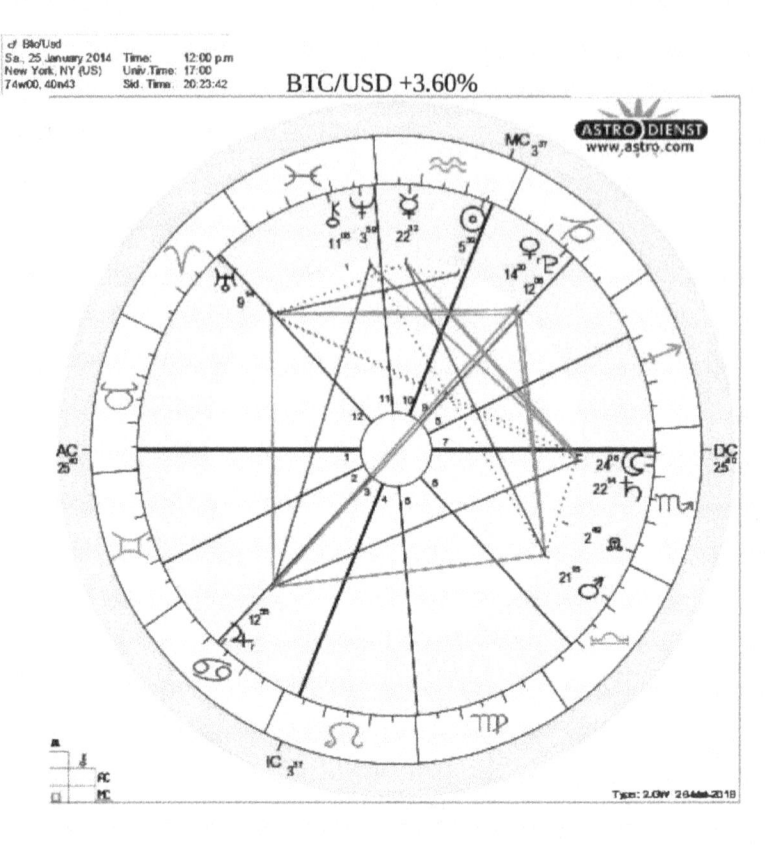

BTC/USD +3.60%

In this chart for Jan 25, 2014, the degree of mercury(22 degrees) is higher than the sun's degree(5 degrees). Therefore, we continue to use **"Figure Set 2"** parameters. When looking at the chart, the last parameter that would have applied from **"Figure Set 2"** would be parameter 8, which says the moon within 1 degree of the degree of mercury after the moon has passed the sun's degree in an earth or water sign brings the value of BTC/USD up. Since the Sun is at 5 degrees, the degree of the sun referred to in this case is the 5th degree of Scorpio, which is a water sign. This prediction would be correct as BTC/USD was up +3.60% for this day.

We will skip to Jan 27, 2014 since that's the next significant price change

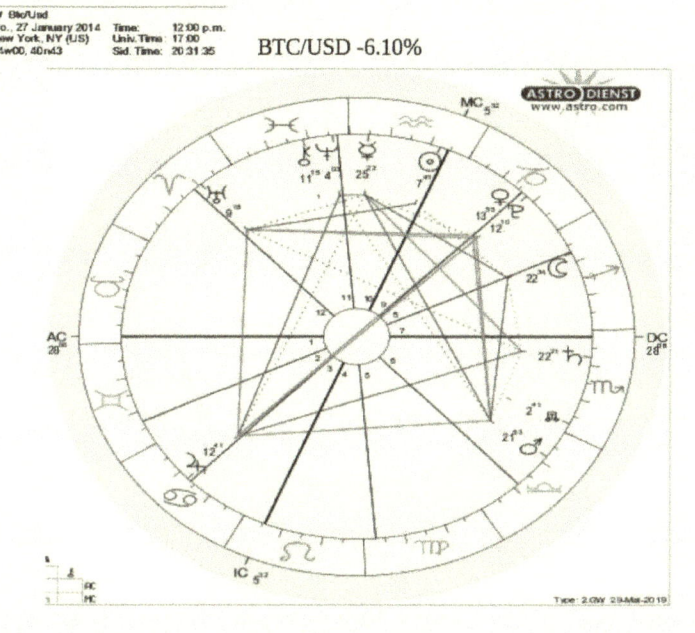

BTC/USD -6.10%

In this chart for Jan 27, 2014, Mercury enters a new sign. Since the 24th degree marks the start of a new sign and Mercury is at 25 degrees in this chart, its now observed for the degree of the mercury to be lower than the degree of the sun. In this case, mercury's degree(25 degrees) is lower than the degree of the sun(7 degrees). Therefore, we stop using the **"Figure Set 2"** parameters and start back again with the **"Figure Set 1"** parameters. These are applied when the degree of mercury is lower than the degree of the sun. When looking at the chart, the last parameter that would have applied from **"Figure Set 1"** would be parameter 2, which says the moon within 1 degree of the degree of the sun in a fire or air sign brings the value of BTC/USD down. Since the Sun is at 7 degrees, the degree of the sun referred to in this case of the moon within 1 degree is the 7th degree mark of Sagittarius, which is a fire sign. Therefore, this prediction would be correct as BTC/USD was down -6.10% for this day.

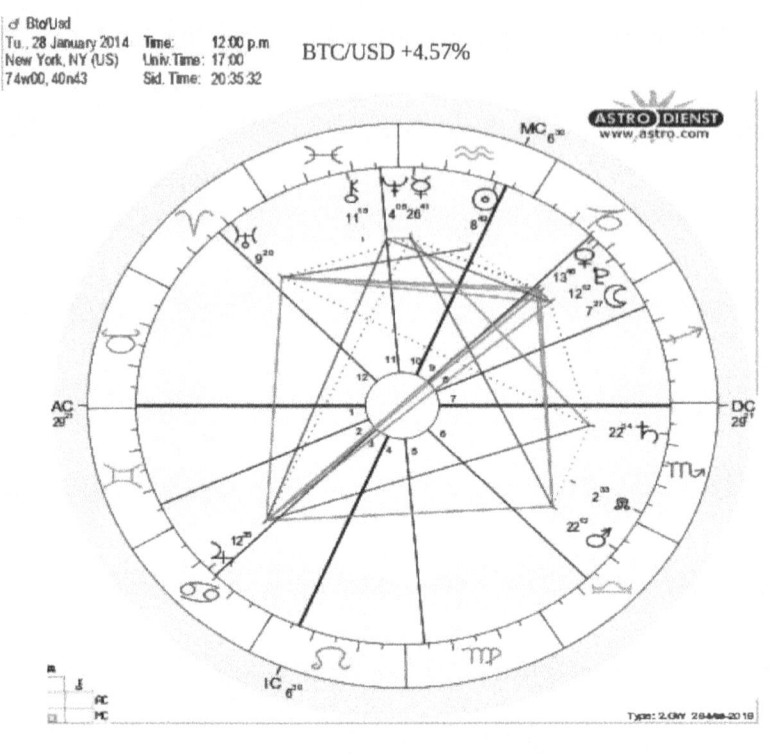

In this chart for Jan 28, 2014, mercury's degree(26 degrees) is lower than the degree of the sun(8 degrees) . Therefore, we use the "**Figure Set 1**" parameters. These are applied when the degree of mercury is lower than the degree of the sun. When looking at the chart, the last parameter that would have applied from "**Figure Set 1**" would be parameter 1, which says the moon within 1 degree of the degree of the sun in an earth or water sign brings the value of BTC/USD up. In this chart, the moon is not exact to within 1 degree of the degree of the sun at 12pm ....so technically in doesn't apply in the way that I was counting it in previous examples---having to be within the exact 1 degree mark down to the superscript(the small number above the number). But since within 1 hour from the time used to calculate the chart, the 1st parameter would eventually end up applying, we use it in this case anyway. Therefore, we can say this prediction would be correct as BTC/ USD was up +4.57% for this day.

We'll end the January there and move onto February to see if the parameters will continue to correlate with the value of BTC/USD. Below are the prices for BTC/USD during the month of February 2014. We will continue with the same algorithm

Date	Price	Open	High	Low	Vol.	Change %	
Feb 28, 2014	565.0	575.5	590.3	544.9	0.34K	-2.42%	
Feb 27, 2014	579.0	592.5	592.5	565.7	0.01K	-0.52%	These are the
Feb 26, 2014	582.0	548.7	594.5	544.0	0.72K	13.01%	prices for the
Feb 25, 2014	515.0	554.0	567.0	425.0	1.91K	-8.43%	BTC/USD for
Feb 24, 2014	562.4	597.3	597.3	562.4	0.01K	-9.14%	the month of
Feb 23, 2014	619.0	597.7	624.1	597.7	0.02K	4.00%	February
Feb 22, 2014	595.2	587.6	602.8	563.7	0.00K	4.79%	2014
Feb 21, 2014	568.0	565.2	591.5	548.5	0.06K	-1.88%	
Feb 20, 2014	578.9	633.0	633.0	574.8	0.04K	-8.17%	
Feb 19, 2014	630.4	634.2	638.0	628.0	0.10K	0.38%	
Feb 18, 2014	628.0	660.0	660.0	622.0	0.05K	-5.40%	
Feb 17, 2014	663.8	626.0	663.8	626.0	0.03K	9.19%	
Feb 16, 2014	608.0	650.0	650.0	608.0	0.11K	-6.95%	
Feb 15, 2014	653.4	652.9	655.7	650.0	0.02K	-4.20%	
Feb 14, 2014	682.0	622.0	724.0	565.2	0.46K	7.53%	
Feb 13, 2014	634.3	671.9	671.9	630.0	0.04K	-7.41%	
Feb 12, 2014	685.0	691.1	691.1	650.0	0.06K	3.97%	
Feb 11, 2014	658.9	739.0	761.7	653.3	0.13K	-6.72%	
Feb 10, 2014	706.3	720.0	739.0	642.0	0.11K	-0.52%	
Feb 09, 2014	710.0	702.6	720.0	702.6	0.10K	2.90%	
Feb 08, 2014	690.0	700.0	716.4	690.0	0.05K	-4.17%	
Feb 07, 2014	720.0	750.3	755.1	677.0	0.28K	-6.68%	
Feb 06, 2014	771.6	793.0	793.0	768.0	0.16K	-2.46%	
Feb 05, 2014	791.0	807.0	808.0	791.0	0.33K	-2.71%	
Feb 04, 2014	813.0	810.8	813.2	808.3	0.12K	0.37%	
Feb 03, 2014	810.0	806.8	814.1	801.7	0.14K	-0.57%	
Feb 01, 2014	814.6	801.9	814.6	801.9	0.01K	1.83%	

Highest: 814.6 Lowest: 425.0 Difference: 389.6   Average: 660.5

Change %: -29.4

BTC/USD +1.83%

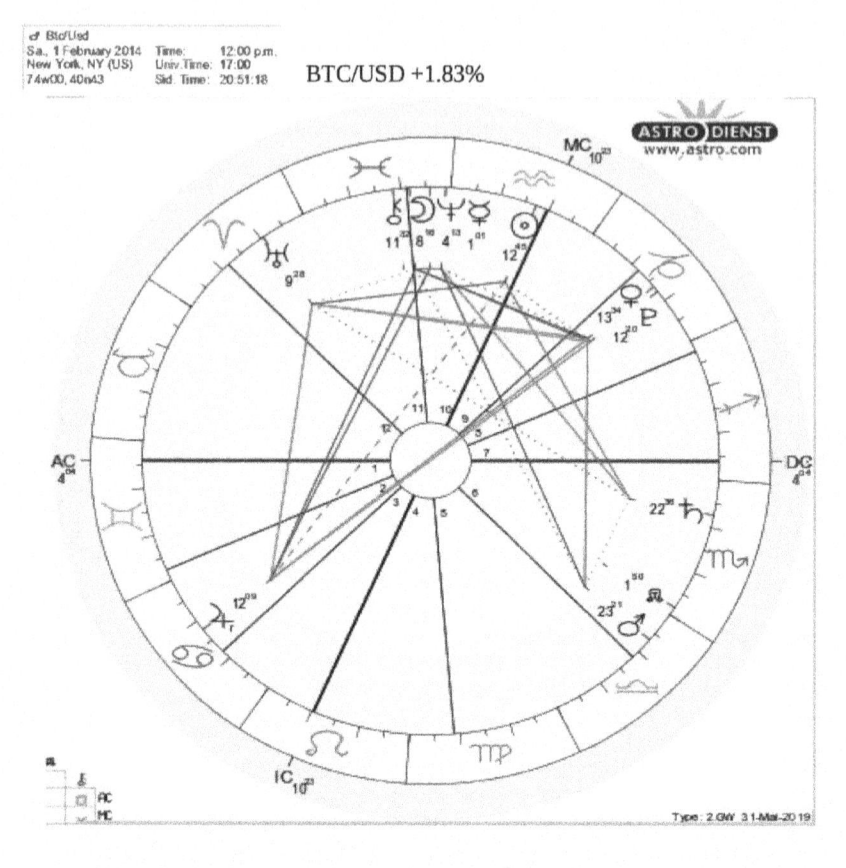

In this chart for Feb 1, 2014, mercury's degree(1 degree) is lower than the degree of the sun(12 degrees). Therefore, we continue to use the "**Figure Set 1**" parameters. These are applied when the degree of mercury is lower than the degree of the sun. When looking at the chart, the last parameter that would have applied from "**Figure Set 1**" would be parameter 9, which says the moon within 1 degree of the degree of mercury after the moon has passed the sun's degree in an air or fire sign brings the value of BTC/ USD up. The last degree of the sun that the moon passed was the 12th degree in Aquarius, which is an air sign. Therefore this prediction is accurate. BTC/USD was up +1.83%.

we'll skip to Feb 5th 2014 since that's the next significant move

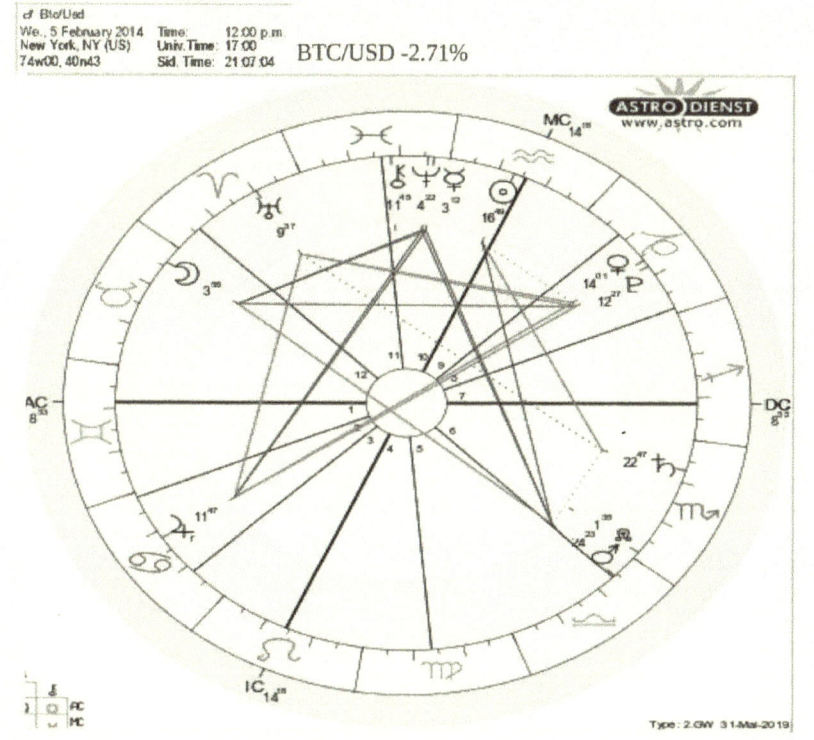

BTC/USD -2.71%

In this chart for Feb 5, 2014, mercury's degree(3 degrees) is still lower than the degree of the sun(16 degrees). Therefore, we continue to use the **"Figure Set 1"** parameters. When looking at the chart, the last parameter that would have applied from **"Figure Set 1"** would be parameter 9, which says the moon within 1 degree of the degree of mercury after the moon has passed the sun's degree in an air or fire sign brings the value of BTC/ USD up. The last degree of the sun that the moon passed was the 12th degree in Aries, which is fire sign. Therefore this prediction is wrong. BTC/USD was actually down -2.71%.

note: there will be days when the parameters will be wrong.

BTC/USD -2.46%

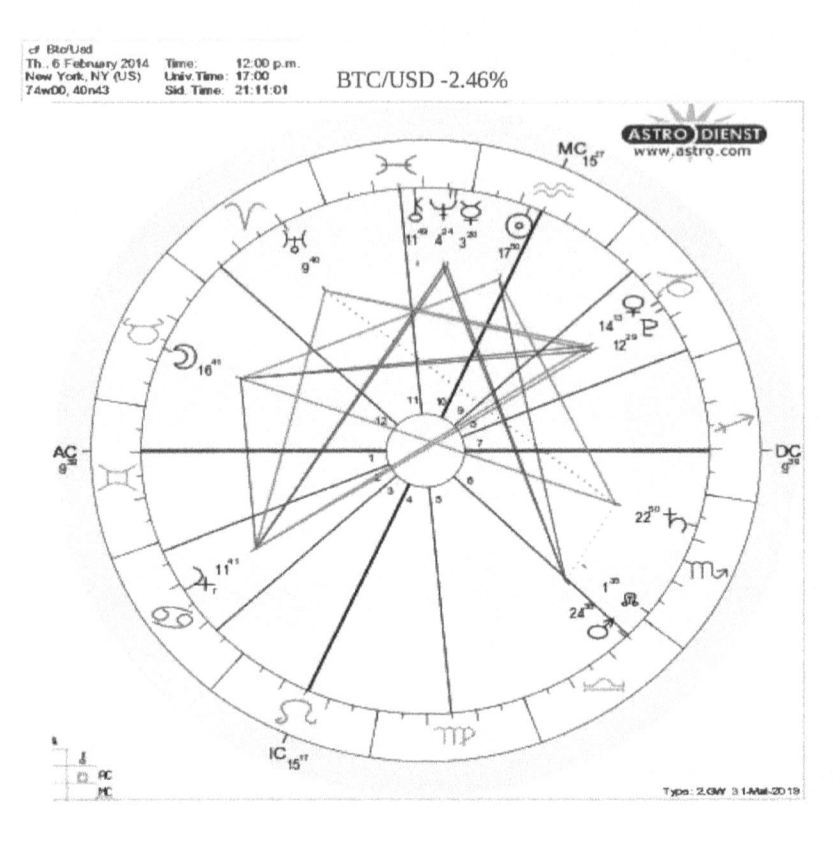

In this chart for Feb 6, 2014, mercury's degree(3 degrees) is lower than the degree of the sun(17 degrees). Therefore, we continue to use the **"Figure Set 1"** parameters. When looking at the chart, the last parameter that would have applied from **"Figure Set 1"** would be parameter 6, which says the moon within 3 degrees of the degree of the sun in an earth or water sign brings the value of BTC/USD down. This prediction is correct. BTC/USD was down -2.46%.

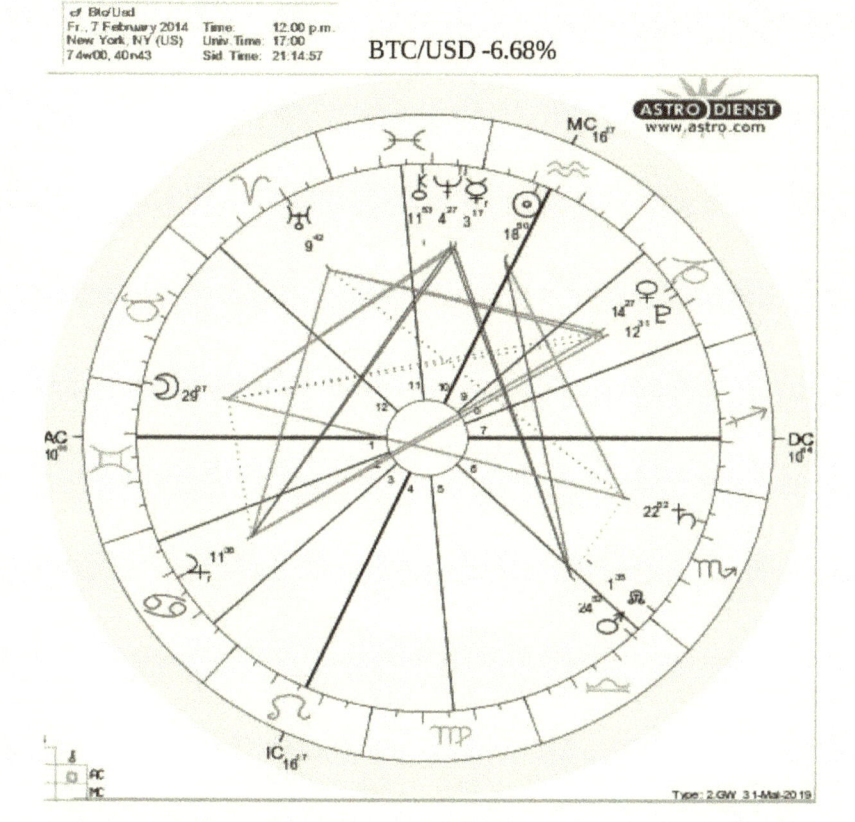

BTC/USD -6.68%

In this chart for Feb 7, 2014, mercury's degree(3 degrees) is lower than the degree of the sun(18 degrees). Therefore, we continue to use the **"Figure Set 1"** parameters. When looking at the chart, the last parameter that would have applied from **"Figure Set 1"** would be parameter 3, which says the moon within 3 degrees of the degree of the lunar node in any sign brings the value of BTC/USD down. The lunar node is at 1 degree and the moon is at 29 degrees. So this applies because the moon is 2 degrees away from the lunar node, which is within the determined 3 degrees to effectuate the prediction. This prediction is correct. BTC/USD was down -6.68%.

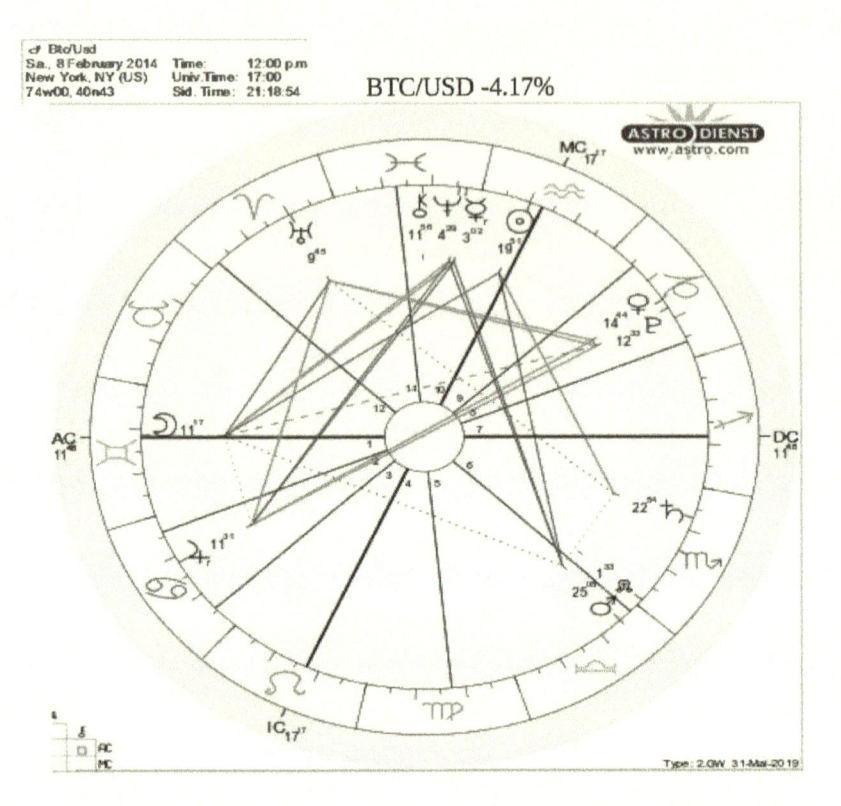

BTC/USD -4.17%

In this chart for Feb 8, 2014, mercury's degree (3 degrees) is lower than the degree of the sun (19 degrees). Therefore, we continue to use the **"Figure Set 1"** parameters. When looking at the chart, the last parameter that would have applied from **"Figure Set 1"** would be parameter 8, which says the moon within 1 degree of the degree of mercury after the moon has passed the sun's degree in an Earth or Water sign brings the value of BTC/USD down. The degree of the sun is 19, and the last degree of the sun passed by the moon in this chart was the 19th degree in Taurus, which is an earth sign. Therefore, this prediction is correct. BTC/USD was down -4.17%.

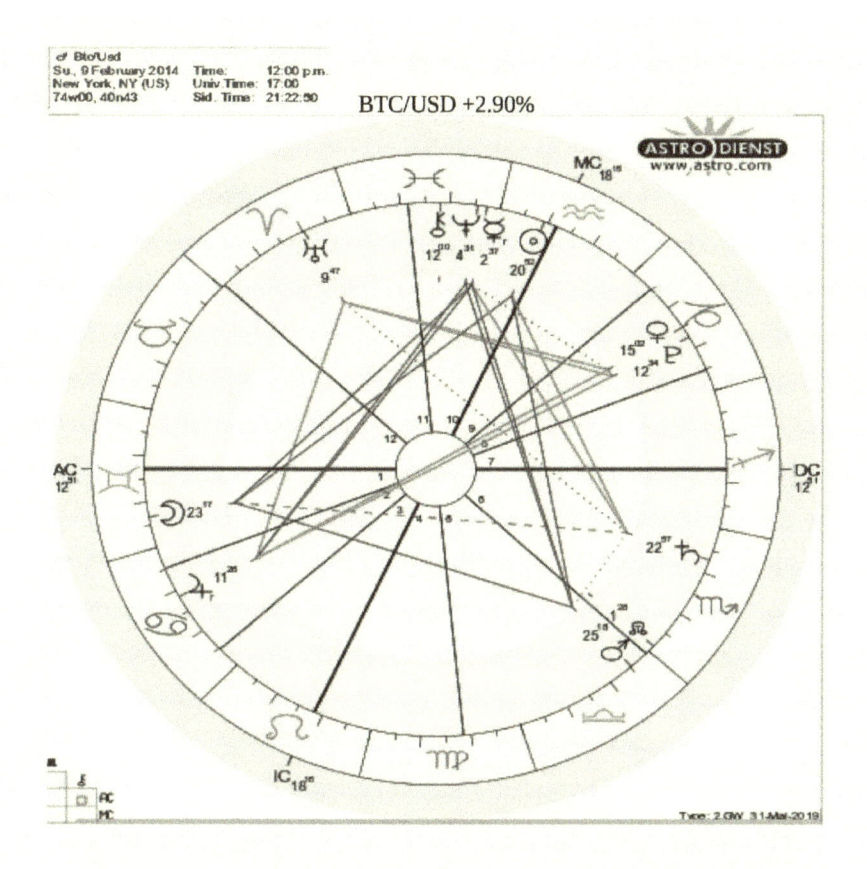

BTC/USD +2.90%

In this chart for Feb 9, 2014, mercury's degree(2 degrees) is lower than the degree of the sun(20 degrees). Therefore, we continue to use the **"Figure Set 1"** parameters. When looking at the chart, the last parameter that would have applied from **"Figure Set 1"** would be parameter 2, which says the moon within 1 degree of the degree of the sun in an Air or Fire sign brings the value of BTC/USD down. Gemini is an air sign Therefore, this prediction is WRONG. BTC/USD was up +2.90% this day. .

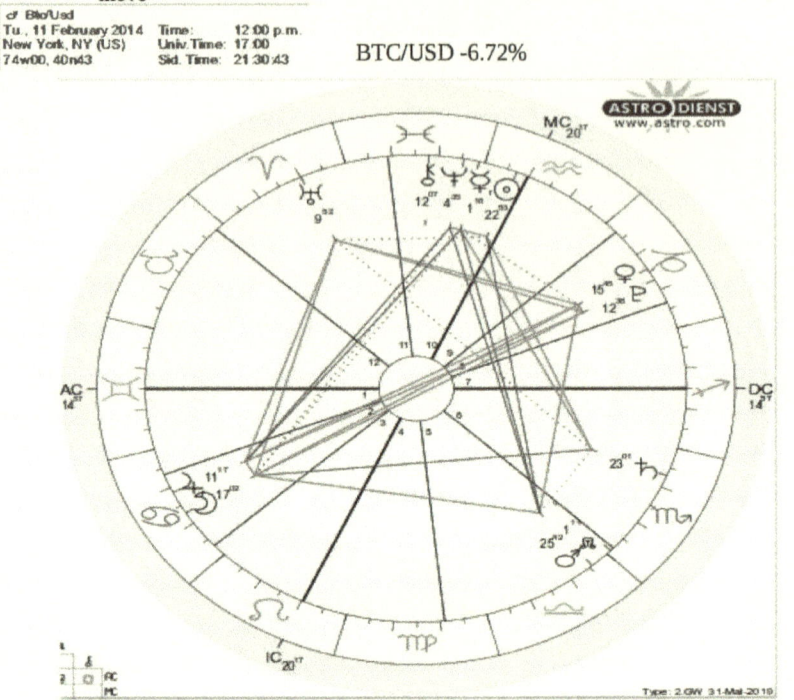

we'll skip to Feb 11ᵗʰ 2014 since that's the next significant move

♂ Btc/Usd
Tu., 11 February 2014 Time: 12:00 p.m.
New York, NY (US) Univ.Time: 17:00
74w00, 40n43 Sid. Time: 21:30:43

BTC/USD -6.72%

In this chart for Feb 11, 2014, mercury's degree(1 degree) is lower than the degree of the sun(22 degrees). Therefore, we continue to use the **"Figure Set 1"** parameters. When looking at the chart, the last parameter that would have applied from **"Figure Set 1"** would be parameter 9, which says the moon within 1 degree of the degree of mercury after the moon has passed the sun's degree in an Air or Fire sign brings the value of BTC/USD up. That last sun's degree of 22 was passed by the moon in Gemini which is an air sign. Therefore, this prediction is WRONG. BTC/ USD was down -6.72% this day. This could only be resolved by the fact that the moon would have been within 3 degrees of the degree of the sun in about 4 hours from the time used to calculate the chart. That would have invoked a prediction for BTC/USD to drop.

BTC/USD +3.97%

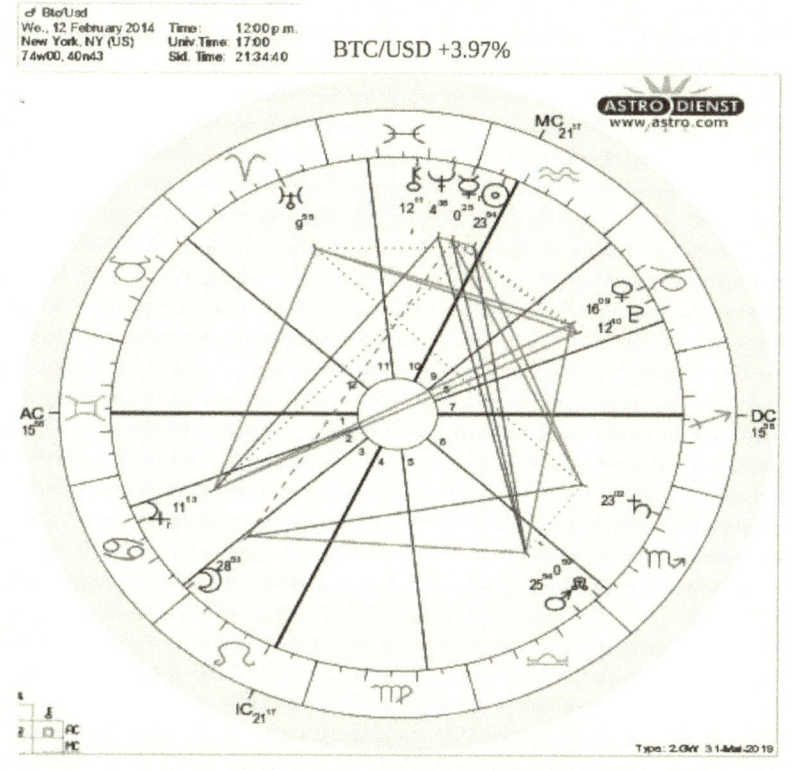

In this chart for Feb 12, 2014, mercury's degree(0 degree) is lower than the degree of the sun(23 degrees). Therefore, we continue to use the "**Figure Set 1**" parameters. When looking at the chart, the last parameter that would have applied from "**Figure Set 1**" would be parameter 3, which says the moon within 3 degrees of the degree of the lunar node in any sign brings the value of BTC/USD down. With the moon at 28 degrees and the lunar node at 0 degrees, we see that the parameter is taking place, however the prediction is wrong again. BTC/USD rose +3.97%. However in about 3 hours from the time used to calculate the chart, the sun would have went into the next sign and the moon would have traveled about 2 degrees. This would invoke another set and another parameter which would predict the BTC/USD to rise.

BTC/USD -7.41%

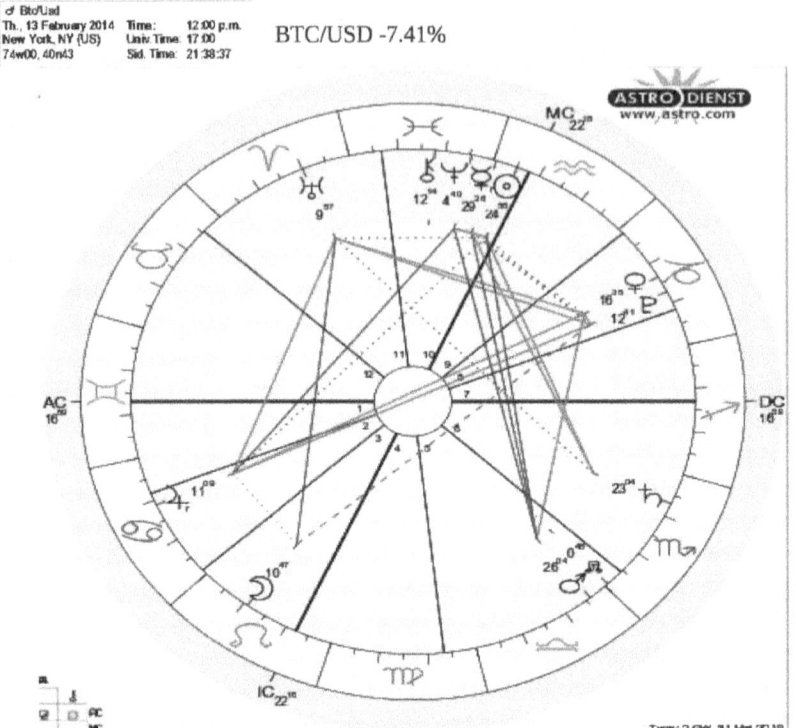

In this chart for Feb 13, 2014, the Sun enters a new sign at the 24 degree mark. This means that mercury's degree(29 degrees) is now higher than the degree of the sun(24 degrees). Therefore, we stop using the "**Figure Set 1**" parameters and start using the "**Figure Set 2**" parameters again. "**Figure Set 2**" parameters are applied when the degree of mercury is higher than the degree of the sun. When looking at the chart, the last parameter that would have applied from "**Figure Set 2**" would be parameter 5, which says the moon within 1 degree of the degree of the lunar node after the moon has passed the sun's degree in an air or fire sign brings the value of BTC/USD down. The 24th degree, which is the degree of the sun in this chart and also the beginning of the next sign, would have been passed by the moon at the 24th degree of Cancer, which is interpreted to Leo, which is a fire sign. Therefore the prediction is correct. BTC/USD was down -7.41%.

BTC/USD +7.53%

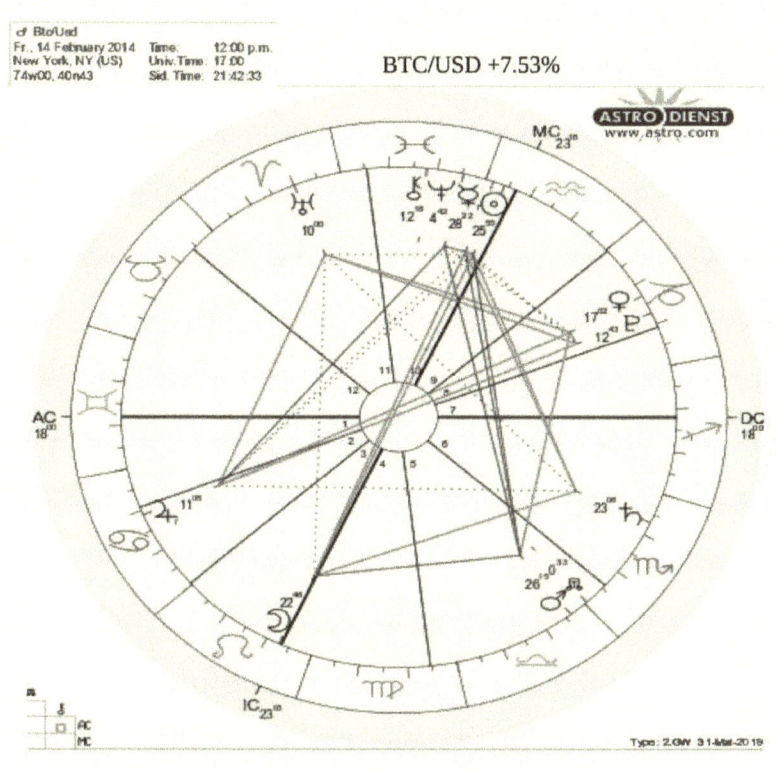

In this chart for Feb 14, 2014, mercury's degree (28 degrees) is higher than the sun's degree (25 degrees). Therefore, we use the "**Figure Set 2**" parameters again. "**Figure Set 2**" parameters are applied when the degree of mercury is higher than the degree of the sun. When looking at the chart, the last parameter that would have applied from "**Figure Set 2**" would be parameter 6, which says the moon within 3 degrees of the degree of the sun in an earth or water sign brings the value of BTC/USD up. The degree of the moon is 22 degrees and the degree of the sun is 25 degrees in Aquarius interpreted to Pisces, which is a water sign. That's within 3 degrees of a water sign as defined by the parameter and therefore results in the correct prediction. BTC/USD was up +7.53%.

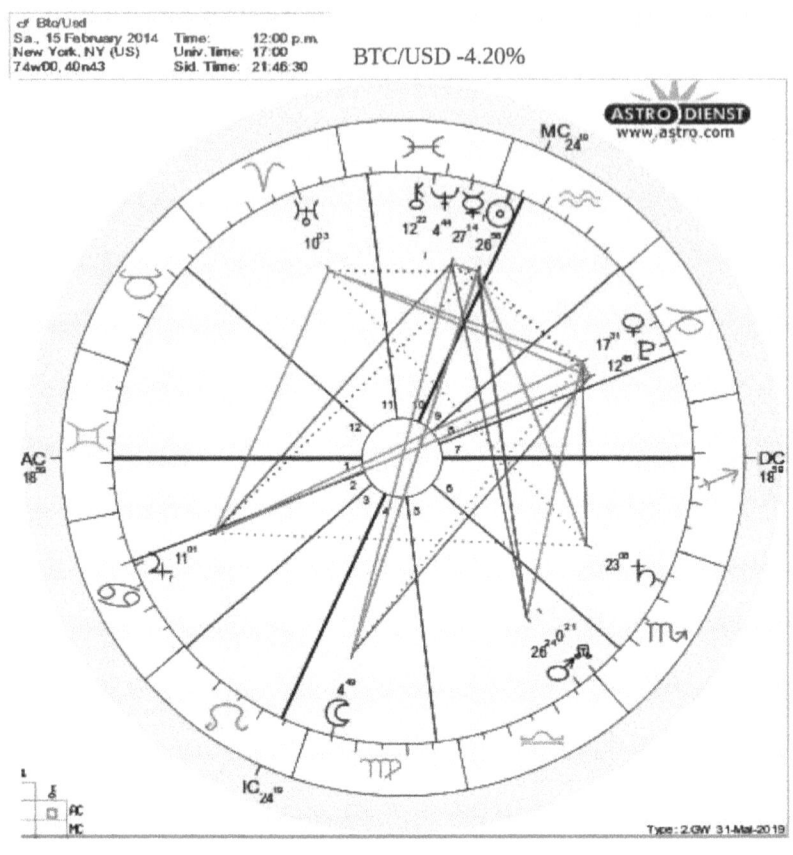

♂ Btc/Usd
Sa., 15 February 2014   Time: 12:00 p.m.
New York, NY (US)   Univ. Time: 17:00
74w00, 40n43   Sid. Time: 21:46:30

BTC/USD -4.20%

In this chart for Feb 15, 2014, mercury's degree(27 degrees) is higher than the sun's degree (26 degrees). Therefore, we use the "**Figure Set 2**" parameters again. When looking at the chart, the last parameter that would have applied from "**Figure Set 2**" would be parameter 4, which says the moon within 1 degree of the degree of the lunar node after the moon has passed the degree of the sun in an earth or water sign brings the value of BTC/USD up. So this prediction turns out incorrect as BTC/USD was down -4.20%. This can be resolved by looking at the fact that mercury, which is in retrograde, would switch positions with the sun that day by going to a lesser degree than the sun and thus invoking "**Figure Set 1**" parameters, which would give the correct prediction.

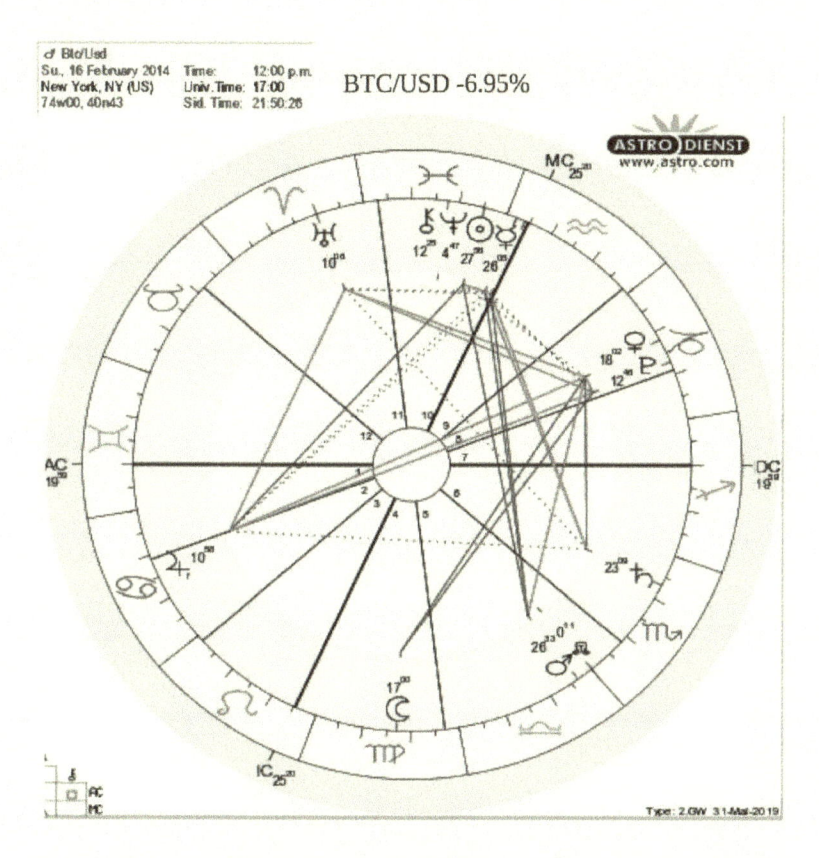

In this chart for Feb 16, 2014, mercury's degree (26 degrees) becomes lower than the sun's degree(27 degrees). Therefore, **"Figure Set 2"** parameters no longer apply here. We now go back to **"Figure Set 1"** parameters. The last parameter from **"Figure Set 1"** that applied in this chart was parameter 4, which says the moon being within 1 degree of the degree of the lunar node after the moon has passed the degree of the sun in an earth or water sign brings the value of BTC/USD down. That occurred here and thus the prediction is correct. BTC/USD was down – 6.95%.

BTC/USD +9.19%

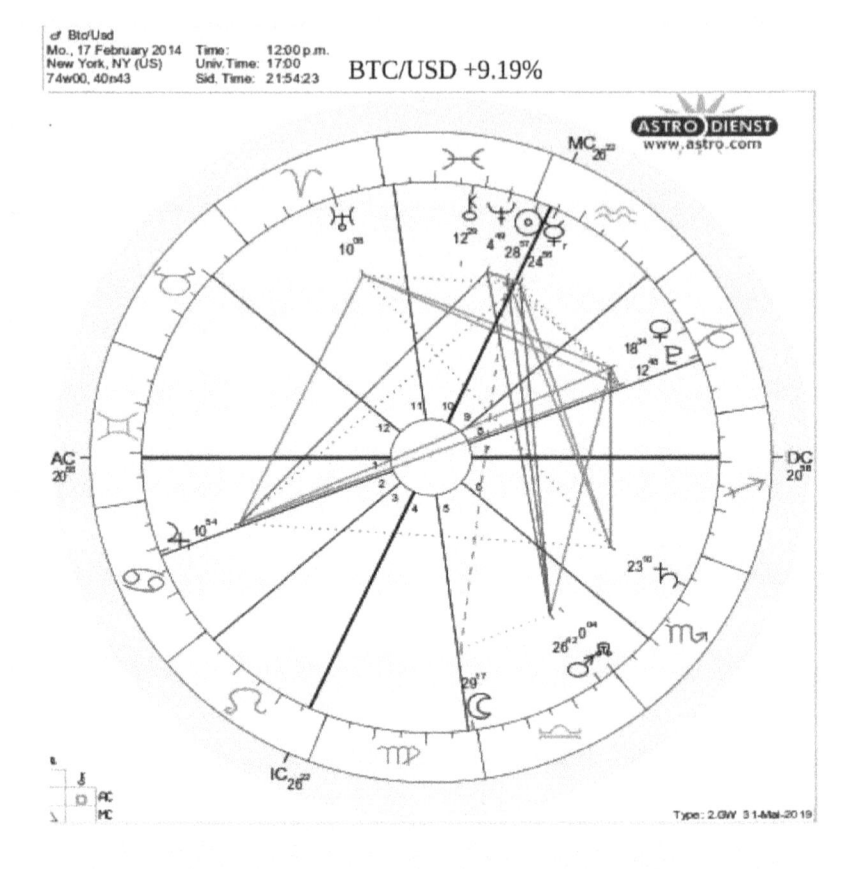

In this chart for Feb 17, 2014, mercury's degree (24 degrees) is lower than the sun's degree(28 degrees). Therefore, **"Figure Set 1"** parameters still apply. The last parameter from **"Figure Set 1"** that applied in this chart was parameter 5, which says the moon being within 1 degree of the degree of the lunar node after the moon has passed the degree of the sun in a fire or air sign brings the value of BTC/USD up. The degree of the moon is at 29 and the degree of the lunar node is at 0. That's within the 1 degree mark stated in the parameter 5 along with the moon having already passed the sun's degree in an air or fire sign as libra is an air sign. This leaves us with another correct prediction. BTC/USD was up +9.19%.

BTC/USD -5.40%

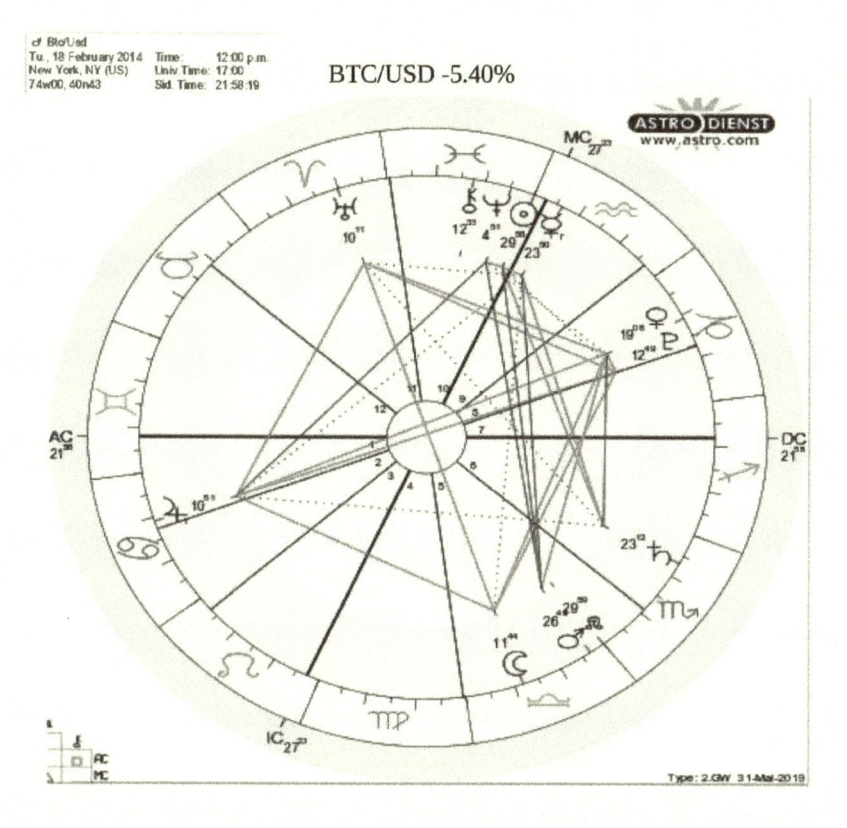

In this chart for Feb 18, 2014, another change in the relationship between the sun and mercury has taken place. Mercury has gone back wards into another sign at the 23rd degree mark. This puts mercury's degree(23 degrees) higher than the sun's degree(29 degrees). (Remember, the 24th degree marks the beginning of a new sign so that makes the 24th degree the lowest numbered degree.) Therefore, **"Figure Set 1"** parameters no longer apply. We go back to **"Figure Set 2"** parameters. The last parameter from **"Figure Set 2"** that would have applied here would be parameter 5, which says the moon being within 1 degree of the degree of the lunar node after the moon has passed the degree of the sun in an air of fire sign bring the value of BTC/USD down. Since Libra is an air sign, this prediction is correct. BTC/USD was down -5.40% this day.

we'll skip to Feb 20th 2014 since that's the next significant

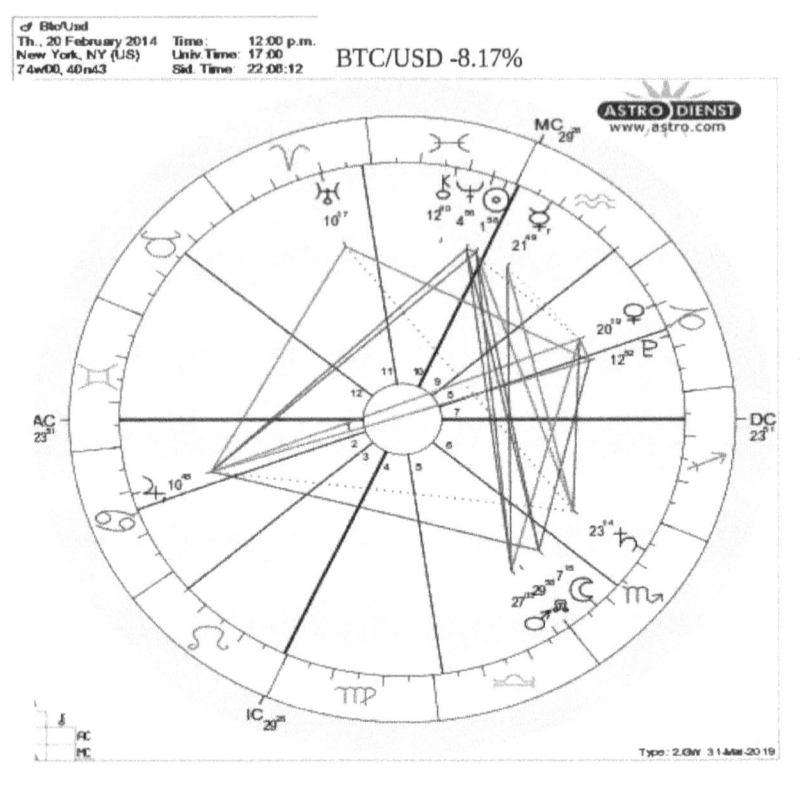

BTC/USD -8.17%

In this chart for Feb 20, 2014, Mercury's degree(21 degrees) higher than the sun's degree(1 degree). Therefore we continue with **"Figure Set 2"** parameters. The last parameter from **"Figure Set 2"** that would have applied here would be parameter 1, which says the moon being within 1 degree of the degree of the sun in an earth of water sign brings the value of BTC/USD down. That degree of the sun would be in Scorpio, which is a water sign. Therefore, the prediction is correct. BTC/USD was down -8.17%.

we'll skip to Feb 22nd and 23rd 2014 since that's the next significant moves

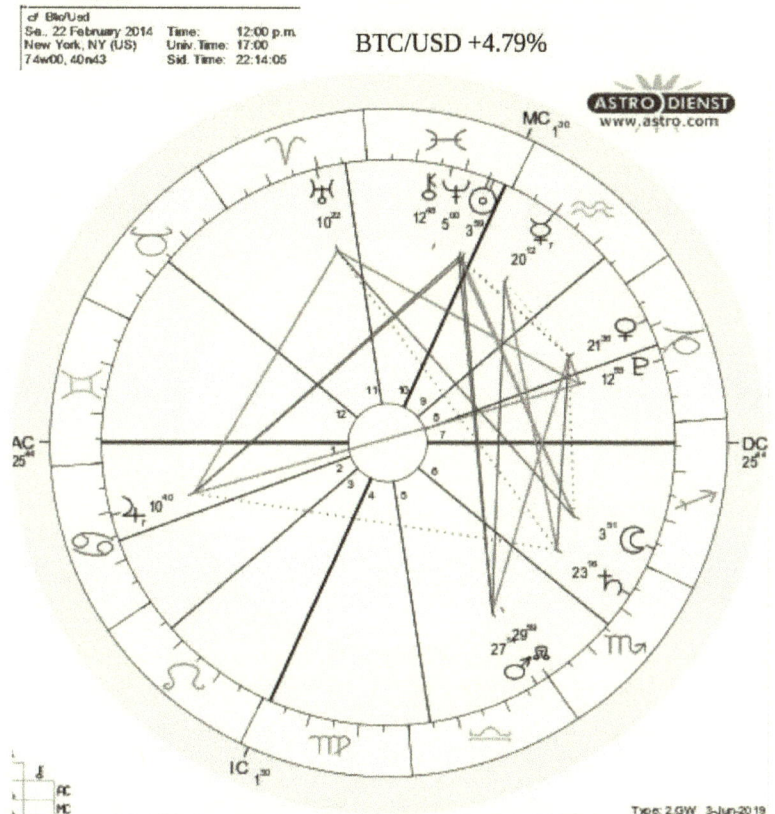

BTC/USD +4.79%

In this chart for Feb 22, 2014, Mercury's degree(20 degrees) is higher than the sun's degree(3 degree). Therefore we continue with "**Figure Set 2**" parameters. The last parameter from "**Figure Set 2**" that would have applied here would be parameter 2, which says the moon being within 1 degree of the degree of the sun in a fire or air sign brings the value of BTC/USD up. That degree of the sun would be in Sagittarius in this chart, which is a fire sign. Therefore, the prediction is correct. BTC/USD was up +4.79%.

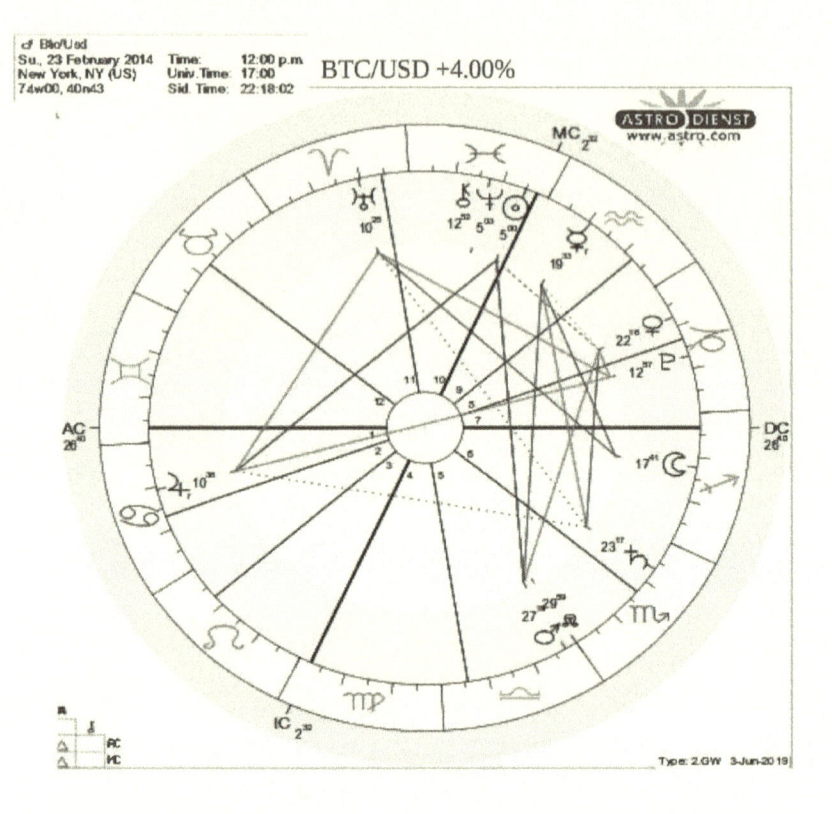

BTC/USD +4.00%

In this chart for Feb 23, 2014, Mercury's degree(19 degrees) higher than the sun's degree(5 degree). Therefore we continue with **"Figure Set 2"** parameters. The last parameter from **"Figure Set 2"** that would have applied here would be parameter 2 again, which says the moon being within 1 degree of the degree of the sun in a fire or air sign brings the value of BTC/USD up. That degree of the sun would be in Sagittarius in this chart, which is a fire sign. Therefore, the prediction is correct. BTC/ USD was up +4.00%.

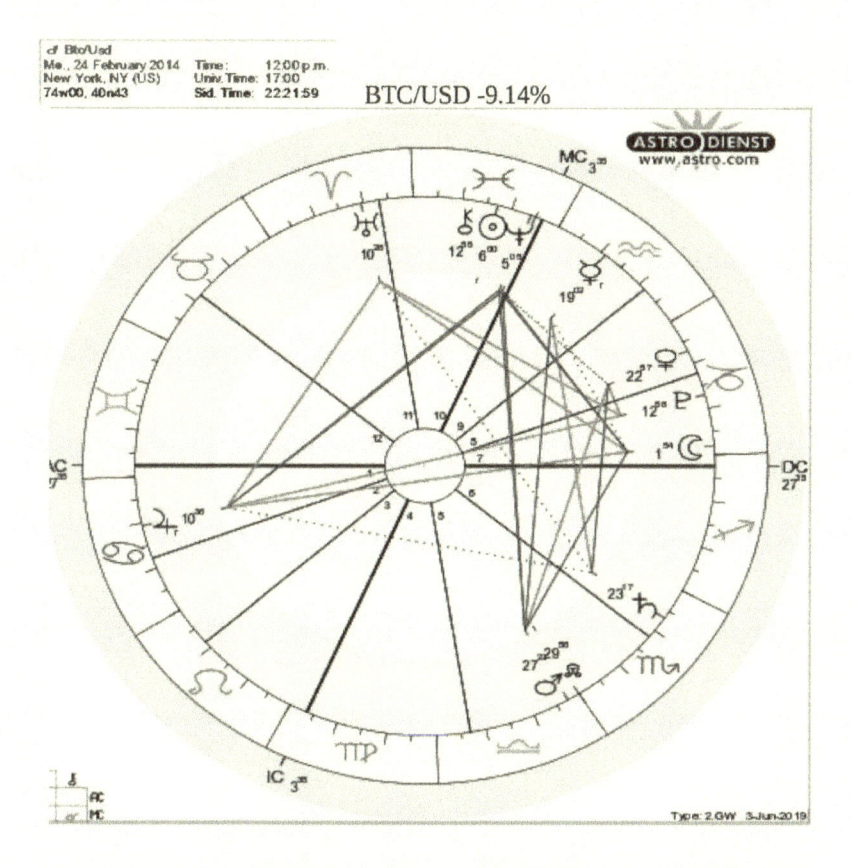

BTC/USD -9.14%

In this chart for Feb 24, 2014, Mercury's degree(19 degrees) higher than the sun's degree(6 degrees). Therefore we continue with "**Figure Set 2**" parameters. The last parameter from "**Figure Set 2**" that would have applied here would be parameter 5, which says the moon being within 1 degree of the degree of the lunar node after the moon has passed the sun's degree in an air or fire sign brings the value of BTC/USD down. Before the moon went to within 1 degree of the degree of the lunar node in Capricorn, it had to last pass the degree of the sun in Sagittarius, which is a fire sign. Therefore, the prediction is correct. BTC/USD was down -9.14% this day.

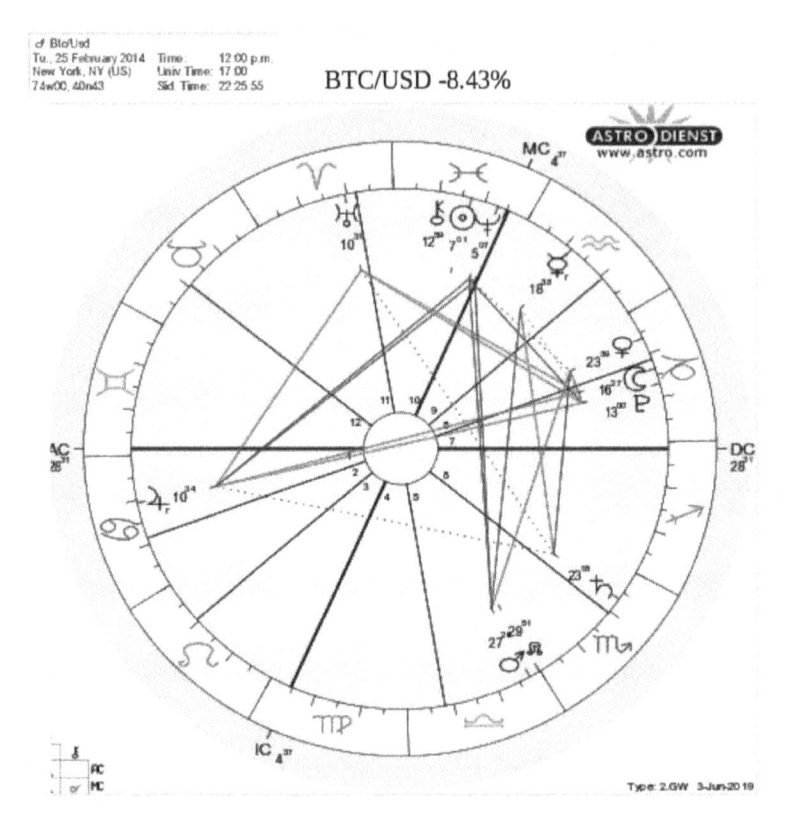

In this chart for Feb 25, 2014, Mercury's degree(18 degrees) is higher than the sun's degree at (7 degrees). Therefore we continue with **"Figure Set 2"** parameters. The last parameter from **"Figure Set 2"** that would have applied here would be parameter 1, which says the moon being within 1 degree of the degree of the sun in an earth or water sign brings the value of BTC/USD down. That degree of the sun would have been in Capricorn because that's where the moon would have crossed it last. Capricorn is an earth sign. Therefore, the prediction is correct. BTC/USD was down -8.43% this day.

```
♂ Btc/Usd
We , 26 February 2014    Time:       12:00 p.m.
New York, NY (US)        Univ.Time:  17:00
74w00, 40n43             Sid. Time:  22:29:52
```
BTC/USD +13.01%

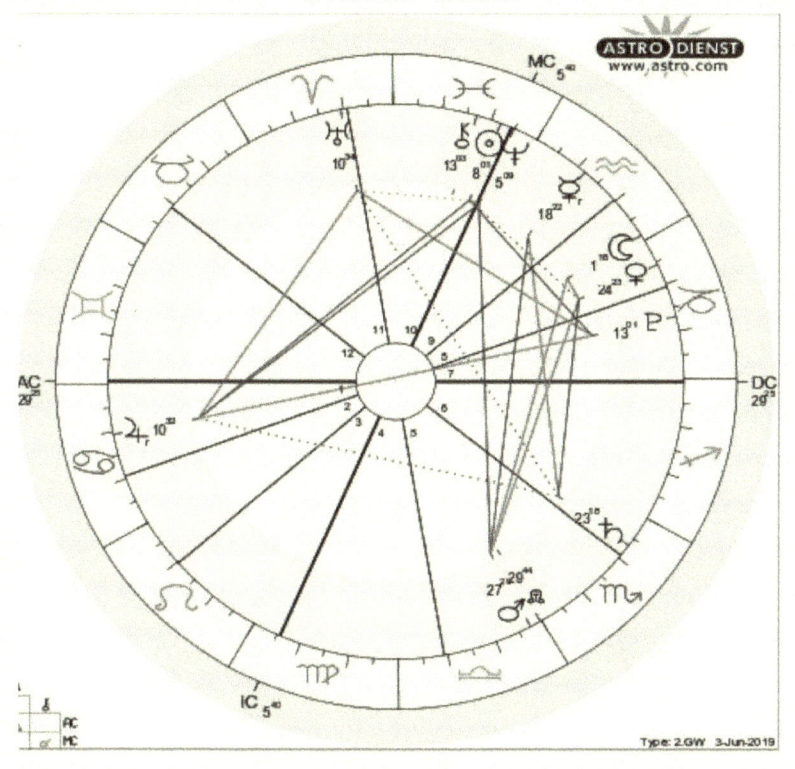

In this chart for Feb 26, 2014, Mercury's degree(18 degrees) is higher than the sun's degree(8 degrees). Therefore we continue with **"Figure Set 2"** parameters. The last parameter from **"Figure Set 2"** that would have applied here would be parameter 4, which says the moon being within 1 degree of the degree of the lunar node after the moon has passed the sun's degree in an earth or water sign brings the value of BTC/USD down. Before the moon went to within 1 degree of the degree of the lunar node in Aquarius, it had to last pass the degree of the sun in Capricorn, which is an earth sign. Therefore, the prediction is correct. BTC/USD was up +13.01% this day.

we'll skip to Feb 28th 2014 since that's the next significant move

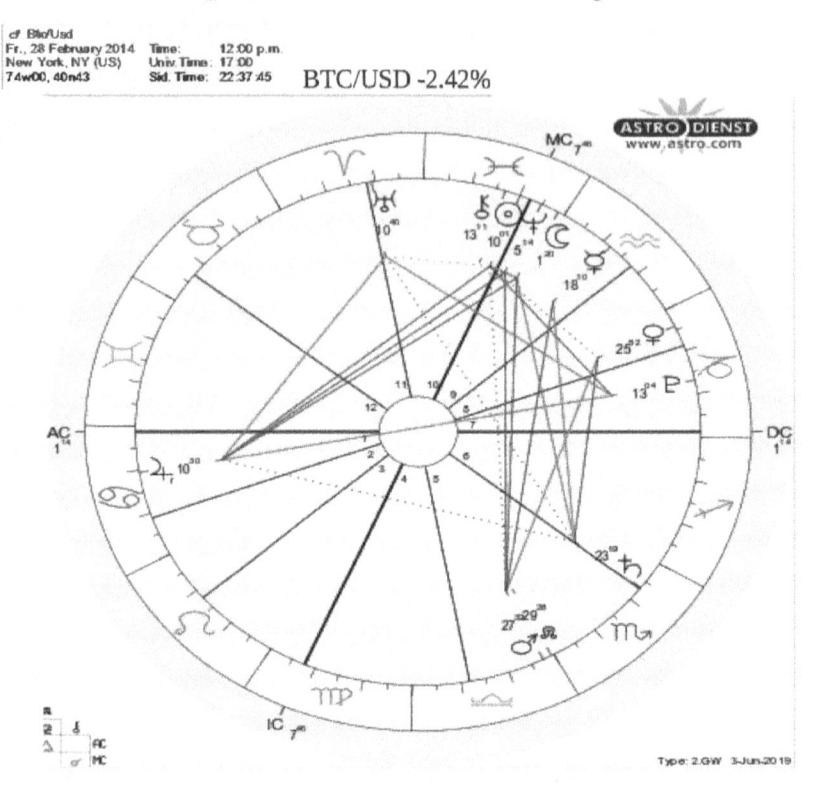

♂ Btc/Usd
Fr., 28 February 2014   Time: 12:00 p.m.
New York, NY (US)   Univ. Time: 17:00
74w00, 40n43   Sid. Time: 22:37:45   BTC/USD -2.42%

In this chart for Feb 28, 2014, Mercury's degree(18 degrees) is higher than the sun's degree(10 degrees). Therefore we continue with **"Figure Set 2"** parameters. The last parameter from **"Figure Set 2"** that would have applied here would be parameter 5, which says the moon being within 1 degree of the degree of the lunar node after the moon has passed the sun's degree in a fire or air sign brings the value of BTC/USD down. Before the moon went to within 1 degree of the degree of the lunar node in Pisces it had to last pass the degree of the sun in Aquarius, which is an air sign. Therefore, the prediction is correct. BTC/USD was down -2.42% this day.

These are the prices for the BTC/USD for the month of March 2014

Date	Price	Open	High	Low	Vol.	Change %
Mar 31, 2014	452.0	478.6	485.0	443.1	0.08K	-2.61%
Mar 30, 2014	464.1	493.0	493.0	440.4	0.14K	-5.66%
Mar 29, 2014	491.9	506.2	507.0	491.0	0.02K	-1.11%
Mar 28, 2014	497.4	525.0	525.0	490.0	0.23K	-0.22%
Mar 27, 2014	498.5	582.4	589.3	498.5	0.24K	-16.21%
Mar 26, 2014	595.0	580.0	595.0	570.0	0.54K	2.23%
Mar 25, 2014	582.0	586.6	586.7	579.1	0.31K	-1.35%
Mar 24, 2014	590.0	560.4	590.0	552.0	0.35K	4.20%
Mar 23, 2014	566.2	570.3	570.3	566.2	0.01K	1.11%
Mar 22, 2014	560.0	560.0	562.9	550.0	0.01K	-1.55%
Mar 21, 2014	568.8	581.0	605.4	568.8	0.70K	-2.52%
Mar 20, 2014	583.5	610.0	639.2	583.5	0.49K	-4.50%
Mar 19, 2014	611.0	622.9	622.9	611.0	0.11K	-1.19%
Mar 18, 2014	618.4	623.1	623.9	610.9	0.49K	-0.95%
Mar 17, 2014	624.3	635.0	635.7	624.0	0.60K	-1.68%
Mar 16, 2014	635.0	640.1	640.1	635.0	0.04K	-1.03%
Mar 15, 2014	641.6	636.9	641.6	636.9	0.00K	1.85%
Mar 14, 2014	630.0	632.9	639.0	630.0	0.56K	-1.87%
Mar 13, 2014	642.0	633.5	645.1	633.5	0.04K	-1.23%
Mar 12, 2014	650.0	615.0	650.0	615.0	0.86K	5.69%
Mar 11, 2014	615.0	615.0	615.0	613.5	0.05K	0.00%
Mar 10, 2014	615.0	621.0	621.0	612.8	0.12K	-0.97%
Mar 09, 2014	621.0	610.5	621.0	609.4	0.05K	1.12%
Mar 08, 2014	614.1	621.0	621.0	600.2	0.06K	-1.11%
Mar 07, 2014	621.0	663.0	663.0	614.0	0.76K	-6.33%
Mar 06, 2014	663.0	673.4	675.0	657.0	0.96K	-1.78%
Mar 05, 2014	675.0	658.0	675.8	658.0	0.49K	1.05%
Mar 04, 2014	668.0	654.7	675.0	652.6	0.47K	1.52%
Mar 03, 2014	658.0	571.5	685.0	569.7	0.67K	17.37%
Mar 02, 2014	560.6	570.9	583.5	560.0	0.01K	-1.34%
Mar 01, 2014	568.2	565.0	571.8	560.0	0.06K	0.57%

Change %: -20.0

BTC/USD -1.34%

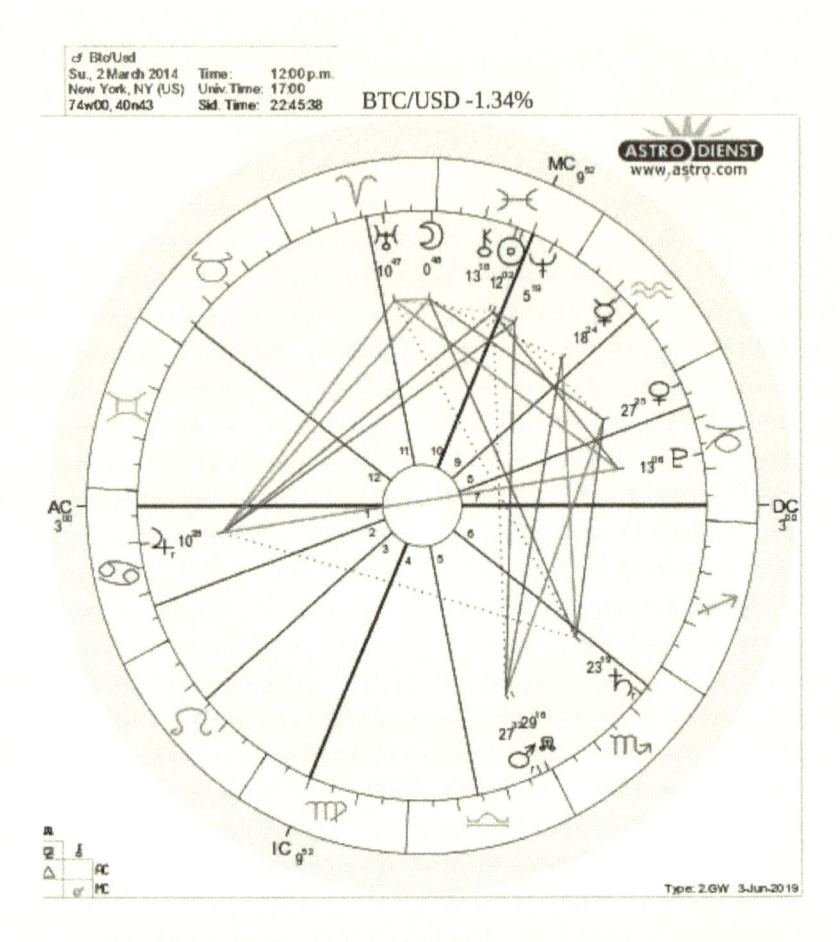

In this chart for Mar 2, 2014, Mercury's degree(18 degrees) is higher than the sun's degree(12 degrees). Therefore we continue with **"Figure Set 2"** parameters. The last parameter from **"Figure Set 2"** that would have applied here would be parameter 4, which says the moon being within 1 degree of the degree of the lunar node after the moon has passed the sun's degree in an earth or water sign brings the value of BTC/USD up. Before the moon went to within 1 degree of the degree of the lunar node in Aries it had to last pass the degree of the sun in Pisces, which is a water sign. Therefore, this prediction is WRONG. BTC/USD was down -1.34% this day.

BTC/USD +17.37%

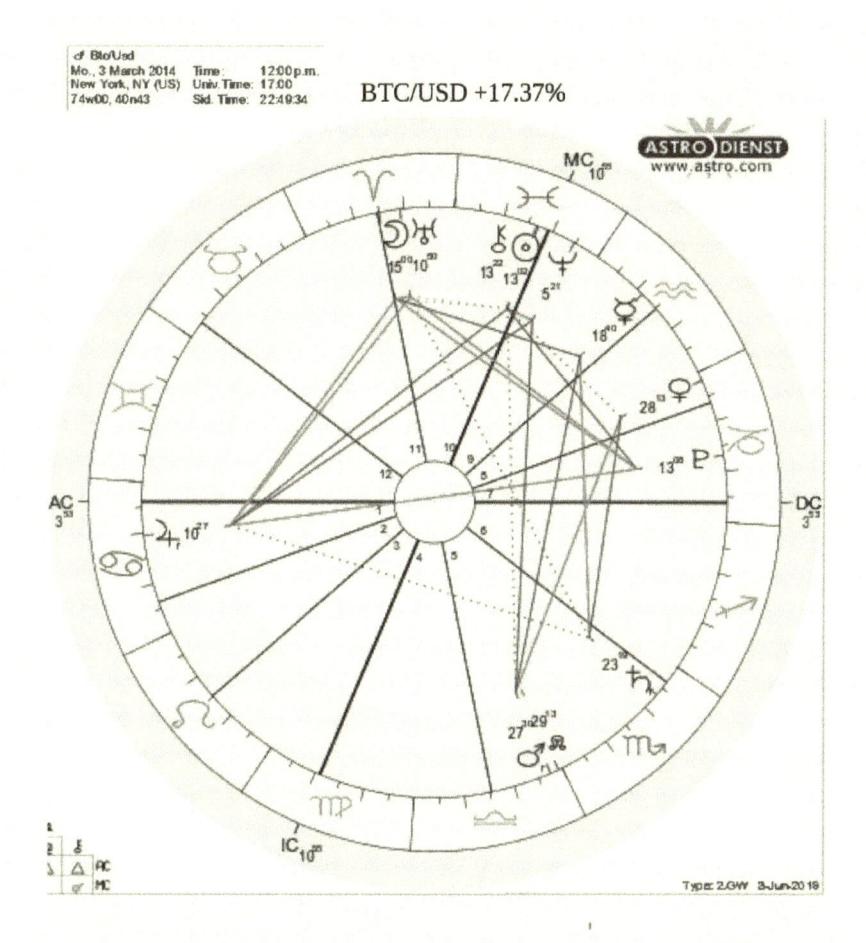

In this chart for Mar 3, 2014, Mercury's degree(18 degrees) is higher than the sun's degree(13 degrees). Therefore we continue with **"Figure Set 2"** parameters. The last parameter from **"Figure Set 2"** that would have applied here would be parameter 2, which says the moon being within 1 degree of the degree of the sun in an air or fire sign brings the value of BTC/USD up. That degree of the sun would be in Aries, which is a fire sign, Therefore, this prediction is CORRECT. BTC/USD was up +17.37% this day.

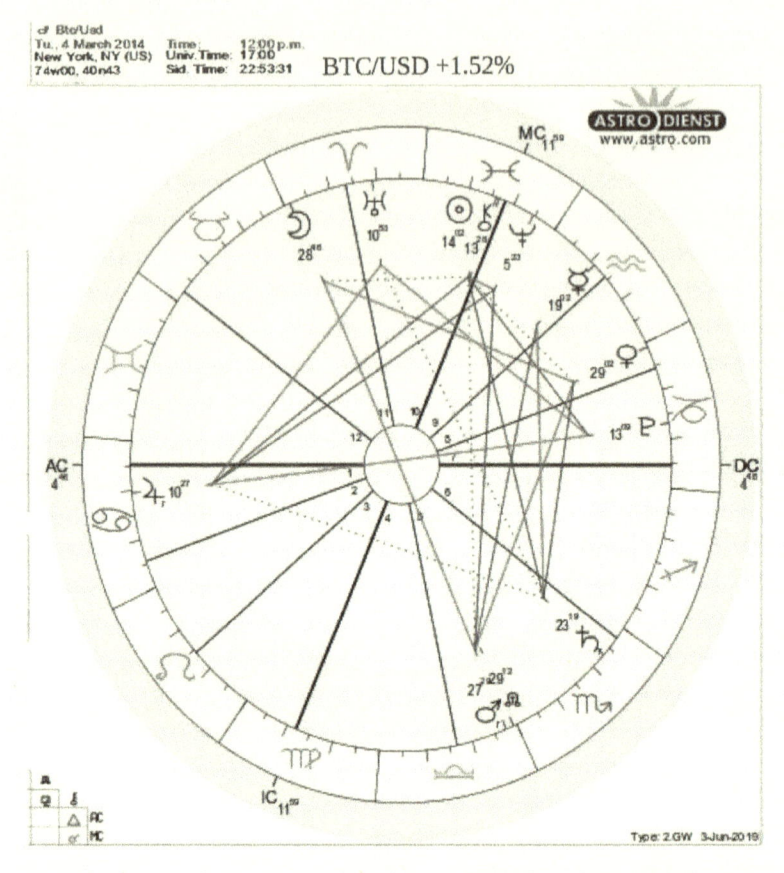

BTC/USD +1.52%

In this chart for Mar 4, 2014, Mercury's degree(19 degrees) is higher than the sun's degree(14 degrees). Therefore we continue with **"Figure Set 2"** parameters. The last parameter from **"Figure Set 2"** that would have applied here would be parameter 5, which says the moon being within 1 degree of the degree of the lunar node after the moon has passed the sun's degree in an air or fire sign brings the value of BTC/USD down. Before the moon went to within 1 degree of the degree of the lunar node in Taurus it had to last pass the degree of the sun in Aries, which is a fire sign. Therefore, this prediction is WRONG. BTC/USD was up +1.52% this day.

Starting March 6th, and continuing with the astro chart calculated for noon in New York, the algorithm that we have been using thus far for BTC/USD will taper off for a few days, as the next 3 major price moves for BTC/USD doesn't correlate with the algorithm. The price on March 6th when BTC/USD dropped -6.33%, the price on March 12th when BTC/USD rose +5.69%, and the price on March 24 when BTC/USD dropped -4.50% are all missed by the algorithm. Its not until March 25 that the algorithm recovers some accuracy and catches that next major price drop that takes place on March 27 , 2014, when the price of BTC/USD dropped -16.21%. Of course one can try to go back and make the algorithm fit by changing parameters around. However, a challenge to that would be keeping the algorithm historically relevant while doing so. When an algorithm tapers off for a few days, it doesn't mean that the algorithm no longer applies historically and vice versa an algorithm that works perfectly for 2 weeks doesn't mean that it will apply historically. There is a bit of game theory involved. Game theory is defined as "the branch of mathematics concerned with the analysis of strategies for dealing with competitive situations where the outcome of a participant's choice of action depends critically on the actions of other participants. Game theory has been applied to contexts in war, business, and biology." In the case of predictive analysis, if one algorithm allows one to be correct for a number of consecutive days but miss extremely important key dates historically or futuristically, then that has to be weighed against another algorithm that is less accurate in those same consecutive days, but at the same time more accurate historically and futuristically.

Applying that to what we have been using through the days in March in which our algorithm tapered of starting March 6th : if we continue with that same algorithm, despite that predictive slump, we eventually get to

March 25, where our algorithm recovers and catches the remaining key dates of BTC/USD price changes for the remainder of the month and also the next month of April. Had we tried to change the algorithm to make it fit more accurate in through that short term slump, we may have lost accuracy for those times the price moved significantly in the later days and weeks. Of course our example is related to an overall assessment of BTC/USD for the entire day. The parameters, however, allow for it to be used in real time. Meaning, one can use the algorithm to make predictions based on the exact time that the parameter applies. Since parameter 1 in "**Figure set 2**" says the moon within 1 degree of the degree of the sun in an earth or water sign brings the value of BTC/USD down, one can calculate the chart to the exact time that happens and predict BTC/USD to start dropping at that time. This also applies for the algorithm in our EUR/USD example in Figure 1a and also our earlier Dow Jones example. I used what I felt applied most historically on key dates, but of course there is room for more analysis on this. There is much flexibility regarding how to apply the algorithm. I do believe, however, that using the Sun, Moon, Mercury and the Lunar node provides a fixed standard for daily prediction reliability over the course of time.

Below are percentage ups and downs of the BTC(Bitcoin)/USD currency pair during times when the Sun and Mercury are in the same sign and also during times when the Sun and Mercury are in different signs. These statistics go back to 2012. My initial observation would conclude that there is a higher prevalence of a rise in BTC/USD when the Sun and Mercury are in different signs and a higher prevalence of a drop when the Sun and Mercury are in the same sign. Mercury retrograde periods, however, seem to reverse that pattern, making it to where the Sun and Mercury in different signs would drive the BTC/USD lower, while the Sun and Mercury in the same sign (during the retrograde) would bring it higher. Any of the stats marked below with an asterisk * are the dates that would be affected by the mercury retrograde.

Here is the algorithm:

1. Sun and Mercury in a different sign = BTC/USD rises (unless there is a mercury retrograde which would then cause it to drop. Mercury retrograde times are marked with an asterisk)

2. Sun and Mercury in the same sign = BTC/USD drops(unless there is a mercury retrograde, which could then cause it to rise. Mercury retrograde times are marked with an asterisk)

Here are the stats staring back in 2012. Astrology charts calculated using western astrology, starting the beginning of a new sign at the 24th degree mark. The charts used to mark off the periods of when the Sun and Mercury are in the same sign and when they are in different signs were calculated for New York, Eastern Time Zone 11pm.

Sun & Mercury in the same sign
Feb 1, 2012 - Feb 9, 2012
BTC/USD down -4.1%

Sun & Mercury in different signs
Feb 10, 2012 - Feb 12, 2012
BTC/USD down -5.5%

Sun & Mercury in the same sign
Feb 13, 2012 - Feb 26, 2012
BTC/USD down -10.7%

Sun and Mercury in a different sign
Feb 27, 2012 - March 13, 2012
BTC/USD up +7.1%

(mercury retrograde Mar 12, 2012 - April 4, 2012)

Sun and Mercury in the same sign*
Mar 14, 2012 - Apr 1, 2012
BTC/USD down -8.3%

Sun and Mercury in a different sign
Apr 2, 2012 - Apr 5, 2012
BTC/USD up + 1.9%

Sun and Mercury in the same sign
Apr 6, 2012 - Apr 12, 2012
BTC/USD down -0.0%

Sun and Mercury in a different sign
Apr 13, 2012 - May 4, 2012
BTC/USD up + 3.0%

Sun and Mercury in the same sign
May 5, 2012 - May 13, 2012
BTC/USD down -2.8%

Sun and Mercury in a different sign
May 14, 2012 - May 20, 2012
BTC/USD up + 3.2%

Sun and Mercury in the same sign
May 21, 2012 - Jun 3, 2012
BTC/USD down +2.4%

Sun and Mercury in a different sign
Jun 4, 2012 - Jun 13, 2012
BTC/USD up +13.0%

Sun and Mercury in the same sign
Jun 14, 2012 - Jun 20, 2012
BTC/USD up +12.5%

Sun and Mercury in a different sign
Jun 21, 2012 - Jul 14, 2012
BTC/USD up +13.0%

(Mercury retrograde Jul 14 2012 - August 7, 2012)

Sun and Mercury in the same sign*
Jul 15, 2012 - Aug 15, 2012
BTC/USD up +75.7%

Sun and Mercury in a different sign
Aug 16, 2012 - Aug 27, 2012
BTC/USD down -17.4%

Sun and Mercury in the same sign
Aug 28, 2012 - Sep 12, 2012
BTC/USD up +3.7%

Sun and Mercury in a different sign
Sep 13, 2012 - Sep 15, 2012
BTC/USD up +3.4%

Sun and Mercury in the same sign
Sep 16, 2012 - Sep 30, 2012
BTC/USD up +5.5%

Sun and Mercury in a different sign
Oct 1, 2012 - Oct 15, 2012
BTC/USD down -4.5%

Sun and Mercury in the same sign
Oct 16, 2012 - Oct 22, 2012
BTC/USD down -1.1%

(Mercury retrograde Nov 6 2012 - Nov 26, 2012)

Sun and Mercury in a different sign*
Oct 23, 2012 - Nov 14, 2012
BTC/USD down -6.5%

Sun and Mercury in the same sign*
Nov 15, 2012 - Nov 17, 2012
BTC/USD up +7.7%

Sun and Mercury in a different sign*
Nov 18, 2012 - Dec 4, 2012
BTC/USD up +13.7%

Sun and Mercury in the same sign
Dec 5, 2012 - Dec 14, 2012
BTC/USD up +1.4%

Sun and Mercury in a different sign
Dec 15, 2012 - Dec 26, 2012
BTC/USD down -1.0%

Sun and Mercury in the same sign
Dec 26, 2012 - Jan 12, 2013
BTC/USD up +5.7%

Sun and Mercury in a different sign
Jan 13, 2013 - Jan 14, 2013
BTC/USD up +0.4%

Sun and Mercury in the same sign
Jan 13, 2013 - Jan 31, 2013
BTC/USD up +42.7%

Sun and Mercury in a different sign
Feb 1, 2013 - Feb 11, 2013
BTC/USD up +20.0%

(mercury retrograde February 23, 2013 - March 17, 2013)

Sun and Mercury in the same sign*
Feb 12, 2013 - Mar 13, 2013
BTC/USD up +90.3%

Sun and Mercury in a different sign
Mar 14, 2013 - Apr 8, 2013
BTC/USD up +299.0%

Sun and Mercury in the same sign
Apr 9, 2013 - Apr 13, 2013
BTC/USD down -50.3%

Sun and Mercury in a different sign
Apr 14, 2013 - Apr 27, 2013
BTC/USD up +37.0%

Sun and Mercury in the same sign
Apr 28, 2013 - May 11, 2013
BTC/USD down -9.7%

Sun and Mercury in a different sign
May 12, 2013 - May 13, 2013
BTC/USD up +2.0%

Sun and Mercury in the same sign
May 14, 2013 - May 26, 2013
BTC/USD up +13.2%

Sun and Mercury in a different sign
May 27, 2013 - Jun 13, 2013
BTC/USD down -22.1%

(Mercury retrograde June 26, 2013 - July 20, 2013)

Sun and Mercury in the same sign*
Jun 14, 2013 - Jul 15, 2013
BTC/USD up -10.4%

Sun and Mercury in a different sign
Jul 16, 2013 - Aug 3, 2013
BTC/USD up +3.8%

Sun and Mercury in the same sign
Aug 4, 2013 - Aug 15, 2013
BTC/USD up +0.9%

Sun and Mercury in a different sign
Aug 16, 2013 - Aug 19, 2013
BTC/USD up +4.9%

Sun and Mercury in the same sign
Aug 20, 2013 - Sep 4, 2013
BTC/USD up +17.9%

Sun and Mercury in a different sign
Sep 5, 2013 - Sep 15, 2013
BTC/USD up +3.3%

Sun and Mercury in the same sign
Sep 16, 2013 - Sep 23, 2013
BTC/USD down -1.9%

Sun and Mercury in a different sign
Sep 24, 2013 - Oct 16, 2013
BTC/USD up +12.4%

(Mercury retrograde October 21 2013 - November 10, 2013)

Sun and Mercury in the same sign*
Oct 17, 2013 - Nov 15, 2013
BTC/USD up +191.1%

Sun and Mercury in a different sign
Nov 16, 2013 - Nov 29, 2013
BTC/USD up +176.4%

Sun and Mercury in the same sign
Nov 30, 2013 - Dec 14, 2013
BTC/USD down -19.3%

Sun and Mercury in a different sign
Dec 15, 2013 - Dec 19, 2013
BTC/USD down -21.8%

Sun and Mercury in the same sign
Dec 20, 2013 - Jan 7, 2014
BTC/USD up +12.7%

Sun and Mercury in a different sign
Jan 8, 2014 - Jan 13, 2014
BTC/USD up +3.5%

Sun and Mercury in the same sign
Jan 14, 2014 - Jan 25, 2014
BTC/USD down -1.0%

(mercury retrograde Feb 6, 2014 - Feb 28, 2014)

Sun and Mercury in a different sign*
Jan 26, 2014 - Feb 11, 2014
BTC/USD down -18.7%

Sun and Mercury in the same sign*
Feb 12, 2014 - Feb 17, 2014
BTC/USD up +0.8%

Sun and Mercury in a different sign*
Feb 18, 2014 - Mar 10, 2014
BTC/USD down -7.4%

Sun and Mercury in the same sign
Mar 11, 2014 - Mar 13, 2014
BTC/USD up +4.4%

Sun and Mercury in a different sign
Mar 14, 2014 - Apr 2, 2014
BTC/USD down -30.9%

Sun and Mercury in the same sign
Apr 3, 2014 - Apr 12, 2014
BTC/USD down -6.4%

Sun and Mercury in a different sign
Apr 13, 2014 - Apr 19, 2014
BTC/USD up +21.7%

Sun and Mercury in the same sign
Apr 20, 2014 - May 3, 2014
BTC/USD down -12.8%

Sun and Mercury in a different sign
May 4, 2014 - May 13, 2014
BTC/USD up +21.7%

Sun and Mercury in the same sign
May 14, 2014 - May 21, 2014
BTC/USD up +9.2%

Sun and Mercury in a different sign
May 22, 2014 - Jun 14, 2014
BTC/USD up +16.7%

(Mercury retrograde June 7, 2012 - July 1, 2012)

Sun and Mercury in the same sign*
Jun 15, 2014 - Jul 15, 2014
BTC/USD up +12.0%

Sun and Mercury in a different sign
Jul 16, 2014 - Jul 27, 2014
BTC/USD down -4.9%

Sun and Mercury in the same sign
Jul 28, 2014 - Aug 11, 2014
BTC/USD down -3.0%

Sun and Mercury in a different sign
Aug 12, 2014 - Aug 15, 2014
BTC/USD down -11.6%

Sun and Mercury in the same sign
Aug 16, 2014 - Aug 28, 2014
BTC/USD up +0.3%

Sun and Mercury in a different sign

Aug 29, 2014 - Sept 15, 2014
BTC/USD down -7.5%

Sun and Mercury in the same sign
Sep 16, 2014 - Sep 19, 2014
BTC/USD down -15.9%

(Mercury Retrograde October 4, 2014 - October 25, 2014)

Sun and Mercury in a different sign*
Sep 20, 2014 - Oct 15, 2014
BTC/USD down -0.5%

Sun and Mercury in the same sign*
Oct 16, 2014
BTC/USD down -3.6%

Sun and Mercury in a different sign*
Oct 17, 2014 - Nov 3, 2014
BTC/USD down -14.7%

Sun and Mercury in the same sign
Nov 4, 2014 - Nov 15, 2014
BTC/USD up +16.4%

Sun and Mercury in a different sign
Nov 16, 2014 - Nov 23, 2014
BTC/USD down -4.2%

Sun and Mercury in the same sign
Nov 24, 2014 - Dec 12, 2014
BTC/USD down -2.1%

Sun and Mercury in a different sign
Dec 13, 2014 - Dec 14, 2014
BTC/USD down 0.0%

Sun and Mercury in the same sign
Dec 14, 2014 - Dec 31, 2014
BTC/USD down -10.1%

Sun and Mercury in a different sign
Jan 1, 2015 - Jan 13, 2015
BTC/USD down -27.5%

(Mercury retrograde Jan 21, 2015 - February 11, 2015)

Market Prediction Algorithms for the US Dollar, the Stock Market and Bitcoin

Sun and Mercury in the same sign*
Jan 14, 2015 - Feb 11, 2015
BTC/USD down -4.4%

Sun and Mercury in a different sign
Feb 12, 2015 - Mar 7, 2015
BTC/USD up +26.0%

Sun and Mercury in the same sign
Mar 8, 2015 - Mar 13, 2015
BTC/USD up +2.3%

Sun and Mercury in a different sign
Mar 14, 2015 - Mar 26, 2015
BTC/USD down -12.0%

Sun and Mercury in the same sign
Mar 27, 2015 - Apr 11, 2015
BTC/USD down -4.9%

Sun and Mercury in a different sign
Apr 12, 2015 - Apr 13, 2015
BTC/USD down -5.0%

Sun and Mercury in the same sign
Apr 14, 2015 - Apr 26, 2015
BTC/USD down -2.4%

Sun and Mercury in a different sign
Apr 27, 2015 - May 14, 2015
BTC/USD up +7.7%

(Mercury retrograde May 18, 2015 - June 11, 2015)

Sun and Mercury in the same sign*
May 15, 2015 - Jun 14, 2015
BTC/USD down -1.3%

Sun and Mercury in a different sign
Jun 15, 2015 - Jul 4, 2015
BTC/USD up +11.6%

Sun and Mercury in the same sign
Jul 5, 2015 - Jun 15, 2015
BTC/USD up +9.5%

Sun and Mercury in a different sign

Jul 16, 2015 - Jul 19, 2015
BTC/USD down -3.6%

Sun and Mercury in the same sign
Jul 20, 2015 - Aug 3, 2015
BTC/USD up +2.3%

Sun and Mercury in a different sign
Aug 4, 2015 - Aug 16, 2015
BTC/USD down -7.6%

Sun and Mercury in the same sign
Aug 17, 2015 - Aug 21, 2015
BTC/USD down -10.7%

Sun and Mercury in a different sign
Aug 22, 2015 - Sep 16, 2015
BTC/USD down -1.4%

(Mercury retrograde September 17, 2015 - October 9 2015)

Sun and Mercury in the same sign*
Sep 17, 2015 - Oct 16, 2015
BTC/USD up +15.7%

Sun and Mercury in a different sign
Oct 17, 2015 - Oct 28, 2015
BTC/USD up +15.6%

Sun and Mercury in the same sign
Oct 29, 2015 - Dec 5, 2015
BTC/USD up +28.1%

Sun and Mercury in a different sign
Dec 6, 2015 - Dec 15, 2015
BTC/USD up +19.6%

Sun and Mercury in the same sign
Dec 16, 2015 - Dec 25, 2015
BTC/USD down -2.4%

Mercury retrograde January 5th, 2016 – January 25th, 2016)

Sun and Mercury in a different sign*
Dec 26, 2015 - Feb 7, 2016
BTC/USD down -18.3%

Sun and Mercury in the same sign
Feb 8, 2016 - Feb 12, 2016
BTC/USD up +2.9%

Sun and Mercury in a different sign
Feb 13, 2016 - Feb 29, 2016
BTC/USD up +14.7%

Sun and Mercury in the same sign
Mar 1, 2016 - Mar 13, 2016
BTC/USD down -6.2%

Sun and Mercury in a different sign
Mar 14, 2016 - Mar 17, 2016
BTC/USD up +1.7%

Sun and Mercury in the same sign
Mar 18, 2016 - Apr 1, 2016
BTC/USD down -0.3%

Sun and Mercury in a different sign
Apr 2, 2016 - Apr 12, 2016
BTC/USD up +2.2%

(Mercury Retrograde April 28th 2016 – May 22nd, 2016)

Sun and Mercury in the same sign*
Apr 13, 2016 - May 13, 2016
BTC/USD up +6.8%

Sun and Mercury in a different sign
May 13, 2016 - Jun 6, 2016
BTC/USD up +28.4%

Sun and Mercury in the same sign
Jun 7, 2016 - Jun 13, 2016
BTC/USD up +20.6%

Sun and Mercury in a different sign
Jun 14, 2016 - Jun 25, 2016
BTC/USD down -5.8%

Sun and Mercury in the same sign
Jun 26, 2016 - Jul 10, 2016
BTC/USD down -2.3%

Sun and Mercury in a different sign

Jul 11, 2016 - Jul 14, 2016
BTC/USD up +1.5%

Sun and Mercury in the same sign
Jul 15, 2016 - Jul 25, 2016
BTC/USD down -0.9%

Sun and Mercury in a different sign
Jul 26, 2016 - Aug 15, 2016
BTC/USD down -13.7%

Sun and Mercury in the same sign
Aug 16, 2016 - Aug 18, 2016
BTC/USD up +1.3%

Sun and Mercury in a different sign
Aug 19, 2016 - Sep 8, 2016
BTC/USD up +10.4%

(Mercury retrograde August 30, 2016 - September 22, 2016)

Sun and Mercury in the same sign*
Sep 9, 2016 - Sep 15, 2016
BTC/USD down -3.2%

Sun and Mercury in a different sign
Sep 16, 2016 - Oct 2, 2016
BTC/USD down -0.4%

Sun and Mercury in the same sign
Oct 3, 2016 - Oct 15, 2016
BTC/USD up +5.1%

Sun and Mercury in a different sign
Oct 16, 2016 - Oct 20, 2016
BTC/USD down -1.2%

Sun and Mercury in the same sign
Oct 21, 2016 - Nov 7, 2016
BTC/USD up +11.3%

Sun and Mercury in a different sign
Nov 9, 2016 - Nov 14, 2016
BTC/USD up +0.47%

Sun and Mercury in the same sign
Nov 15, 2016 - Nov 27, 2016

BTC/USD up +2.5%

Sun and Mercury in a different sign
Nov 28, 2016 - Dec 14, 2016
BTC/USD up +6.08%

(Mercury retrograde December 19th, 2016 – January 8th, 2017)

Sun and Mercury in the same sign*
Dec 15, 2016 - Jan 12, 2017
BTC/USD up +3.9%

Sun and Mercury in a different sign
Jan 13, 2017 - Feb 2, 2017
BTC/USD up +25.0%

Sun and Mercury in the same sign
Feb 3, 2017 - Feb 11, 2017
BTC/USD down -0.5%

Sun and Mercury in a different sign
Feb 12, 2017 - Feb 21, 2017
BTC/USD up +12.9%

Sun and Mercury in the same sign
Feb 22, 2017 - Mar 9, 2017
BTC/USD up +5.4%

Sun and Mercury in a different sign
Mar 10, 2017 - Mar 13, 2017
BTC/USD up +4.0%

Sun and Mercury in the same sign
Mar 14, 2017 - Mar 25, 2017
BTC/USD down -21.5%

Sun and Mercury in a different sign
Mar 26, 2017 - Apr 12, 2017
BTC/USD up +26.3%

(Mercury retrograde April 9, 2017 - May 3, 2017)

Sun and Mercury in the same sign*
Apr 13, 2017 - May 13, 2017
BTC/USD up +48.3%

Sun and Mercury in a different sign

May 14, 2017 - Jun 2, 2017
BTC/USD up +32.3%

Sun and Mercury in the same sign
Jun 3, 2017 - Jun 13, 2017
BTC/USD up +11.2%

Sun and Mercury in a different sign
Jun 14, 2017 - Jun 17, 2017
BTC/USD down -2.5%

Sun and Mercury in the same sign
Jun 18, 2017 - Jul 1, 2017
BTC/USD down -10.0%

Sun and Mercury in a different sign
Jul 2, 2017 - Jul 15, 2017
BTC/USD down -15.8%

Sun and Mercury in the same sign
Jul 16, 2017 - Jul 19, 2017
BTC/USD up +13.9%

Sun and Mercury in a different sign
Jul 20, 2017 - Aug 15, 2017
BTC/USD up +84.3%

(Mercury retrograde August 12, 2017 - September 5, 2017)

Sun and Mercury in the same sign*
Aug 16, 2017 - Sep 15, 2017
BTC/USD down -10.9%

Sun and Mercury in a different sign
Sep 16, 2017 - Sep 25, 2017
BTC/USD up +6.3%

Sun and Mercury in the same sign
Sep 26, 2017 - Oct 12, 2017
BTC/USD up +38.1%

Sun and Mercury in a different sign
Oct 13, 2017 - Oct 16, 2017
BTC/USD up +6.2%

Sun and Mercury in the same sign
Oct 17, 2017 - Oct 31, 2017

BTC/USD up +12.1%

Sun and Mercury in a different sign
Nov 1, 2017 - Nov 15, 2017
BTC/USD up +12.7%

Sun and Mercury in the same sign
Nov 16, 2017 - Nov 23, 2017
BTC/USD up +9.6%

Sun and Mercury in a different sign
Nov 23, 2017 - Dec 9, 2017
BTC/USD up +83.8%

(Mercury retrograde December 3 - December 22, 2017)

Sun and Mercury in the same sign*
Dec 10, 2017 - Dec 14, 2017
BTC/USD up +11.8%

Sun and Mercury in a different sign
Dec 15, 2017 - Jan 5, 2018
BTC/USD up +3.3%

Sun and Mercury in the same sign
Jan 6, 2018 - Jan 13, 2018
BTC/USD down -16.1%

Sun and Mercury in a different sign
Jan 14, 2018 - Jan 26, 2018
BTC/USD down -22.0%

Sun and Mercury in the same sign
Jan 27, 2018 - Feb 11, 2018
BTC/USD down -27.1%

Sun and Mercury in a different sign
Feb 12, 2018 - Feb 13, 2018
BTC/USD up +5.5%

Sun and Mercury in the same sign
Feb 14, 2018 - Mar 1, 2018
BTC/USD up +28.3%

Sun and Mercury in a different sign
Mar 2, 2018 - Mar 13, 2018
BTC/USD down -16.4%

(Mercury retrograde March 22 - April 15, 2018)

Sun and Mercury in the same sign*
Mar 14, 2018 - Apr 12, 2018
BTC/USD down -13.4%

Sun and Mercury in a different sign
Apr 13, 2018 - May 8, 2018
BTC/USD up +16.1%

Sun and Mercury in the same sign
May 9, 2018 - May 13, 2018
BTC/USD down -5.5%

Sun and Mercury in a different sign
May 14, 2018 - May 25, 2018
BTC/USD down -14.1%

Sun and Mercury in the same sign
May 26, 2018 - Jun 8, 2018
BTC/USD up +2.1%

Sun and Mercury in a different sign
Jun 9, 2018 - Jun 14, 2018
BTC/USD down -12.9%

Sun and Mercury in the same sign
Jun 15, 2018 - Jun 24, 2018
BTC/USD down -7.3%

Sun and Mercury in a different sign
Jun 25, 2018 - Jul 15, 2018
BTC/USD up +3.2%

(Mercury retrograde July 25, 2018 - August 18, 2018)

Sun and Mercury in the same sign*
Jul 16, 2018 - Aug 15, 2018
BTC/USD down -1.2%

Sun and Mercury in a different sign
Aug 16, 2018 - Sep 1, 2018
BTC/USD up +14.8%

Sun and Mercury in the same sign
Sep 2, 2018 - Sep 15, 2018

BTC/USD down -9.5%

Sun and Mercury in a different sign
Sep 16, 2018 - Sep 17, 2018
BTC/USD down -4.0%

Sun and Mercury in the same sign
Sep 18, 2018 - Oct 5, 2018
BTC/USD up +6.2%

Sun and Mercury in a different sign
Oct 6, 2018 - Oct 16, 2018
BTC/USD up +1.6%

Sun and Mercury in the same sign
Oct 17, 2018 - Oct 25, 2018
BTC/USD down -3.3%

Sun and Mercury in a different sign
Oct 26, 2018 - Nov 15, 2018
BTC/USD down -11.9%

(Mercury retrograde November 16, 2018 - December 06, 2018)

Sun and Mercury in the same sign*
Nov 16, 2018 - Dec 14, 2018
BTC/USD down -42.8%

Sun and Mercury in a different sign
Dec 15, 2018 - Dec 30, 2018
BTC/USD up +21.2%

Sun and Mercury in the same sign
Dec 31, 2018 - Jan 13, 2019
BTC/USD down -9.7%

Sun and Mercury in a different sign
Jan 14, 2019 - Jan 19, 2019
BTC/USD up +4.7%

Sun and Mercury in the same sign
Jan 20, 2019 - Feb 5, 2019
BTC/USD down -6.6%

Sun and Mercury in a different sign
Feb 6, 2019 - Feb 11, 2019
BTC/USD up +4.8%

Sun and Mercury in the same sign
Feb 12, 2019 - Feb 23, 2019
BTC/USD up +14.4%

(Mercury retrograde March 5, 2019 to March 28, 2019)

Sun and Mercury in a different sign*
Feb 24, 2019 - Mar 13, 2019
BTC/USD down -6.3%

Sun and Mercury in the same sign*
Mar 14, 2019
BTC/USD up +0.0%

Sun and Mercury in a different sign
Mar 15, 2019 - Apr 10, 2019
BTC/USD up +34.5%

Sun and Mercury in the same sign
Apr 11, 2019 - Apr 13, 2019
BTC/USD down -4.0%

Sun and Mercury in a different sign
Apr 14, 2019 - May 2, 2019
BTC/USD up +12.2%

Sun and Mercury in the same sign
Apr 11, 2019 - Apr 13, 2019
BTC/USD up +35.5%

Sun and Mercury in a different sign
May 14, 2019 - May 17, 2019
BTC/USD down -4.4%

Sun and Mercury in the same sign
May 18, 2019 - May 31, 2019
BTC/USD up +15.1%

Sun and Mercury in a different sign
Jun 1, 2019 - Jun 14, 2019
BTC/USD up +1.8%

Sun and Mercury in the same sign
Jun 15, 2019 - Jun 19, 2019
BTC/USD up +15.1%

Sun and Mercury in a different sign
Jun 20, 2019 - Jul 15, 2019
BTC/USD up +16.3%

(Mercury retrograde July 7, 2019 to August 2, 2019)

Sun and Mercury in the same sign*
Jul 16, 2019 - Jul 30, 2019
BTC/USD down -11.4%

Sun and Mercury in a different sign*
Jul 31, 2019 - Aug 1, 2019
BTC/USD up +8.4%

Sun and Mercury in the same sign
Aug 2, 2019 - Aug 16, 2019
BTC/USD down -0.3%

Sun and Mercury in a different sign
Aug 17, 2019 - Aug 25, 2019
BTC/USD down -2.3%

Sun and Mercury in the same sign
Aug 26, 2019 - Sep 9, 2019
BTC/USD up +1.8%

Sun and Mercury in a different sign
Sep 10, 2019 - Sep 16, 2019
BTC/USD down -0.2%

Sun and Mercury in the same sign
Sep 17, 2019 - Sep 28, 2019
BTC/USD down -20.0%

Sun and Mercury in a different sign
Sep 29, 2019 - Oct 16, 2019
BTC/USD down -0.2%

Sun and Mercury in the same sign
Oct 17, 2019 - Oct 22, 2019
BTC/USD up +0.5%

Sun and Mercury in a different sign
Oct 23, 2019 - Nov 6, 2019
BTC/USD up +16.1%

(Mercury retrograde October 31 2019 to November 20 2019)

Sun and Mercury in the same sign*
Nov 7, 2019 - Nov 15, 2019
BTC/USD down -9.2%

Sun and Mercury in a different sign
Nov 16, 2019 - Dec 3, 2019
BTC/USD down -13.7%

Sun and Mercury in the same sign
Dec, 4 2019 - Dec 15, 2019
BTC/USD down -2.5%

Sun and Mercury in a different sign
Dec 16, 2019 - Dec 24, 2019
BTC/USD up +1.7%

Sun and Mercury in the same sign
Dec, 25 2019 - Jan 11, 2020
BTC/USD up +10.4%

----------------------Results of algorithm for the year 2020----------------------

Sun and Mercury in a different sign
Jan, 12 2020 - Jan 14, 2020
BTC/USD up +10.0%

Sun and Mercury in the same sign
Jan, 15 2020 - Jan 29, 2020
BTC/USD up +5.3%

Sun and Mercury in a different sign
Jan 30, 2020 - Feb 12, 2020
BTC/USD up +11.0%

(Mercury retrograde February 18 2020 to March 9 2020)

Sun and Mercury in the same sign*
Feb 13, 2020 - Mar 13, 2020
BTC/USD down -45.9%
please note that BTC/USD dropped 38.18% on March 12th after mercury retrograde already ended.

Sun and Mercury in a different sign
Mar 14, 2020 - Apr 7, 2020
BTC/USD up +28.0%

Sun and Mercury in the same sign
Apr 8, 2020 - Apr 13, 2020
BTC/USD down -4.8%

Sun and Mercury in a different sign
Apr 14, 2020 - Apr 24, 2020
BTC/USD up +9.7%

Sun and Mercury in the same sign
Apr 25, 2020 - May 8, 2020
BTC/USD up +30.5%

Sun and Mercury in a different sign
May 9, 2020 - May 13, 2020
BTC/USD down -5.2%

Sun and Mercury in the same sign
May 14, 2020 - May 23, 2020
BTC/USD down -1.3%

Sun and Mercury in a different sign
May 24, 2020 - Jun 13, 2020
BTC/USD up +3.2%

(Mercury retrograde Jun 18 2020 to Jul 11 2020)

Sun and Mercury in the same sign*
Jun 14, 2020 - Jul 15, 2020
BTC/USD down -2.9%

Sun and Mercury in a different sign
Jul 16, 2020 - Jul 31, 2020
BTC/USD up +23.2%

Sun and Mercury in the same sign
Aug 1, 2020 - Aug 15, 2020
BTC/USD up +4.5%

Sun and Mercury in a different sign
Aug 16, 2020 - Aug 16, 2020
BTC/USD up +0.5%

Sun and Mercury in the same sign
Aug 17, 2020 - Sep 1, 2020
BTC/USD up +0.1%

Sun and Mercury in a different sign
Sep 2, 2020 - Sep 15, 2020
BTC/USD down -9.5%

Sun and Mercury in the same sign
Sep 16, 2020 - Sep 21, 2020
BTC/USD down -3.4%

Sun and Mercury in a different sign
Sep 22, 2020 - Oct 15, 2020
BTC/USD up +10.4%

(Mercury retrograde Oct 14, 2020 to Nov 3 2020)

Sun and Mercury in the same sign*
Oct 16, 2020 - Nov 14, 2020
BTC/USD up +39.4%

Sun and Mercury in a different sign
Nov 15, 2020 - Nov 26, 2020
BTC/USD up +7.2%

Sun and Mercury in the same sign
Nov 26, 2020 - Dec 14, 2020
BTC/USD BTC/USD up +2.9%

Sun and Mercury in a different sign
Dec 15, 2020 - Dec 16, 2020
BTC/USD BTC/USD up +10.6%

Milton Keynes UK
Ingram Content Group UK Ltd.
UKHW010722070823
426447UK00001B/158